'This memoir is about a lost sister, but also things that touch us all: the weight of love, loss and guilt; families and their means of survival; how possessions define a life and where they scatter after death. Simpson's writing … fillets the little details that reveal the profundity and bravery of her sister's weakening struggle with mental illness: even, near the end, the way Tricia painstakingly dressed up in elegant outfits to attend the local church … It sticks with me'

JENNY MCCARTNEY, *Mail on Sunday*

'Beautifully understated memoir … A startling, elegiac portrait of farming life in modern Britain'

HAYLEY MAITLAND, *Vogue*

'There are moments here of heart-stopping poignancy and unbearable sadness, but it is never maudlin or sentimental. Simpson is too good a writer for that, and it is her restraint and phlegmatic humour which lend the book its tremendous power. A deeply engaging, courageous and human work'

GRAEME MACRAE BURNET, author of *His Bloody Project*

WHEN I HAD
A LITTLE SISTER

*The Story of a Farming Family
Who Never Spoke*

CATHERINE SIMPSON

4th ESTATE • *London*

4th Estate
An imprint of HarperCollins*Publishers*
1 London Bridge Street
London SE1 9GF

www.4thEstate.co.uk

First published in Great Britain in 2019 by 4th Estate
This 4th Estate paperback edition published in 2020

1

A catalogue record for this book is
available from the British Library

ISBN 978-0-00-830167-5

Printed and bound in Great Britain by
CPI Group (UK) Ltd, Croydon

MIX
Paper from
responsible sources
FSC™ C007454

This book is produced from independently certified FSC™ paper
to ensure responsible forest management.

For more information visit: www.harpercollins.co.uk/green

For
Cello
Nina & Lara

Mum, Dad
Elizabeth & Tricia

WHEN I HAD
A LITTLE SISTER

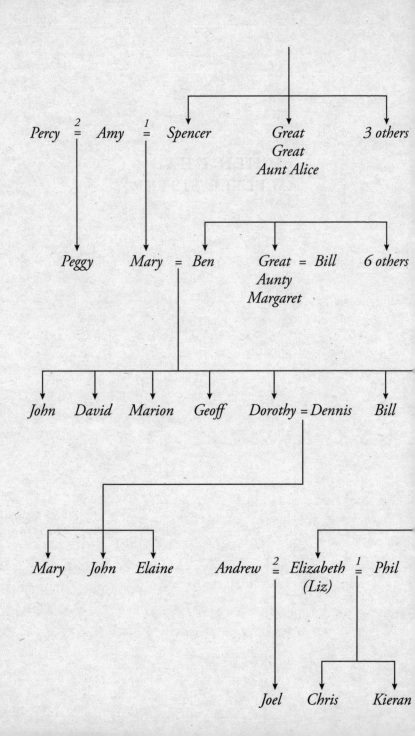

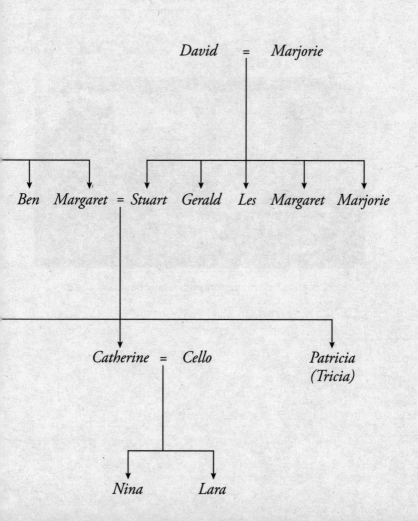

New House Farm, the Simpson family home since 1925

CHAPTER ONE

Saturday 7th December 2013,
late afternoon

I peer into the bathroom and from here the room looks like a tableau with the main character removed. On the wooden floor is a striped mug half-full of cold coffee. I move closer and see the milk cold and pale, risen to the top. Beside the mug is a packet of opened cigarettes, not Tricia's usual baccy and Rizla papers, and next to that her blue plastic lighter. There are four floating dog-ends in the toilet bowl.

It is dark outside and gloomy in, and the house is filled with a terrible quiet.

Tricia must have sat on the bathroom floor with her back to the radiator long enough to smoke four cigarettes, dragging hard, taking the smoke deep into her lungs and holding it, holding it, for long seconds at a time, before blowing it out of the side of her mouth, eyes squint, then when she'd got down to the filters grinding out the butts and dropping them in the toilet bowl one after the other. She was smoking in the bathroom to help her cut down – she had banned herself from smoking anywhere else in the house because she wanted to be healthy.

On the night she died she was still trying to be healthy.

When did she decide to die? Was it before midnight on Friday the 6th, because she couldn't face another night, or was it before dawn on Saturday the 7th, because she couldn't face another day?

Did she think about us? Did she think about her dog, Ted, or her cat, Puss, sleeping on Grandma Mary's old sofa in the conservatory and who would be waiting for her to feed them in the morning? What about her horses in the stable – Billy and Sasha – who she called her 'babies'? Did she think about them? Did she imagine Dad finding her? It would have to be Dad, after all. It couldn't be anyone else.

Did she know what she was doing?

Saturday 7th December 2013,
earlier that day

A late start for the Christmas shopping. I call a friend and say let's not bother buying for each other this year – I need to simplify. I'm tired; only back a day or two from a trip with my elder sister, Elizabeth, and 87-year-old father to the First World War battlefields at Ypres to see where my grandad fought in 1917. We'd planned it for Dad – he'd always wanted to go. We thought it would give him time away from the farm and be a break from worrying about our younger sister, Tricia – although he worried about her constantly anyway.

Now I am worn out and too tired for Christmas.

My husband Marcello, known as Cello, drives me to Haddington, a market town in East Lothian, to begin the Christmas shopping.

I choose turquoise leather diaries for both my sisters. I also pick out art supplies for Tricia: paints and pastels and a sketch pad. She likes painting and drawing. She is good at it.

There is a café in the shop and as a reward for starting the Christmas shopping Cello and I tuck into coffee and scones. We enjoy what I think of afterwards as the last bit of normal life for a long time.

As we leave the shop my mobile rings. I dump my carrier bags on the pavement and root through my rucksack. I can never find my phone. I hate my phone. I have an autistic daughter and over the years I have come to associate a ringing phone with trouble.

My screen flashes up 'Johnny', Elizabeth's new boyfriend. I have only met Johnny a handful of times. I smile as I say hello.

'Bad news, I'm afraid.' His voice is urgent and there is scuffling at the other end as the phone is handed to Elizabeth. I prickle with fear and my body goes onto high alert. My breathing stops, my scalp fizzes.

What is it? I can feel my voice rise. *What is it?* It must be Dad.

Or Tricia. Which one is it? Dad? Or Tricia?

We have been living on a knife-edge for so long I know this is something big.

Elizabeth struggles to speak but eventually says, 'I think something's happened to Tricia.' *What's happened?* Elizabeth's voice wavers. 'Paramedics phoned from the farm. I think Tricia might be dead.'

It's as though a great boot has caught me hard under the ribs – a knockout blow to the solar plexus – and my knees buckle. There is no breath left in me. I grip the shop's windowsill and I am aware of the tinsel in the Christmas display twinkling at the corner of my eye as my face hangs over the pavement. The world sways and I have an urge to get onto the ground to feel secure, but do not. My husband grabs my arm. 'What is it? What's happened?'

'It's Tricia,' I say, 'Elizabeth thinks she's dead,' and I am unaware whether I am whispering or wailing.

'Oh no,' I hear Cello say again and again. 'Oh no.'

Shock and grief are very physical and it will be weeks before I lose the sensation of reeling backwards, of staggering, unable to grasp onto anything sure and safe that will enable me to regain my balance and find my footing again.

For years it will take nothing but the sight of tinsel in a window or the feel of Christmas in the air to bring me crashing back to this moment when my heart was broken.

* * *

The family farm where Tricia lives, near Dad, is in Lancashire. I am in Scotland. Elizabeth is in the Midlands. The world seems impossible and chaotically out of control.

I am panic-stricken and fight the desire to tear at my hair. I sob as I stumble to the car, aware that all around me shoppers still shop, shopkeepers still sell, and for everyone else Christmas continues.

Cello drives us home and I say, 'I hope Tricia is alive and this is a horrible mistake; if not, I hope she is dead.' I cannot bear the thought of Tricia in a coma, Tricia in a hospital bed, Tricia suffering any more than she already has over so many years.

We arrive home and I throw things into a suitcase, folding on top a black funeral dress and black shoes. I also put in my iPod which I think may help us choose the funeral music. Everything is in a state of confusion and turmoil and uncertainty but a part of me has gone hard, cold and distant. I have begun to organize, to plan, to try to wrest some control from a world turned ugly and terrifying.

Over and over I try to reach Elizabeth. Does she know anything else? Have I imagined this whole nightmare? But I can't get through. There is no answer at Dad's house. There is no answer at Tricia's farmhouse. Where is everyone? I sit at the kitchen table with my coat fastened up to the chin waiting for Cello to drive me 170 miles to the farm. I am icy, I am shaking and my ears are full of a high-pitched ringing. I am not fully in the room; I am here but I am not here. For the moment I have been removed from my body.

My mobile rings and I grab it. It's Johnny again: there has been no mistake. The worst has happened. Tricia is dead.

CHAPTER TWO

I expect my dad to die. I do not think he can survive the discovery of the body of his youngest daughter.

After the three-hour drive from Scotland I walk into Dad's living room, breathless and dizzy.

It has not killed him.

He is sitting in his armchair. He looks at me and shakes his head and he is crying. 'Poor lass, she didn't know what she was doing. Poor lass.' He will repeat this many times over the next few weeks.

I gather the story, about how Dad knocked on the farmhouse door this morning to ask did Tricia want a newspaper? He was going to the shop. Did she want her usual tin of tuna? Soup? When he got no answer he didn't go to the shop. He went home for his lunch but could barely eat – he felt something was wrong. It wasn't unusual for Tricia not to answer the door. She had poor sleep habits and was often in bed at odd hours. Still, Dad sensed something was very wrong.

Phoning was no use – Tricia's phone was out of order. The last thing she'd said to him yesterday was: 'Don't worry; I'll sort out the phone tomorrow.' He'd dropped her at the farm-house yesterday evening after taking her for a new prescription because the psychiatrist had been out to the farm and upped her medication. A new prescription had pleased Dad. It meant things were being done. We all lived in hope of new pills and revised prescriptions because then we could imagine that *something was being done*. Dad drove her for the new pills – pleased he could also do this to help since the doctors had taken away Tricia's driving licence. He dropped her back at the farmhouse afterwards where she'd said, 'Don't worry, we'll sort everything out tomorrow.'

While forcing his lunch down he resolved to break in – he was now convinced she was lying in bed too ill to get up. He knew which windowpane in the conservatory could be forced from the outside and he went straight back to the farmhouse to gain access.

Knocking the window open caused the whole sill of plants to crash to the floor, some smashing, all spilling soil and grit onto the lino. He stepped through the window, crunching over the pot fragments and scattered plants, and went into the house.

This is when he found the body of his youngest daughter.

He could not call an ambulance because of the broken phone so he dashed back to his own house, four hundred yards up the lane, to dial 999. Then he returned to the farm-house and sat there, waiting.

I cannot imagine the world at this time. I cannot imagine Dad in the house alone with Tricia's body.

Twenty minutes later the police arrived, and then an air ambulance landed in the field opposite. As the paramedics ran inside Dad said, 'I'm afraid you're too late.'

After they confirmed Tricia was dead the paramedics tried to contact family members for Dad, using an old mobile of Tricia's with barely any charge or signal. Dad couldn't use a mobile because of his hearing aid and the paramedics said they weren't allowed to explain the situation to Johnny when he answered Elizabeth's phone. Elizabeth was in the shower and as Johnny tried to get her attention and hand her the phone it got cut off. This is what caused the chaotic half-messages that Chinese-whispered their way to me.

Sometime after the paramedics left the farmhouse Tricia's mental-health worker drove into the yard for an appointment. Tricia had a history of acute depression and visits from the mental-health or crisis teams were daily by then. The policeman went outside to explain what had happened. The woman did not come in to speak to Dad but stayed in her car writing notes before driving off.

Mrs Smith, a neighbour from up the lane, had seen the helicopter land and ran down to the farm. She poked her head into the farmhouse and asked the policeman, 'Is it Stuart or is it Tricia?' The officer was relieved to hand Dad over to a friendly face but Dad didn't want to leave Tricia alone in the house with police searching through her bedroom and her private belongings, tramping up and down the stairs looking for a suicide note.

Mrs Smith eventually coaxed him away. The policeman stayed on in the house, waiting for the ambulance to take her body to the mortuary.

The countryside can be enveloped in a heavy silence and, as the policeman waited alone with Tricia's body, the quiet must have seemed crushing.

An hour later, when Elizabeth and Johnny arrived at the farmhouse, they told the policeman who they were and Elizabeth made Johnny go and check on Tricia first. She was covered in a blanket. Johnny went to look – this was only the third time he had ever seen Tricia – and he reassured Elizabeth: it's OK. Elizabeth went to see her but afterwards said she wished she hadn't.

By the time I arrived, Tricia had gone.

I saw her on the Monday morning. The mortuary was tucked down the side of Lancaster Royal Infirmary in a single-storey, white building. I knocked on the door and a small man in late middle age answered. He ushered me and Elizabeth in. He looked sad even though he must greet bereaved relatives every day. He hesitated outside the door to the viewing room and looked at us, from one to the other; he clearly saw a family resemblance between us and Tricia. 'She was very young,' he said.

She was forty-six. Three years younger than me, and six years younger than Elizabeth.

Elizabeth hung back for a second. 'Take a minute; whenever you are ready,' he said, but I was keen to see Tricia. I felt I'd let her down by not being able to make contact with her sooner – she'd now been dead two days.

I pushed the door open.

Her hair had been brushed away from her face in an unfamiliar style but otherwise it was Tricia lying there on a table wearing her work clothes – the dark blue jacket and jeans she wore to feed and muck out her horses.

Her hand was chilled. I touched it and asked her, out loud, 'Oh, Tricia, what have you done? What have you done?'

CHAPTER THREE

The dash south on the day Tricia died was an echo of a similar journey when my mother was on her deathbed seven years before. After hearing she'd taken a turn for the worse there had been the frantic packing of a suitcase followed by the same three-hour hiatus on the M6, but as familiar sights flew by – the bleak stretches over Shap, the promise of Tebay Services, the elegant verdigris dome of the Williamson Memorial – the familiarity was overridden by a surreal feeling of travelling into the unknown and the knowledge that *everything* in the world had changed.

I was raised in a family of five. Mum's death had taken that to four; now we were down to three.

Mum had died in the scorching summer of 2006, six years after being diagnosed with non-Hodgkin's lymphoma. Her final years were a white-knuckle ride of scans, hospital appointments, inpatient, outpatient, chemotherapy, sickness and terror – hers and ours – with short reprieves when we dared to hope it was all behind us and that we'd be able to re-close our eyes and our ears to death and pretend it hadn't come so close we could smell it.

We buried her in the outfit she'd worn for a Buckingham Palace garden party she'd been invited to through Dad's work with the Royal Lancashire Show: a silky blue dress bought from a boutique rather than a catalogue or being home-made which would have been more typical. I took her perfume, her glasses and her handbag to the undertaker's. I put an ironed lace handkerchief inside her handbag. I took her lipstick and her face powder.

I drew the line at her fascinator.

I put everything in a carrier bag because I had seen someone else leave clothes at the undertaker's and *their* underwear and skirt and blouse were left exposed, draped over the back of a chair in the waiting room. I could only imagine my mother's tight-lipped, you-can't-trust-anyone-to-do-anything eye-roll if her underskirt and tights were left draped *for all the world to see*.

Her five grandchildren wrote notes to put in the handbag and did drawings. They wanted to because they loved her. She had never complained when they turned her house into an obstacle course or her entire living room into a den. Unlike when we were kids and she had berated us for making a mess, yelling, 'When you're grown up I'm going to come and jump on your settee and see how you like it!' It always looked as though she enjoyed being a grandma more than a mother.

The day after she died we tried to impose some order on her chaotic kitchen – sorting out, putting away, making space to put stuff down – things we were not allowed to do when she was alive. We'd been embarrassed the evening before when the nurses arrived with the morphine and couldn't find anywhere to assemble the morphine driver. They'd looked at us, questioning, disapproving, maybe thinking we'd created this mess and obviously wondering why we didn't sort the place out. Elizabeth and I had kept quiet, aware how ridiculous it would sound for two middle-aged daughters of a dying woman to gaze helplessly round the chaos and say: 'But we're not allowed!'

I found her platinum wedding ring in the bottom of a jug in the kitchen. It had worn smooth and thin since her wedding forty-seven years earlier and was cut and misshapen – she must have severed it with wire cutters or pliers to remove it from her left hand when her finger swelled with the cancer treatment or her skin became too sensitive for jewellery.

Dad and Elizabeth said she must be buried with the ring so I took it to the undertaker's even though I wanted to keep it. I wanted to repair it, to make it into a complete circle again and to wear it. I did not want it forever lost underground.

She did not have an engagement ring to bury because she was the only woman I ever knew who rejected a diamond ring as nothing but a nuisance. She thought engagements were meaningless. You are either married or you are not married – what is *engaged*? My mother could infuse a single word with such contempt.

I visited Mum several times in the days leading up to her funeral. I accompanied my nephews and my father to the viewing room to make sure everything had been done right; that the wedding ring had been placed on the third finger of her left hand and the handwritten notes and her glasses and lipstick were in her handbag which nestled beside her in the coffin.

As I checked the grandchildren's notes I slipped my fingers into the silken pocket inside her handbag and found, sunk and hidden at the bottom, a thick gold chain and engraved locket that once belonged to my great-grandmother. I drew it out. My mother did not like sharing. Even though she found jewellery cumbersome and irritating she didn't want anyone else to have it. Maybe it was growing up as the oldest of eight siblings during the Second World War. When she died she would have taken everything with her if she could. I held the chain up and the locket swung and spun and I felt a fleeting, incongruous moment of triumph. 'You nearly got away with that one,' I said and I fastened the chain around my neck.

Later, as I went through her jewellery box, I again felt that reversal of power; I was here and she was not. Her things had been out of bounds when she was alive but now they were not. As children we had longed to sit at her dressing table and try on her beads and gold chains and rub scent on our wrists.

Now all these treasures were ours. There was no one's permission to ask.

I examined her dressing table, half-expecting to hear: 'Stop rooting! I've got eyes in the back of my head, you know!' I discovered the perfume was congealed and most of the jewellery was broken. I got her pearls restrung but I never wore them. I saw on the television that you can tell real pearls by rubbing them against your teeth. If you feel tiny bumps they are real, if not they are fake. I went to the jewellery box and took out the pearls and tested them. My mother's pearls were fake.

I was reminded of when we were children and the biggest bedroom was out of bounds because the roof leaked. It was full of stacks of material, wool and haberdashery, with the odd bucket to catch the drips. When Mum went shopping we sneaked into this room to root among the treasures. We discovered a doll still in her packaging behind moulded plastic; staring eyes, solid hair, her own little kitchen sink behind the plastic too. How we longed to play with this doll but we could not mention it without admitting we'd been where we shouldn't. Over the years as we visited the doll the plastic packaging got grubbier and more opaque as her staring eyes disappeared behind the dirt. Then one day Mum brought the doll out but by this time we were too old for it. When we took it from its plastic we discovered the doll was so cheap she didn't even bend at the hips. We threw both her and her kitchen sink in the bin.

My mother had particular hands – hands I would recognize anywhere, with flat almond-shaped nails always cut short. Several days after her death her fingers had gone a creamy pale blue but they were still recognizably, uniquely hers. I touched them and they were deathly cold. It took me a visit or two to realize that the chill was caused by her body being refrigerated in between because, in fact, death is room temperature.

I photographed her hands.

Weeks later I was flicking through the photographs on my camera and unwittingly came face to face with the close-up of my mother's mottled hands. I was shaken and a bit embarrassed. What would people say if they knew I was keeping a picture of my mother's dead hands?

I studied the photo and noticed the exact shape of her fingernails, the way her wedding ring had worn a smooth groove in the flesh of her finger before she'd cut the ring off, and I noticed the knobs of arthritis in her thumb joints as her hands rested against the blue silk pattern on her dress.

Then I deleted the photograph.

Death is a thousand tiny losses and each loss is a thousand tiny details.

* * *

Why was it important to get everything right for my mother as she lay in her coffin? It was guilt, I think – guilt that I couldn't do anything else for her, guilt that I couldn't bring her back, guilt that I had not been able to stop her dying in the first place. My mother had an enormous ability to make me feel guilty even when I had no idea what I should feel guilty about.

Years later I discovered that items placed in a coffin have a name: grave goods. Apparently people tuck all sorts around the dead: jewellery, photographs, sealed letters, rosary beads, spectacles, hats, mints, walking sticks, cigarettes, football strips, teddy bears, comfortable shoes and money.

For whose benefit are grave goods? Maybe mourners believe the item will help the dead on the journey to the afterlife – the walking stick, money, glasses and shoes. Or perhaps some items are considered part of the deceased's identity, things that they should never be parted from – in particular the glasses. Or do grave goods in the coffin give the living a sense of comfort?

I think so.

In fitting my mother up with a bag and glasses and notes and her fanciest dress I took comfort from having done the best I could.

* * *

We arranged to bury Mum in the local village churchyard, a row further on from her own mother and father. We explained this to the undertaker at a meeting in Dad's kitchen. The undertaker took notes on a clipboard and my father said, 'Dig it deep and leave enough room for me,' and Tricia, speaking up for the first time since the meeting began, said, 'Dig it even deeper and leave enough room for me too.'

CHAPTER FOUR

Every wall, every gateway and every tree on the lane leading to the farmhouse held a memory of Tricia. On my right was the wooden fence we leaned on to watch the mating ducks when she was five or six. 'What they doing?' she asked. 'Makin' friends,' I said. On my left was the verge where our neighbour parked his flatbed truck – our stage for the plays I wrote, heavily influenced by Enid Blyton, in

Me and Tricia in front of the wall we used as a stage and a catwalk

which I cast Tricia and Janet-from-next-door, mainly as dolls or fairies. (Play: *A Lot of Rice for Tea*; Characters: Rag Doll, Dancer Doll, Fairy Doll, Dolly Doll and six 'Chinease' Dolls.)

Past the verge was the head-high yard wall we balanced along for 'playin' bally', never having had a ballet lesson. We took turns wearing a dog-eared 1950s evening dress donated to the dressing-up box by Great-Aunty Margaret and we 'did twizzers'– arms outstretched and on tiptoes – until we legged ourselves up. At right angles was the stone garden wall we used as a stage to play 'Miss World', during which we draped ourselves in stuff from Mum's ragbag. Elizabeth was compère and held a spoon or a drumstick for a microphone – 'And in national dress, please welcome Miss Guam' – as I set off down the wall wearing a 1940s tea-dress tied round with a tablecloth. 'Next up, in her evening frock, it's Miss Ceylon,' and Tricia tottered down the wall wearing her vest, with a 1920s shawl around her waist and bits of broken chain-belt in her hair. On one occasion we used the wall as a catwalk for a fashion show with dresses we made from old cow-feed sacks, with holes cut for heads and arms and tied up with bale twine. The sacks made a 'mini' for Elizabeth, a 'midi' for me and a 'maxi' for Tricia, and left us covered in hundreds of tiny insect bites. We sampled the cow food-pellets – finding them salty and gloopy when chewed – but tried to forget about that fifteen years later when mad cow disease was all over the papers.

Tricia beside the knicker bush, dressed as 'Miss Ceylon'

The day after Tricia died I was drawn back down the lane from Dad's to the farmhouse, by a sense of disbelief, I think – a sense heightened by the many surrounding memories. The mortuary was closed for the weekend so I had not yet visited her body and I needed evidence it had happened; to see Tricia's world without her in it, to check she was really gone.

Inside, the house smelled of stale tobacco – a smell that hit me then like a punch and still does. To me the smell of stale tobacco is the smell of anguish and hopelessness.

I stood at the door of the bathroom with its cold coffee and cigarettes on the wooden floor by the radiator. I moved about the house where I was born, a place that since yesterday had become the place Tricia had chosen to die.

In the living room I saw the lights were lit on the CD player. It was playing with the volume turned down – Tricia must have left it on a continuous loop. I squatted down to turn it up and the room filled with the pure, clear voice of Alison Krauss singing 'When You Say Nothing At All'. The suddenness knocked me over and from a squatting position I plumped sideways onto the carpet.

In the kitchen I found the bin full of her long dark hair. I stared at it; so unexpected. She must have chopped it off last thing before she died because there was nothing thrown on top. *Why* had she cut her hair off? I did not reach into the bin and rescue a lock because the sight of her lovely hair there among the teabags and the soup tins reeked of despair and I couldn't bear to touch it. Her long hair had been one of her trademarks ever since her early teens. There had been the occasional perm in the 1980s and it got shoved into a woolly hat when she was milking the cows or working with the horses, but it had never been anything other than long and dark and glossy, and now here it was tossed in the rubbish.

On the kitchen surfaces I found boxes and boxes of lotion for getting rid of hair lice. Tricia did not have hair lice; at that stage she didn't have close enough contact with anyone to catch hair lice. I examined the boxes, baffled and heartbroken because these boxes reeked of despair too.

I learned later that a symptom of psychosis can be the sensation of a crawling on the skin that is impossible to alleviate. Memories of those boxes, and knowledge of the effort it must have taken Tricia to get out of the house and buy them for a problem she believed she had, swim into my mind often and have crystallized into the very image of loneliness.

I went into her bedroom but hated to look at her bed with the sheets and quilt in a tangled heap and some of the last items of clothing she had worn discarded on the floor. Signs of activity made her seem so close and underlined how recently she had been alive, how recently we *should* have been able to save her. The finality of death and the knowledge – although still not the belief – that she had gone shocked and re-shocked me over and over again every time my eyes alighted on some other personal item: her bedside glass of water, her toothbrush, her gum shield for stopping her grinding her teeth as she slept. The air was thick. It was as though the house itself was holding its breath.

I pushed open the door of my childhood bedroom – the familiar rattle of the latch, the whoosh of the door over the old shag-pile carpet – only to discover it had become a dressing room full of beautiful clothes. Tricia had been a farmer and a horsewoman; I remembered her in jeans and jumpers and grubby jackets with bits of straw clinging to them or maybe in a boiler suit, the top pulled down and tied round her waist as she wore a T-shirt in summer. This room used to contain two single beds and an ugly chest of drawers; now it appeared to contain a wardrobe and hanging rail stuffed with posh frocks. I found it hard to take in. I walked into the room and touched the hanging clothes. I could see a black satin halter-neck covered in red and yellow orchids and a black chiffon minidress with beaded cuffs, and alongside them were linen skirts, wool coats, silk blouses, fitted jackets, piles of scarves in every shade and texture, shelves of extraordinary shoes: gold sandals, red silk sandals, purple suede peep-toes, silver wedges and sparkly stilettos.

There were other items folded in big stiff carriers with the names of local boutiques on the side and with their labels still attached along with handwritten invoices for hundreds of pounds. So this was how Tricia had been spending her inheritance from Mum. There were clutch bags, large and small, in every colour. The wardrobe was full, as was the hanging rail which stood beside a full-length tilting mirror. It was a room devoted to glamour and beauty and femininity. I knew my sister was beautiful but I had not realized she possessed all these lovely things, or that she cared so much about her physical appearance.

Over the following months Elizabeth and I picked out pieces and took them home. Tricia was taller and more willowy than us, though, and one by one most of the outfits ended up at the charity shop.

My sister had shocked me by killing herself but maybe there were many things I didn't know about her even though I had known her all her life, and almost all of mine. I had loved her. Things had been difficult as her mental health deteriorated, but I had always loved her.

All my life one gauge I used to decide if someone was acting unreasonably towards me was to ask myself: 'Would I let them treat Tricia this way?' I had always felt protective of her but in that I had clearly failed. I sat on the bed gazing in amazement at all these unfamiliar possessions – the possessions of a different woman altogether from the one I thought I knew – and I wondered: how well had I known her? How well can we ever know anyone?

As I sat in the farmhouse, dazed, the telephone engineer arrived to mend the phone. He thought the problem was a fault with an overhead wire, he said. He was standing at the back door and I told him what had happened the day before. His face became stricken and his eyes flickered over my shoulder as though drawn to witness the trauma. He picked up his enormous toolbag and headed into the garden to do the repair. An hour later he reappeared. It was all fixed, he said, but in future could we get Dad to build his enormous bonfires somewhere else. He gave me a meaningful look and cast a furtive glance towards the orchard, then mouthed the words 'or they'll charge him a fortune', and with a tap on the side of his nose he was gone. An act of kindness from the telephone man seemed enormously significant. In those first raw days I latched onto all small acts of kindness and humanity.

* * *

We buried Tricia in her dressage gear – jodhpurs, fitted dark blue jacket, white shirt with a stock around the neck – and we put her riding crop in her hand. I never saw Tricia practising dressage, even though she had been doing it for some years, because she was shy about being watched. But I knew how much pride she took in it. I knew, on a good day, how enthusiastically she'd tell you about her 'perfect trot–canters' and her 'flying changes'. My memories of Tricia riding were of the less-controlled variety. For instance, the first time she was put on the back of a friend's horse, aged six or seven, and the horse bolted down the lane. I remember the screams of the friend's mother and the panic followed by the relief when the horse was captured and led back – with Tricia still in the saddle, an enormous grin on her face.

As we prepared Tricia's outfit, Alice, a lady from the village, showed me how to tie the stock so I could explain it to the undertaker. We couldn't find Tricia's stock pin so Alice went home and brought back a gold stock pin with a little horseshoe on it which strangely looked like a symbol of good luck. Elizabeth spent hours polishing Tricia's riding boots to a glassy sheen, all the time aware that the undertaker might have to slice right up the back to get them on.

There was a line of framed photographs along Tricia's mantelpiece in the farmhouse kitchen showing her Labrador, Ted, and her old collie, Roy, alongside pictures of her long-gone mare Hattie shoving her head over the denim-blue stable door. We took these photographs, and one of Dad sitting on the old water trough with Roy smiling at his feet, and placed them around her in the coffin.

It was months before I realized that the only photograph we left behind on the mantelpiece was one of the whole family together: my mum (Margaret), dad (Stuart), Elizabeth, Tricia and me, at a family wedding smiling in our Sunday best.

Maybe in choosing the photographs of her animals to go in her coffin – as her 'grave goods' – we had unconsciously acknowledged that animals were a constant source of

Dad, Mum, Me, Tricia and Elizabeth at Cousin Mary's wedding

comfort to her and had never let her down whereas we, her family, had.

The eventual emptying of the farmhouse after Tricia died, a job we put off again and again for months, was a huge task because my grandparents, David and Marjorie, had moved into the farm in 1925 and it seemed little had been cleared out since; consequently generations of belongings had composted over the years and it felt as though we were unearthing an architectural dig. The process of untangling our past called for decision after decision which seemed to accumulate in weight as we progressed.

In fact some of the clearing *had* been done, in 2005, eight years before Tricia died, when we sold the old barns for development. At that time the great hay barn, the cowsheds, the old stables and pig pens had to be emptied of what amounted to my mother's 'overspill'. My mother was a shopper. In particular she was a shopper of wool and cloth, sewing paraphernalia and gadgets. She loved gadgets for cleaning, gadgets for cooking, gadgets for sewing and knitting. My mother had an eagle eye for advertisements featuring anything newfangled that came with an instruction book – things that made big promises about saving time and labour – and she would seek out these expensive gadgets and buy them. Her idea of a birthday outing was a drive to Lakeland Plastics in its original Lakeland home to buy more gadgets.

When it came to the clearing of the barns in 2005 we were faced with chest freezers and suitcases and cardboard boxes full of mouldy wool and bolts of cloth still with their labels attached showing the size and price – which was always startlingly high – plus baffling gadgets that had never been assembled: gadgets for cleaning windows, steaming carpets, cutting out dress patterns, assembling quilts and knitting complex designs.

Anyone would think my mother enjoyed cleaning and housework, but this was not true; in fact she despised the excessively house-proud. She liked to declare that only boring women had tidy houses. I suppose her constant purchase of gadgets for cleaning was a way to make housework more interesting, or at least put it off for a while in favour of another shopping trip. But she adored handicrafts and, after packing the farmhouse to the gunwales with cotton bobbins, buttons on cards, zips in every colour and endless dressmaking patterns, as well as the wool and cloth, she set to filling the barns and outhouses with her haberdashery as well.

In the year 2000 Mum and Dad moved out of New House Farm to a newly built dormer bungalow up the lane. Tricia was left to live alone in the farmhouse, much to her satisfaction, although she was less thrilled when she realized the house was to be left still packed with stuff because, as it turned out, although my mother had moved she still reigned supreme – now over two houses – and her possessions left behind in the farmhouse and barns (until the barns were sold) *must not be touched*. Meanwhile Mum set about filling her new house with stuff too.

My mother's mood – often low and downbeat – could be transformed by 'newness'. She was excited by technology and innovation. She bought shares in the Channel Tunnel as soon as it was possible, went to 'computer classes' before I ever did, and invested in bio-tech companies, enthusiastically telling you which diseases her investments were about to cure. She was dismissive of self-appointed gurus who advised you on how to live your life ('Huh! Who says? Experts!') but admired inventors and scientists.

She didn't like to see me hand-sewing even though I found it satisfying. When I was twelve years old I stitched a patchwork quilt and she would watch me, her hands twitching, frustrated. 'You'd do it much quicker on a machine,' she kept saying. My needle and thread flew over the quilt in a ham-fisted front to back motion, producing stitches so neat and tiny they were barely visible. 'Leave her,' said Dad. 'Let her do it if she likes it.'

When we sold the barns in 2005 we also sold the outhouse that had been used by my Grandad David – Dad's father – who we always called 'Gran'. This outhouse, known as 'Gran's Dairy', was Edwardian red-brick and had been used by Gran's wife, Marjorie, to make cheese in the 1920s and 30s. Inside it was floor to ceiling white tile with a monumental cheese press. When I was growing up in the 1970s the back room of the dairy was Gran's den and he spent every evening in there sitting in his old armchair, with his fuzzy black and white television, his wireless set, his crate of brown ale and his stack of Westerns from the mobile library.

The farm collie and next door's terrier and our half-feral cats joined him in front of his two-bar electric fire and under the halogen pig lamp that shone orange on his white hair to keep him warm. Cats draped themselves about his shoulders and perched on his head to share the warmth and he didn't

David ('Gran') and Grandma Marjorie married
and moved to New House in 1925

mind a bit. He would chew lumps of bacca he had cut off rope-like tobacco he called 'twist' with his penknife, eventually spitting the stuff out on the stone floor, like some character from the Wild West, where the dog would eat it.

Gran had retreated to his den when my mother and father married in the late 1950s. By then he had been widowed many years following Grandma Marjorie's death in childbirth. Gran lived with us almost until his death, outliving Marjorie by fifty years.

He was known to almost everyone as Gran, possibly because Elizabeth couldn't say Grandad as a toddler, although in fact no one really knew, and we didn't bat an eyelid to hear 'Gran's having a shave' or 'Gran needs more bacca' or 'Gran's checking his mowdy traps'. One of Gran's hobbies was catching moles ('mowdies'). He set vicious claws into the ground to crush the creatures as they burrowed between molehills which ruined the grass. I once discovered a mole rooting up the seedlings in a tray of baby lettuce on the back yard. My schoolfriend and I raced to save it as Gran hovered nearby shouting 'Kill it! Kill it!'

He used the same penknife for cutting bacca, paring his nails, peeling apples and setting his mowdie traps. The penknife lived in the pocket of the old coat he always wore over his ancient trousers and jacket, and which was wrapped round at the waist with a length of baling twine.

* * *

By the 1970s Gran's Dairy was lined with Marjorie's old cheese shelves which were packed with the flotsam and jetsam of his farming life: decoy ducks, empty milk bottles and rolls of wire, all coated in a thick layer of aged dust. Pushed up against them was his armchair, ingrained with grime and packed with newspapers where the springs used to be.

Bit by bit Gran's Dairy filled up with broken furniture that Mum wouldn't have in the house: legless chairs, chairless dining tables, overwound clocks and a wooden fire surround, all dating from Marjorie's day and too precious to Gran to throw away. The only things my mother seemed to want to get rid of were things that were precious to other people.

When one of the cats died on a sofa in there, another cat flattened the body and turned it into a bed before anybody noticed.

One day a barometer slid from the wall and smashed. Mercury rolled around the stone floor and we stamped on it watching it shatter and gather itself like the quicksilver it was until it finally splintered and was lost down the joins and the cracks.

Gran came into the farmhouse to sleep and to eat his meals. He would peer through the kitchen door to see what was on the table and if it had a crust or a hard skin he'd go back for his teeth. He ate everything; fat, gristle, the lot, both courses from the same plate, wiping it clean in between with a slice of bread. 'You don't know you're born,' he'd say if he caught me wrinkling my nose at the sight of custard covering traces of gravy.

Visiting children found Gran intimidating but he had a sense of humour – as dry as dust and well hidden. One time I remember hearing his rumbling chortle was when a caterpillar, boiled in its entirety, rolled out of a cauliflower floret I'd just chased round my dinner plate.

On our birthdays he gave us fifty pence. He'd root through his pockets, sorting handfuls of washers and bits of straw, until he found a silver coin which he'd look closely at then hand over with a faint chuckle. Life was tough and we'd better get used to it.

He was a veteran of the trenches at Ypres where he was shot through the shoulder. In hospital in Boulogne he learned to thank the nurses – *mercy boo coo*.

When he was an old man he said little. Aged twelve I went out to his dairy with my notebook and pencil to ask him questions for a school project about 'The Olden Days'.

'Gran, when you were little what did you do on a Sunday?'

He tamped his pipe and puffed a bit to get it going.

'Put on me fustian breeches and watched tide, 'appen.'

I wrote: 'watched tide'.

'What did you do during the war?'

He did a silent kind of a snort, thought about it a minute then put his head back.

'War … huh.'

Gran fought in the trenches at Ypres
in the First World War

As an adult when I reminisced about Gran spending time in his dairy, my dad's sister, Aunty Margaret (another one), was upset that he should be remembered thus. She recalled him during her childhood as 'a smart man' whose successful efforts to keep his family together, despite the death of his wife, were nothing short of heroic.

Not all the furniture from Marjorie's day ended up in Gran's Dairy. A mahogany glass-fronted cabinet stacked with silver tea services, dating from David and Marjorie's wedding, and with drawers full of sepia photographs, remained in the farmhouse sitting room. If we opened the drawers and asked about the people in the photographs, Mum told us: 'Shut that drawer and stop rooting.'

Years later, when we took the photographs from the drawer and tried to work out who they were, there was nobody left to ask and all we had was a sea of sepia strangers whose lives and stories were lost to the past.

Gran kept leather-bound farm diaries detailing animals that went to market, crops planted and cheese produced. On 15th May 1938, the day his wife died in childbirth, it says only 'M died' and after that there are no more entries. He found my dad who was milking the cows that day and, shaking his head, said, 'Never mind,' then with another four children to think about, including a newborn baby, he left my dad to finish the milking.

My twelve-year-old dad never went to school again. The truant officer poked his head into the barn every so often as my dad forked hay or fed the calves. 'Try to get to school today, eh?'

Eighty years later my dad keeps a postcard in his desk, addressed to 'Master Stuart Simpson', sent by his mother from hospital in Preston as she waited to give birth. The card shows a painting of a spaniel. 'Wasn't Preston lucky on Saturday. I heard it on the wireless. Hope you are doing your best for Daddy.'

He still cries when he sees it.

Also in his desk is the bill from the hospital for the maternity services his mother received. A bill issued to her husband after her death.

Grandma Marjorie was survived by her baby girl, who was also named Marjorie. As a girl, Young Marjorie was red-haired and sparky. She worked on the farm, throwing herself into everything – baking with gusto and covering herself and the kitchen with flour, chopping logs and accidentally hacking her finger-end off with the axe. She got engaged to a local undertaker called John but Young Marjorie had a digestive disorder and no one realized how serious it was until she collapsed and died. Instead of being married in

Young Marjorie, aged 21, the year she died

1959 she was buried. This was four years before I was born. She was twenty-one.

I think it was in 2005 that the Kilner jars of damsons, picked from the orchard and bottled by Young Marjorie, and that had been lining the far-pantry shelves my entire life, were finally thrown out.

It took me a long time to realize that Grandma Marjorie was so scarcely mentioned I didn't have a proper name for her and had settled on 'Dad's Mum'. Stories about her were rare not because nobody cared but because Dad and Gran cared so much. On this subject, as on so many others, we were dumbstruck.

In my lifetime the cupboard halfway up the farmhouse stairs had been painted shut with layer upon layer of thick gloss paint. As a child I pressed my eye to the keyhole, shone in a torch and saw book spines untouched for more than twenty years.

Books were my escape from a world with the wrong kind of drama in it. I hungered for stories and books to make reality fall away.

I read to find circuses, wild animals, long dresses, castles, enchanted forests and magic faraway trees. Re-entering real life after being lost in a book was painful and disorientating.

At the table I read the back of the cereal packet. I read the primary-school library over and over again. I read the set texts Elizabeth brought home from secondary school: *Animal Farm*, *White Fang*, *The Otterbury Incident*. I read the *Daily Express*. I read the *Radio Times*. When I ran out of stories I read the dictionary. I compiled my own dictionary of words I didn't understand. 'Tippet: a woman's shawl; Brougham: a horse-drawn carriage; Stucco: plaster used for decorative mouldings' reads the list, in what must have been a Georgette Heyer phase.

Until sixth-form college my reading was unguided so I read *Tender is the Night* but not *The Great Gatsby*, *Anna Karenina* but not *War and Peace*, *Lady Chatterley's Lover* but not *Women in Love*. I chose books from Garstang Library purely on covers and titles. I read the entire works of P. G. Wodehouse and Agatha Christie, fascinated by their versions of English country houses. I read everything Catherine Cookson wrote and pronounced 'whore' with a 'w'.

My mother brought back library books in the Ulverscroft Large Print series for me, knowing I wore glasses without understanding they were for distance not for reading. Producing a child who needed glasses was perturbing for my mother: 'I fell down stairs when I was expecting. I didn't make such a good job of you.' I never told her I could read small print perfectly well, because I liked getting lost in the great big words.

But my mother did give me occasional random compliments. 'Your ears lie good and flat. The back of your head is well shaped. Your eyebrows suit your face.'

I was short of books and often panicked about it, so one day I prised open the cupboard door on the stairs as the hinges made sharp cracking sounds and splinters of paint flaked off. Inside were dusty and faded hard-backed books. I inched one out and shut the door, pressing the cracked paint on the hinges back into place. The book was *Sue Barton, Senior Nurse* and was signed on the flyleaf 'Marjorie Simpson, 1956'.

I took it downstairs and sat on the hearthrug in front of the open fire. My mother said: 'What's that? It looks like rubbish.' I struggled through a few pages but there was no adventure here; it seemed to be about nothing but a nurse in trouble with 'Sister' for being on the ward with her 'slip' showing. My mother was right, it *was* rubbish. I squeezed my hand again between the painted-up doors, scraping my knuckles as I put Aunty Marjorie's book back in the past.

I have wanted to be a writer for as long as I've been able to read. I wrote my first book aged nine in a hard-backed Silvine notebook with marbled endpapers. It chronicled the adventures of 'Sandra' and 'Barbara' – two girls who apparently went everywhere (mainly to dancing lessons) on horseback and had a sworn enemy called Mr White. My best friend, Alex, and I acted out the adventures of Sandra and Barbara every day in the school playground.

My writing ambitions faltered after that because writing became embarrassing; self-indulgent and pointless, particularly after a boyfriend found something I'd written when I was a teenager and flicked through with a sneer on his face. 'What is this? What do you think you are – *a writer*?' Later I discovered he had scrawled in the margin 'This is stupid', in case I hadn't got the message.

My mother read gardening books, dressmaking books, yoga books and recipe books, but no fiction. She referred to fiction as 'made-up stuff', and asked 'why do you read *that*?'

I left school at eighteen with dismal A-level results and became a bank clerk then a civil servant, jobs taken for the sake of taking a job – because that's *what you did*. I also had to pay the mortgage I'd saddled myself with aged nineteen – because buying a house was something else *that you did*. In my mid-twenties I retrained as a journalist because that seemed an acceptable way to earn a living with words. My mother died when I was forty-two and shortly after that I began to write pieces of fiction and memoir. It took me until my first novel was published, when I was fifty-one, to realize the death of my mother and the birth of my writing were linked – that in losing my mother I had acquired the right to write my own life.

CHAPTER FIVE

After Tricia died the thought of what would be involved in clearing the farmhouse was terrifying.

A few years earlier I had viewed a house for sale in which the owner had died of a heart attack only days before and I had been appalled to see bread on the kitchen units that was still in date and the dead owner's appointments on the calendar for the following week: *Coffee with Bernard, 2 o'clock*.

Families move at different speeds. Tricia had been dead six months when Dad said, 'What about doing something wi' yon house?' and we knew we couldn't put it off any longer. At first I thought we'd get a skip, but no, Dad built another enormous bonfire in the orchard – this time away from the telephone wires – and, bit by bit, we ferried generations of possessions onto what was in effect a funeral pyre.

Not knowing what to do with many things with sentimental value, we threw them into a 'Memory Box', actually a yellow cardboard box in which my new boots had just arrived.

These were the things we saved:

Tricia's childhood jewellery: tangled silver chains, little charms and bent and twisted earrings; her drawings and paintings, watercolours of cats and dogs and horses and self-portraits; photographs of Tricia with friends we didn't know in places we didn't recognize. I studied her face, scanning her expression for signs of distress – did she want to be there? Was she enjoying herself or was she desperate to be alone, smoking? Was that a false smile? Was she suffering? Was that one of her good days or one of her bad?

We saved stacks of her notebooks and diaries that I couldn't bear to read – including the notebook that the police officer had removed along with her body. 'She wrote a lot, didn't she?' he said the following day when he returned to take down more details. Elizabeth was angry. *We* did not know what she'd written in that notebook so why should *he*? Apparently, though, the book did not shed any light on her thoughts on her last night on this earth – it did not contain a suicide note. We were allowed to have it back after the inquest, except by then it was lost. Incensed they had been so careless with her things, we asked the Coroner's Office to chase it up until the police found it and hand-delivered it to Dad's in a sealed envelope to stop him reading it and getting upset.

We saved Tricia's soft toys. How do you burn a teddy bear you remember from childhood, no matter how filthy? We saved a home-made sheep, a rock-hard badger and a gangly Pink Panther. Who made these? Nobody could remember.

It was probably Mum's mum, Grandma Mary, who took up handicrafts with a passion after her husband, Grandad Ben, died – sublimating her grief in patchwork dogs, hessian dolls and punched leather work.

We saved Tricia's one-legged Tiny Tears doll called Karen who we found naked except for a bikini drawn on in green felt pen and wrapped in Mum's old fox fur with its flat nose and glass eye. Karen and the toys were rescued from the farmhouse only to be flung on a rocking chair in a corner of Dad's house where they remain, described by my teenage daughter, Lara, as 'that pile of old weird shit'.

We saved sherry glasses – stacks of sherry glasses in styles ranging from the delicately etched of the 1930s to the clunky and chunky of the 1970s – even though we had never drunk sherry except at Christmas. Where had all these sherry glasses come from? Dead great-aunts? Grandma? No one could remember but we took to drinking Harveys Bristol Cream before supper.

I saved a page of doodles I discovered with the words 'My name is Nina, and I am brilliant and I must not forget it' written on, surrounded by trees and hearts, shoes and cats. I framed it and hung it on my daughter, Nina's, wall.

Although many items had been removed in the weeks after Tricia died, there were still plenty of things dangling in the wardrobe. I saved clothes that would never fit me and would never be worn again even if they did but that I remembered Tricia wearing, including the twenty-year-old bridesmaid's dress she wore at my wedding. We saved a flow-ery skirt that I turned into a cushion, a dress I turned into a jumper and a jumper I turned into a hat. We saved broken beads to be made into Christmas decorations. We saved her piano certificates. We saved her swimming badges, from 50 metres to bronze lifesaving, which were still attached to her red stripy swimsuit. Going to 'the baths' at Lancaster had been a big deal. The first time we went I must have been about seven and expected it to be one big claw-foot bath like we had at home. I wore a swimsuit with polystyrene floats fitted round the waist – a costume rejected by Tricia. I gazed, fascinated, at the sign NO RUNNING, PUSHING, SHOUTING, DUCKING, PETTING, BOMBING, SMOKING with its helpful cartoon illustrations and I clung to the side as Tricia set off on tiptoe, splashing across the shallow end seemingly unconcerned by water lapping at her nostrils. It was similar to the only time we went ice skating. Then I'd gripped the safety rail while Tricia's game spirit was spotted by a stranger – a middle-aged woman – who led her around the rink. By the end of a torturous hour for me they glided serenely back, side by side with crossed hands, like something off a Victorian Christmas card. Tricia was always braver than me.

Some things were easy to burn: the piles of medication in blister packs, which went straight on the bonfire, as did stacks of appointment letters from the mental-health services. We burned her last packet of fags – the pack of ten with the four missing that we found on the bathroom floor – but by then I regretted we hadn't put these with her in the coffin. Tobacco had been a good friend to Tricia.

Many things were hard to burn; for instance her socks. Cello cried as he emptied her sock drawer onto the bonfire and watched Dad stopping the balled-up socks from rolling out of the flames with his big stick.

Sometimes we got cavalier. I tossed a toilet bag into the fire without checking carefully enough what was inside, only to discover too late that it contained aerosols and sealed tubes that exploded and sent my father diving for cover behind the giant bamboo.

During the weekends of clearing, the flames burned bright throughout Saturday afternoon and if they began to flag Dad would douse them in diesel and they'd soon be ten feet high again. The bonfire would still be smouldering on Sunday morning which meant we could continue; sofas, mattresses, damp quilts and bedspreads, all the velvet curtains, carpets, lino, on they went.

It felt cleansing and became addictive; you'd find your eyes scanning a room for flammable materials. A battered screen! Dried-flower arrangements! More wool! Let's drag them out and burn them!

Once the rooms were empty we started pulling off wallpaper that hung loose and damp in places – great lengths of woodchip painted in shiny turquoise and mauve that came away bringing layers of plaster with it. We'd bang the flaking plaster with a brush until it all fell and we had at last got back to a sound surface. We wrenched off sheets of plasterboard that had been used to box in original features in the 1970s, to reveal wallpaper from the 1950s with hand-painted roses and lily of the valley.

To watch dusty, neglected, largely unloved items set alight, burn, smoulder and turn to ashes felt right. It also felt very warm and, despite it being summer when we did the clearing, the heat on my face was comforting and gazing into the heart of a fire consuming my family history was mesmerizing.

As a seven-year-old, I had watched the disposal of my Great-Great-Aunt Alice's things and been fascinated by the dismantling of a life, fascinated to see someone's life story being taken apart into its bits and pieces and each one being held up to the light, valued in some way, then kept or discarded.

There were legends about Great-Great-Aunt Alice: she was a suffragette; she founded her own bus company between Manchester and Blackpool; she was a 'man-hater' who married a much younger man only to pay for him to go to Australia and never come back. It was said she was so tight with money she reused old stamps. She was a hoarder whose bungalow was only navigable via narrow corridors between the piles of junk. She nearly killed herself by keeping warm with an electric fire placed on the bed because there was nowhere else to put it and which then set the bedding alight; and, as recalled by one uncle, 'she had a dirty parrot who shit everywhere'.

But you only heard these legends if you asked, because Great-Great-Aunt Alice had no children and so when she died she began to fade fast into history.

I have her photograph on my living-room wall in my gallery of ancestors. The picture dates from around 1914 when she was in her mid-twenties. She is wearing a high-necked Edwardian blouse and two thick gold chains with pendants of amethyst and quartz. She has a cameo brooch pinned on one side and a gold nurse's-style watch on the

Great-Great-Aunt Alice: suffragette, businesswoman and hoarder

other. Her hair is swept up into a chignon and she stares past the camera with a determined expression. She is clearly a woman who amounted to something.

When I was six or seven she was very old and dying and she came to stay for a few weeks with Grandma Mary. Mum and I went upstairs to take her a bowl of prunes on a tray. The air hung heavy in the bedroom where Great-Great-Aunt Alice was a small hump under the bobbly candlewick counterpane. Her little grey head turned as we entered.

She struggled to get her tiny shoulders up onto the pillow so she could taste the prunes in their sticky brown juice. The spoon shook in her hand and clacked against the rim of the bowl and dribbles of juice trickled down her chin. In a loud and forced-cheery voice Mum said, 'We've come to have a look at you,' which was the usual greeting in our family, but Great-Great-Aunt Alice said nothing; all her fading energy was concentrated on getting the prunes onto the spoon and up into her toothless mouth.

Being so infirm, taking so much effort to raise a spoon to your mouth, and to suck and to swallow, to not be able to talk, to want to eat prunes at all – this looked to me like somewhere between life and death, but nearer to death.

A week or two later we went to Grandma Mary's for the usual Sunday afternoon visit and Great-Great-Aunt Alice was nowhere to be seen. Instead there were Great-Great-Aunt Alice's things; boxes and boxes of shoes and handbags and petticoats, so many things that the big farmhouse kitchen was like a jumble sale. I particularly remember the petticoats in satin and silk and watching Tricia and Cousin Elaine clop past wearing one each, lifting them up like Cinderella's ball gowns as they clattered and wobbled by in Great-Great-Aunt Alice's shoes. There was a reek of mothballs.

One of my uncles held up a great pair of white bloomers and said, 'Run *them* up a flagpole and folks'll know you've surrendered,' and everybody laughed.

We poked through drawers that had been removed from chests and dressing tables, which must have been brought from Great-Great-Aunt Alice's bungalow after her death and dumped on Grandma Mary's kitchen table. They were filled with the usual stuff that accumulates in drawers: dried-out pens, purses with the odd sixpence inside, bottles gummed up with the residue of sticky yellow cologne, tickets for long-forgotten trips, postcards from long-lost friends. In the grime in the corner of one drawer an aunt found a garnet and seed-pearl ring and trilled, 'Is it finders keepers?' Grandma, who was standing at the kitchen unit slicing boiled eggs for tea with a plastic and wire contraption, didn't look round and said, 'Take what you want.'

I left with a bracelet of coloured stones and an evening bag all silky inside and infused with a lingering scent of a long-ago perfume. I was delighted to own such glamorous things, and, as both the bracelet and the bag were considered rubbish by my mother, I was at liberty to drag them around the farmyard with me until both the bag and the bracelet were broken and lost.

Many years after the disposal of my Great-Great-Aunt's things I read Mrs Gaskell's *Cranford*. In it Miss Matty burns her parents' love letters.

> 'We must burn them, I think,' said Miss Matty, looking doubtfully at me. 'No one will care for them when I am gone.' And one by one she dropped them into the middle of the fire, watching each blaze up, die out, and rise away, in faint, white, ghostly semblance, up the chimney, before she gave another to the same fate.

I ask myself now: is it possible to dispose of a person's effects with dignity?

Some months after writing this I discussed these memories with my Cousin Mary. She remembered all the stories of Great-Great-Aunt Alice; yes, she did indeed buy her husband a one-way ticket to Australia, writing 'liar, thief and all that is bad' on the back of his remaining photograph. And yes she was a suffragette and made money in stocks and shares and in business, and tried to keep warm by putting the electric fire on the bed – and she did set the bed on fire. But here my memory proved faulty. The bed-fire had in fact killed Great-Great-Aunt Alice after a short hospital stay. So who was the tiny grey-haired lady eating prunes whose stuff we had shared out? It turned out to be another unmarried, childless great-great-aunt called Annie. And this underlined for me that after death not only do we disappear and our belongings become scattered, but our stories begin to blend with the stories of others and meld and shapeshift like a flock of murmurating starlings.

A few years after Great-Great-Aunt Alice (or, as it now seems, Annie) died, my Great-Aunty Margaret died too, also leaving no children, so the contents of her seaside bungalow went up for public auction. I had moved away by then and didn't go and afterwards I asked Mum what had happened to Great-Aunty Margaret's most prized possession – her silver epergne, an elaborate candelabra centrepiece that she displayed on her sideboard, proudly telling everyone it had once belonged to Rochdale Town Hall. My mother said, 'She'd polished it so much she'd worn the silver plate off.' She shrugged. 'Somebody must have bought it, I suppose.'

Great-Aunty Margaret suffered from dementia and as it progressed she told us the same stories over and over again. The one she recounted most often was how she got up on her twelfth birthday to be told she was never returning to school and there was a job waiting for her in a Rochdale cotton mill. 'I did cry,' she repeated. 'Oh, I did cry.' She spent the last months of her life in a home. Her upright piano, and the sheet music for 'I'm Forever Blowing Bubbles' and 'I Wonder Who's Kissing Her Now', went to the home with her in the hope she would play for the other residents. On arrival she declared she had never set eyes on that piano before and it most certainly was not hers. She never touched it again.

Some of Great-Aunty Margaret's more personal effects, which in her handwritten, home-made will she had earmarked for particular old friends, were brought to our farm in a black bin liner for my mother to distribute. They included her fur three-quarter-length, her astrakhan coat and her engagement ring – a small flower set with diamonds.

My mother dumped the bag in Gran's Dairy – I don't know why, the farmhouse was big enough for umpteen bin

Great Aunty Margaret left school at 12
to work in the cotton mill

bags – and my father mistakenly, but inevitably, dragged it out for the bin men. Within days it was flung in the dustcart and that was the end of Great-Aunty Margaret's legacy. Mum and Dad made a mad dash to the council tip at Fleetwood to try to retrieve the bag of Great-Aunty Margaret's treasures but arrived to find a sea of similar black plastic bags stretching to the horizon and realized the furs and diamonds were gone for ever.

As a young woman Great-Aunty Margaret had wanted a family. There was a story that she once thought she was having a baby. She got fat. She made preparations. Unfortunately she stayed pregnant for more than nine months, at which point the phantom baby faded away.

We emptied the farmhouse over many weekends during spring and summer, 2014.

It was filthy, dusty work. I dug through the dead weight of Tricia's vinyl records and found a Roy Wood album from forty years ago and played it at full blast. 'Look Thru the Eyes of a Fool' crackled and slurred and jumped and blurred under the blunt needle and vibrated the stagnant air in the house just a little. As fire was cleansing, so was noise.

I found a load of washing Tricia had done months before still in the machine mouldy and rotting and loaded it straight into a bin bag.

I took photographs to remember the things we burned and to feel I was keeping a part of them: the fusty Disney picture books of *Cinderella* and *Bambi* and *Alice in Wonderland* from the 1970s, the disintegrating 1950s Vogue pattern for evening gloves, the handbook for a 1960s wringer, a 3d pattern for a crocheted hat that would 'only take one hour to make', hard-backed books with titles like *Ezra the Mormon* and *The Major's Candlesticks*, rotting, mildewed Sunday-school prizes signed in fading ink and in a formal script 'for Stuart, for regular attendance, 1934'. From under the stairs we dragged out half-made rag rugs from the 1950s and a romantic print of a Regency couple marked on the back 'Christmas 1908'.

Growing up surrounded by all this lingering stuff, with the past and the present and the living and the dead tangled and colliding, it's hardly surprising that as a child I looked out of my bedroom window and glimpsed Grandma Marjorie, dead since 1938, carrying a basket of washing across the back yard.

By taking photographs of what we were removing, I believed I was in some way keeping the spirit of the thing. It was unthinkable that I should forget. What if I suddenly needed to know the *exact* shade of blue of Grandma Mary's old beaded evening gown? The one she wore in the 1970s to meet the Queen. Was it sky blue or was it nearer royal blue? Or what if it was important to recall the *precise* swirling pattern on the sitting-room carpet? The carpet that was being fitted when half our feral cats climbed in the back of the fitter's van and were driven off and lost for ever.

I took photographs of Dad's mummified football boots which had hung on the garage wall for seventy years, of the view from every window, of the texture of the brickwork, the rust on the outhouse window locks, of the flaking paint on the barn door, of the weeds sprouting between the cobbles and the ivy coiling round the fence posts. Turning these story fragments and half-memories into photographs meant the past was not completely lost nor the memories obliterated. All these things were part of our lives here and might in some small way explain how that story ended as it did.

I snapped away and heard Lara whisper to Cello, 'Mum's just taken a photo of the ground.'

Me and Dad, discovering *Ezra the Mormon*
and *The Major's Candlesticks*

If things could be saved – if they weren't stinking of mould or half-eaten by moths – we sometimes packed whatever it was into a box and dumped it in Dad's garage to create a whole new problem for another day, saying to ourselves, 'Well, you never know.'

I framed a certificate I discovered in the sealed-up cupboard halfway up the stairs that still housed Aunty Marjorie's Sue Barton books, the paint on the cupboard doors finally cracking from top to bottom as I wrenched them fully open. The certificate was from the Ministry of Agriculture's '1944 Victory Churn Contest' and had been awarded to the 'farmers and farm labourers of New House Farm' for increasing the farm's milk yield by over 10 per cent during the country's 'time of need'.

I took tarnished silver spoons home to Scotland and polished them until they shone, only to let them blacken again without using them. I put the headless dressmaker's dummy, still set to Mum's exact measurements, to stand vigil in Dad's spare bedroom. I gathered stacks of photographs of unnamed, unknown people and tried to persuade aunts and cousins to identify them and take them away, largely without success. Some were marked but the markings left more questions than answers; on the back of one black and white photograph of a man in a suit and spectacles and bowler hat who looked like a bank manager, written in Grandma Mary's hand was 'Uncle Percy; cut his throat on a park bench', or another of a woman in a 1930s dress, written in an unknown hand: 'My mother.' When I asked around about 'Uncle Percy', no one seemed to know.

As Mum had not liked sharing her things, she had been equally unwilling to share information. Family anecdotes were treated like state secrets and any request for details was greeted with tight lips and a *Stop mithering* or a *What do you want to know THAT for?* Telling stories was 'gossiping', even if the people involved had been dead for a generation – which meant stacks of photographs were left untethered from their stories.

There was a white box of wedding photographs showing my mother and father on the day they married in 1959; my mother beautiful without make-up and in a home-made dress – a lace and duchesse satin creation that could have come from a couture house. A dress I was disappointed as a child to discover she had chopped up to make satin cot quilts for us as babies – a decision that I now see makes perfect sense. In the black and white wedding photographs my father is handsome in a bespoke suit and white carnation and, in some, with what must be a bright red 'L for Learner' sign pinned to his back by my mother's brothers.

As a child I would have revelled in the glamour of these photographs and listened rapt to the details of the day, but those details were never divulged by my mother who kept the pictures out of sight at the bottom of the wardrobe with stacks of wool and material on top. We'd get tantalizing glimpses of the white box but were strictly forbidden to

Mum and Dad married in 1959

'root'. And now it was too late. Now my mother's memories of the day were lost for ever. My mother wasted an opportunity to talk and to share and it still makes me mad with her, even though she has been dead ten years. What was the point of having these photographs at all if they were to be abandoned to moulder out of sight?

By contrast my father keeps the brochure for their honeymoon in his desk drawer. He takes out the small blue booklet, *Cook's Motor Coach Tour to the Sunny French and Italian Rivieras, Taking in London, Grenoble, Nice, Monte Carlo, San Remo and Paris*, at every opportunity to tell us again about the casino in Monte Carlo and the 'Paris by Night' coach tour on the way home. This must have been quite some tour in 1959; the brochure's instructions hint at the novelty of the trip: 'It is not practice for hotels to provide toilet soap and it is recommended that you take your own soap and at least one hand towel … Cameras can be taken on the Continent, and films purchased quite easily … As there may be opportunities for bathing you may wish to pack a bathing suit … Sunglasses will add to your comfort … Baths (unless you have booked a room with private bath at a supplementary charge) and afternoon teas are not included.' Torquay or, God forbid, Blackpool would not have done for my mother, but whenever Dad talked about their glamorous trip she'd respond with a dismissive wave of the hand. *Who wants to know about that?*

When we were left with only heavy furniture in the farmhouse we called a house clearance cum antique dealer who sent along a pair of rough-looking blokes called Pete and Trev. Pete and Trev pulled up outside with a van already packed, and with no apologies for being two hours late. The things we wanted them to take included the enormous bedroom suite my father's parents, David and Marjorie, had arrived with in 1925 as newly-weds. This suite was heavyset mahogany elaborately carved with leaves and flowers and smelling of camphor. There were four pieces: a wardrobe with an arched bevelled mirror, a marble-topped washstand, a dressing table and a bedside cupboard with a shelf for a chamber pot.

As Pete and Trev sauntered about the farmhouse their eyes never looked where we pointed but flickered around each room, alighting briefly on everything else. Furniture was touched, smoothed, handled, turned upside down, and pronounced upon with a shaking head. 'Brown furniture, you can hardly give it away these days,' said Pete or Trev. 'It's all IKEA now.' Pete or Trev grimaced. 'A piano? It'd cost me more to take it than to leave it. The last one – I couldn't give it away – had to get it dropped from a crane to break it up.' Cupboard doors were opened and shut; drawers were slid in and out, out and in, removed, twizzled round. 'Where are the drawers for this Georgian chest?' asked Pete or Trev. Unfortunately the answer was 'on the bonfire'. 'Where is the other table from this G Plan nest?' We looked at each other; maybe our eyes flickered to the window with the view of the bonfire. Nest? Was there *another* table as ugly as that one? Eventually Pete or Trev brought out a roll of banknotes from a trouser pocket and rapidly peeled off several. 'Three-fifty and it's off yer hands.'

There was almost a hysteria by now about finishing this task which had been generations in the making. The decisions we made were hasty and getting hastier because Elizabeth and I lived hundreds of miles apart and so we did the job in bursts at weekends. It felt at times as though we would never get to the end of it. I had the sensation of trying to free myself from a sticky cobweb that clung relentlessly, refusing to let go and entangling me further no matter how hard I grappled.

Not long after Pete or Trev paid us for the bedroom furniture we found a list of wedding presents, handwritten by Marjorie in 1925, headed up 'Walnut Bedroom Suite – given by Mother and Father'. So it was walnut not mahogany. I felt a guilty stabbing – what were we doing? – before common sense reasserted itself.

As the house became emptier and brighter it seemed physically to lighten and relax. When David and Marjorie's enormous bedroom suite was finally removed by Pete and Trev ninety years after it arrived, it was as though the house had lost its anchor or had its roots severed. The farmhouse was now empty and echoing and it seemed there was every chance that, unencumbered by our family detritus, I might return to it one day and find it had gone – that it had floated entirely away.

CHAPTER SIX

My sisters and I were born at New House Farm in the sitting room; the same room in which my dad was born thirty-eight years before me; a room otherwise only used on Christmas Day to watch films and eat Quality Street; a room that would one day have Pete and Trev strolling round it talking about pianos and cranes and brown furniture as they weighed up brass pots and pieces of china and searched for marks on the silver.

Me and Elizabeth 'helping' Dad mend a puncture around 1966

On the day I was born, Nurse Steele came with her canister of gas and air to deliver me, as she had done three years earlier when Elizabeth arrived and as she would do three years later for the birth of Tricia.

On that occasion Elizabeth and I were not told what was happening in the sitting room directly below our bedroom. We woke one morning to discover our bedroom door so firmly shut it was impossible to open. Was it locked? Were we trapped? We hammered and screamed 'Help! Help! Mummy! Mummy!' until Dad wrenched the door open. 'Sssh!' An aunt took us downstairs and gave us Chocolate Fingers and milky coffee in front of the kitchen fire to keep us quiet until we were eventually taken into the sitting room for the first sight of our new sister.

We were led through the lobby and the sitting-room door, past the grand piano, until I was on eye level with the bed that my father had brought downstairs the week before for the arrival of this baby. Mum was propped up against the pillows, smiling a little, wearing a crocheted bed jacket with satin ties. Tricia was lying on the counterpane wrapped in a white blanket. I think Mum probably decided not to be cuddling Tricia as we came in for our first look so we wouldn't be jealous.

Nurse Steele said, 'Isn't she lovely?' and I stared at this red-raw mewling thing moving in slow motion. I looked sidelong at the smiling nurse – was she laughing at me? Why was she saying it was lovely? I felt betrayed. This was not the playful, chubby-cheeked baby I had been promised – the one I could be 'good' with and share my toys with; I was doubtful it was even a baby at all. It reminded me of new kittens when you first found them in the barn in the nest; eyes shut and rooting for milk. Nurse Steele gave a tinkling laugh and I looked at the carpet.

Someone had played a dirty trick on me.

Years later Tricia claimed she could remember being born – the violence of it, the darkness, the eventual light. When I told Mum she snorted and rolled her eyes. *As if!*

She banged her *Daily Express*, with an expression like Whistler's mother, and that was the end of it. Perhaps the act of childbirth was below my mother's dignity and she didn't want anyone remembering *that*.

In our family, it seemed sitting rooms were for Christmas, for being born or for dying. This was the first room you saw, and the last.

The first dead person I saw was in 1973 when I was nine years old and I was taken to see my maternal grandad lying in an open coffin in the best sitting room of my grandparents' farmhouse. We rarely got to see the inside of this room but there was no time today to examine the upright piano or the cabinet of china ornaments – including a china cat about to kill a cowering china mouse – or the eight black and white wedding photographs of my mother and her seven siblings framed and hanging on the wall like a catalogue of wedding styles through the 1950s and 60s.

No, today the settee had been pushed back against the piano to make room for the coffin, which was shiny oak, top of the range, and resting on some kind of stand. Grandad Ben was wearing a white satin shroud and was surrounded by white satin padding. He had died of lung cancer after being ill for only two months. He had rapidly grown thinner and weaker and his cheeks had sunk but nobody had told me he was dying.

His bed had appeared unannounced and unexplained in the living room of my grandparents' farmhouse where the old sofa used to be – the one we sat on to watch *The Golden Shot* and *Randall and Hopkirk (Deceased)* on a Sunday after-noon while we ate finger rolls with mashed egg and salad cream followed by Great-Aunty Margaret's jam slice – and he had gathered ever-more bowls and containers around him to cough and spit into; but still nobody told me he was dying.

Illness was frightening; adults whispering and shaking their heads was frightening. Frustrated that he looked worse every week and puzzled when Grandma smiled a little too brightly and said, 'He did so well!' when all Grandad had done was walk to the bottom of the yard and back, I asked my mother: 'When's Grandad going to get better?' She was stirring a pan of gravy with a wooden spoon and kept her eyes on it and said, 'Maybe he won't.'

Shock trickled from the top of my head to the tips of my toes like a bucket of iced water. I had never considered there were important things grown-ups could not fix.

I wondered if my mother would ever have told me if I hadn't asked.

When he died my mother asked me and my sisters if we wanted to go and see him. Grandad was six feet tall, a strong farmer with a forceful personality, and now here he was in his coffin looking like a waxwork. We were told his body had been embalmed so he would never change. This, I understood, was because Grandad was a Very Important Person; someone his family looked up to and respected without question. Grandad was a Worshipful Master in the local lodge of the Freemasons; Grandad was a Duchy of Lancaster tenant and had been invited to meet the Queen at St James's Palace more than once; Grandad had played rugby for the Rochdale Hornets and as a young man had been sparring partner for professional boxer Jock McAvoy, known as the Rochdale Thunderbolt; Grandad was a personal friend of Gracie Fields and on the marble mantelpiece by the television was a postcard from the island of Capri to prove it, curling at the edges and a little singed from when it had drifted into the open fire, but still legibly signed 'best wishes, Gracie'. Grandad was all-knowing, all-powerful and immortal.

We edged towards the coffin. I could see Grandad's profile; it was him and yet not him. I wasn't sure that embalming was such a good idea if it meant he would look like this for ever. His hands lay white and frozen on the shiny satin shroud. They looked different; they looked very clean. A farmer's hands never look very clean, no matter how much they scrub them with globs of Swarfega. I learned years later when my own father was ill in hospital with the first of his bouts of cancer that if a farmer's hands are not ingrained with soil he is either dangerously ill or he is already dead.

My mother leaned over the coffin and kissed Grandad's cheek and I watched, horrified. I'd never seen my mother kiss anyone before, let alone a dead person.

I'd been reluctant to kiss Grandad when he was alive because he and my uncles had a habit of grabbing your face and rubbing their stubbly chins on you. This painful experience was known as a 'chin pie' and was supposed to be funny. It certainly made my uncles roar with laughter but it had made me wary. I knew on this occasion Grandad was not going to give me a chin pie but I still didn't want to kiss him.

Elizabeth, Tricia and I inched nearer the coffin, side by side, halting at a safe distance. Grandad had been a generous man who regularly went to the cash-and-carry to buy sweets in wholesale quantities for his grandchildren and handed them out like Father Christmas every Sunday, yet bellowed at me for switching on the stair light in the farmhouse to find my way to the loo because I thought the turn in the creaking stairs was haunted. Grandad was a man who read *Titbits* yet disapproved of many things including a child using the word 'pregnant' ('don't let your grandad hear you saying that word'). Grandad travelled the world with Grandma Mary, including cruising to South Africa, yet I once saw him pluck a partially sucked sweet off my cousin's jumper, say 'waste not, want not', and eat it. I had joined in games where he sat beside a doorway and tried to whack you with a rolled-up newspaper as you ran past, partly excited but mainly terrified.

'Say goodbye to your grandad,' my mother said. She started to cry. I watched, frozen.

I'd never seen my mother cry before either.

I learned when Grandad died that certain rituals follow a death; relatives gather together and speak in undertones and drink tea, but as kids my twenty-odd cousins and I had not yet learned to respect these rituals. On the Sunday after Grandad's death, but before his funeral, we played Blind Man's Buff along the farmhouse corridor like on any ordinary Sunday; except this time not only were we trying to evade the blindfolded 'blind man', we were trying not to touch the sitting-room door because it had dead-Grandad behind it. If one of the younger cousins stumbled against the door an older cousin would chant, 'You're haunted! You're haunted!' and the younger cousin would start blubbering, whereupon an aunt would poke her head out of the kitchen and hiss, 'Ssssh! Don't you know your grandad's dead?' as though there was a danger our racket would wake him up.

I wanted to go to Grandad's funeral but was told, 'No, and don't ask again.' Neither Elizabeth nor Tricia expressed any interest in going. My mother was knocked sideways by the death of her father and she probably thought she had enough on her plate without taking me. I considered this unfair – especially as this was not the first funeral I had been banned from attending.

Five years earlier, when I was four, I'd asked to go to my first funeral when Old Jack died.

Old Jack was our neighbour and looked like a manifestation of God himself – if God ever wore fustian breeches and lived in a red-brick cottage in the middle of Lancashire. He had white hair, a white moustache and a mahogany desk full of chocolate.

We took up his dinner (his midday meal) every day on the tractor the quarter of a mile from our farm. My dad drove and Elizabeth and I bounced along clinging to the tractor cab, struggling to keep the plate straight to stop the gravy and the peas from dribbling into our wellies.

We'd find him sunk in his armchair by the open fire. He wore a jacket and weskit and trousers shiny with age and of an indeterminate colour best described as 'old'. He had pockets of mint imperials and barley sugars.

He was glad to see us and would greet us with a 'How do' and creak out of his chair and root around in his antique desk to find each of us an Aero bar. The desk had shiny black knobs down each side and soft fraying leather on top and a secret drawer. Old Jack showed us how to slide out one of the knobs to open the secret drawer.

Old Jack's cottage had no running water, no electricity and no gas. It was 1968, and by then his wife had been dead more than thirty years. Old Jack had lived there on his own since his brother Old Jem died of lung cancer in 1962. Old Jem had never smoked but had spent every night huddled over the coal fire in the cottage to keep himself warm. Old Jack had had two brothers and a sister, all unmarried, who had lived with him after his wife died and who themselves then died at seven-year intervals – Agnes was the first to go in 1948. She was a woman with an 'erratic mind' who 'fizzled out somehow or other', as my father remembers it. Seven years later Bob shot himself with a 12-bore shotgun on the back cobbles of the cottage. Bob was seventy years old, newly retired and unable to face life without his job on the dykes.

My dad had been visiting Old Jack every Sunday evening since the 1940s and for years there had been games of Nap and Pontoon, with Agnes, Bob and Old Jem, playing for pennies; the oil lamp rocking on the table as they excitedly slapped down the cards.

By the time Old Jack died in 1968 we'd been delivering his meals by tractor every day for ten years and we were the closest thing he had to family.

A year or two earlier when Old Jack was well into his eighties, he'd turned up at our farm on his bike with his Last

Will and Testament shoved in his weskit pocket. He was leaving the lot to my dad and another neighbour, he said; his tiny cottage, its contents and his ten-acre meadow with his cow in it. To Elizabeth he was leaving his ebony and gold antique chiming clock, to my baby sister Tricia he was leaving his Edwardian sofa, and to me he was leaving the loveliest thing I have ever been given – the beautiful antique writing desk with the shiny black knobs and the secret drawer full of chocolate.

Old Jack died 'of old age' in his sleep when he was eighty-six and he was laid out in an open coffin in the cottage's tiny sitting room. I was four years old and wanted to go and see him.

'I want to see Old Jack.'

'No.'

'I want to see him.'

'Stop mithering.'

'What does he look like?'

'Like he's asleep. Now stop mithering.'

'Is he in bed?'

'No, he's in a coffin.'

'What's a coffin?'

(Sigh.) 'It's a box you get buried in. Now that's enough.'

'What kind of a box?'

'Oak with brass handles. It's a box that's oak with brass handles.'

I thought about this. A few years later I would learn about oak boxes with brass handles; I would see them on *The Dave Allen Show* where they were usually balanced on the cross-bars of bikes or slithering out of vans and sliding down hills chased by the vicar. But at the age of four I had never seen one and they intrigued me.

'Can I go to the funeral?'

'No.'

'Why not?'

'You're too young.'

'Why?'

'Children don't go to funerals. Don't ask again.'

'Why?'

'Ask again and you'll go to bed.'

Dad brought the antique desk from Old Jack's with the tractor and trailer. He wrapped his long arms round it and staggered into the house with his knees bent. Unlike with Great-Great-Aunt Alice's bracelet and evening bag, my mother did not consider the desk rubbish. She said, 'That desk's mahogany, it's a Davenport – put it straight in the sitting room.' That meant I'd only see it on Christmas Day or if somebody was born or if somebody died.

It was not going in my bedroom because it would get ruined. It was too good, my mother said. It was too good to get scribble gouges and felt-pen marks and cup rings on it.

The mahogany desk was going in the sitting room and that was that.

Occasionally over the years I would turn the brass knob on the sitting-room door and push the door over the thick carpet and stare at the mahogany desk wedged between the grand piano and Tricia's Edwardian sofa. It was a long way away; acres away over the swirling turquoise and gold carpet and flanked by tarnished photograph frames and piles of sheet music and china vases that I wasn't allowed to touch either. It was far, far away – much farther away than it had been in Old Jack's living room. It was not covered in scribble gouges or felt-pen marks or cup rings. It was not ruined, but its secret drawer was never opened and no one ever stroked its frayed leather top. No, the mahogany desk may not have been ruined but it was dusty and fading and empty of chocolate and so far away it was lost to me.

One way or another there seemed to be a lot of death about as we grew up – Old Jack, Great-Great-Aunt Alice, Grandad, endless farm cats, sickly piglets and occasional calves born dead, which is possibly why I was obsessed with ghost stories – tales of people coming back, people who were dead but not truly gone. I read and reread Aidan Chambers's *Ghost Stories* and *More Ghost Stories* and, when all else failed, my Sunday-school prize, *Saints by Request*.

One afternoon *Wuthering Heights* came on the television. Mum said, 'You might like this, it's a ghost story.' I watched, enraptured by Merle Oberon and Laurence Olivier. The following day Mum went specially to John Menzies in Preston and bought me the book. I was ten years old and sat on the hearthrug doggedly reading it although I did not understand many words and had to skip Joseph and his broad Yorkshire dialect altogether (even though Joseph was basically Gran). Over several evenings I immersed myself in the passion and the brutality, the obsessive revenge, the jealousy and the violence of a story about a girl called Cathy that took place largely in a Northern kitchen. Mum recalled me finishing the book, turning to the front, reading the introduction, asking 'What's incest?' (pronounced *in-kest*), getting no answer and starting the book again. This was a wild world where life and death were close to each other; where it was better to commune with somebody even if they were dead than not commune with them at all.

Elizabeth, Tricia and I attended a Church of England primary school and we regularly went to Sunday school at the village church. Sunday school mainly consisted of Mr Herbert, the vicar (or 'parson' as my father called him), reminiscing about being bombed in Coventry during the Second World War and did not seem to have much to do with God – or at least did not address the interesting questions like did God really look like Old Jack and where, exactly, was heaven.

As a child I did not think to question the existence of God and took comfort in both the idea of a Gentle Jesus

Meek and Mild Looking Upon this Little Child, and the vague notion of a heaven – which, I supposed, hovered somewhere or other full of all the dead people and animals I had ever known. At Christmas, God and Father Christmas became rolled into one – a jolly-faced old man who knew exactly what you'd been up to. The Father Christmas version of God was more worrying than normal-God because he could punish you by failing to bring the selection boxes, talc and bath-cube sets and embroidered hankies that appeared under the tree every year.

My Aunty Dorothy gave me a white King James Bible when I was confirmed aged ten which contained photographs of the Holy Land; of barren rocks, entitled *In the Wilderness*, and silhouettes in a boat upon sparkling water, called *Fishermen on the Sea of Galilee* – photographs I half-believed were taken in the time of Jesus Christ himself. There was also a 'Births, Deaths and Marriages' section for me to fill in. I was proud of my Bible and found it considerably more interesting than the Book of Common Prayer I received at the same time. I noticed there was a chapter in the Bible that was never mentioned at school or Sunday school – the Revelation of St John the Divine. I wondered if perhaps the vicar didn't want to jump ahead and spoil the end of the story.

I asked my mother what it was like when we were dead. She said, 'Ask Mr Herbert.' Mr Herbert had white hair that stood on end and waved like a dandelion clock, he wore thick black-rimmed glasses and a dog collar and his hands shook. I once met him on the way back from a trip to the grocer's. He was carrying a wicker basket in which a lone half-sized tin of spaghetti hoops in tomato sauce rolled forlornly back and forth.

Mr Herbert came to school every Friday to tell us a story from the Bible but he did not engage in casual conversation with the pupils so I did not feel able to ask him anything. Instead I made up my own idea of heaven and decided heaven was a party in the village hall. I pictured the wooden chairs lined up around the edge of the dance floor, George the disc jockey getting his records ready, unseen ladies in the kitchen cutting sandwiches, arranging slices of Battenberg cake and over-diluting orange juice, the coloured lights glowing and the disco ball throwing sparkles hither and thither as it gently rotated – just like before the annual children's WI Christmas party, in fact. But, this being heaven, it was a party only for the dead. Early doors Old Jack was there by himself but by the end of the 1970s all the empty spaces on the 'Deaths' page in my Bible were complete and the party was in full swing.

One night lying in bed in our freezing bedroom I asked Elizabeth whereabouts in the sky this heaven might be and she said, 'Guess.' I pointed up into the blackness somewhere over the milking parlour. 'Nope,' she said, pointing over the back garden towards the hen cabins, 'other way! I win! That means you've got to get out of bed to put the light out!'

* * *

As a child there were a lot of people in my world and many of them were old.

I remember the moment I realized not everyone lived a life like mine, not everyone lived on a farm or even in a village. I was three or four years old and standing on the pavement in the local town waiting for the Whit Monday parade. Crowds two or three deep waited for the marching bands, the floats covered in crêpe paper and the festival queens with their retinues from all the surrounding villages – but I faced away from the road and stared at the toy-town houses behind me. I could tell they were tiny even though my head barely reached the door handles.

These houses were not like farmhouses; their front doors opened onto a pavement not a garden path or a farmyard, they had windowsills that I – somebody who didn't even live there – could sit on, and they had windowpanes that I could press my forehead against and see right through. I stared harder. Yes, I could definitely see somebody's ornaments and their settee and their fireplace.

Everybody I knew lived on a farm, usually down a long lane, surrounded by fields and woods and ponds and a yard and a garden and an orchard. Nobody could sit on *our* windowsills or look through *our* windows at our ornaments or our settees or our fireplaces.

'Turn round,' my mother said. I didn't. I kept staring. Were these houses for old people, people who couldn't walk and who sat in armchairs all day, like Old Jack? They couldn't be for children, surely; not children like me and my sisters and my gaggle of cousins who could run as hard as we liked for as long as we liked and still not reach the neighbours.

I couldn't believe how unlucky other children were not to have their own farms. All my relations had farms and each family was known by the name of their farm: 'Sharples are here!' 'Crookhey have landed up!'

Each farm was popular for a different reason. 'Sharples' had a wood, 'Crookhey' had a pony, 'High House' had a brook, 'Hookcliffe' had a mountain, 'Throstle Nest' had a grassed-over gravel pit, 'New House' (us) had a great stone barn with the world's best rope swing and an old hen cabin filled with discarded furniture – tables and chairs riddled with woodworm, cupboards with warped doors that wouldn't open and then wouldn't shut again, an old camp bed with creaky springs, and everything coated in dust – which was the best den in the world. Farms were chock-a-block with hiding places and climbing trees and animals and it was easy to escape the adults while you created whatever world you wanted, but the people who lived in *these* houses, these tiny houses right beside the pavement, apparently all sat together in cramped little spaces, with strangers staring at them through the window.

Despite having so many cousins, my sisters and I were thrown together a lot without the company of other children. I knew I was lucky to have Tricia from very early on.

I was maybe six years old. It was dinner-time (the meal we ate at midday). We had set places at the kitchen table: Dad at the head, me and Tricia with our backs to the lumpy Artex wall, Elizabeth and Mum with their backs to the kitchen fire, Mum near the cooker, and Gran at the bottom. On this day I was upset and left the table – did I ask for permission? I don't remember – but asking for permission was considered important in our family. *Please may I leave the table?* Table manners were some of the few rules I remember my parents explicitly teaching us – presumably so other people would think we'd been brought up right.

Don't put your elbows on the table; Don't talk with your mouth full; Always put your knife and fork together when you have finished; Never lean in front of other people; Don't scrape your knife on your plate; God forbid don't lick your knife; Don't say 'God Forbid'; and always chew with your mouth closed.

I was once sent away from the table for laughing.

I can't remember what upset me on this particular day but I left my place and curled into a ball on the living-room carpet, forehead pressed to knees, crying. I heard Mum and Dad laugh and I looked up. Next to me Tricia – only a toddler at the time – had curled into an identical ball to keep me company. I sat up, my face wet and cold with tears and with bits of dust stuck to it from the carpet. Tricia sat up too and looked at me with her solemn brown eyes. I of course did not know the word 'empathy' but I thought: Tricia is here. Tricia is with me. Tricia understands. Tricia is the one who loves me.

Tricia was the most loving and lovable child, so sweet-natured it was easy to take advantage of her. She was co-operative and eager to please – not in a needy way but in a happy way.

Elizabeth and I were good at giving her orders: get this, get that, fetch this, fetch that, go for this, go for that, play this, play that, watch this, watch that. I made her play 'Schools' before she knew what a school was and had no idea about bells and desks and lessons, and stared at me baffled as I kept ringing an imaginary bell in her face expecting her to line up for playtime. I made her play 'Hospitals' when she was small enough to be crammed into the dolls' cot and be fed 'medicine' of sugar and water. She wasn't keen on the sugar and water but she wanted to play so much she went along with it. Tricia was always game – we'd realized that when she suddenly stood up and walked at nine months old.

Inevitably, as two's company and three's a crowd, Elizabeth and I fought over Tricia and, with me being younger than Elizabeth, I often lost. When all three of us played 'Houses' in the old hen cabin, Elizabeth was 'mother' in the best cabin with all the best junk furniture and Tricia was her baby while I got to live in the rubbish cabin (the cabin next door filled with logs and chicken wire) and be the nasty neighbour, Mrs Crab-Apple.

Me, Elizabeth and Tricia, centre front, at the
WI Christmas party – my idea of heaven

I liked to get Tricia to myself and on Tuesday evenings,
when Elizabeth went off in the car with Mum for her piano
lesson, Tricia and I had our own game to play: 'Hiding from
the Germans'. This entailed dashing around the farm from
one hiding place or vantage point to another – from among
the hay bales in the loft to the back of Gran's Dairy, from
behind the dog kennel (a metal barrel on its side) to the top
of the great stone cheese presses in the farmyard we sprinted
here and there, flinging ourselves onto our bellies, 'Ssssh!
Keep your head down. Keep quiet!' as we tried to evade

capture and spot the enemy before they spotted us. As a rule we were not a film-watching family and nobody bar Mr Herbert, the vicar, talked about the war (although this was only twenty-five years after the end of the Second World War) so I can only think this game stemmed from watching *The Guns of Navarone* or *The Great Escape* or something similar in the sitting room with Uncle George one Christmas Day.

The farm provided great reading hideaways – up trees, on roofs, inside a stack of straw bales with a torch, where I'd read and itch and sneeze. I enjoyed finding a hidden place to escape into a book. Unseen among the branches of a tree or high up on a building I'd watch and think and feel safe. I always knew if Dad or Gran were near by the rattle of buckets.

At other times I'd lie on the back lawn staring into the sky at the white vapour trails from Manchester Airport. Sometimes the longing to be on board a flight was so strong it was an out-of-body experience. It didn't matter where it was going, anywhere was better than here. Second only to flying away was the dream of a road trip. I watched wagon drivers jealously when they visited the farm, imagining the freedom of the road. Sometimes they'd turn up with a girl-friend slumped in the passenger seat looking bored, chewing gum with her bare feet up on the dashboard among the toffee wrappers and under the rabbit's foot dangling from the rear-view mirror, and I'd know those girls were truly blessed.

Freedom for me meant wearing no shoes. My sisters and I were never bothered by dirt and as we ran about the farm I never wore shoes, just socks, and I could leap from one dry patch to another, from one clean, flat stone to the next, avoiding mucky puddles and nettles and sharp stones. For many years I half-believed I could fly, just a little, if I willed it hard enough. That is the sort of thing I told Tricia; that I could fly and that she could too if she tried hard enough; if she ran fast enough and didn't breathe and only touched the ground with her very tippy toes she would fly. I can see her face now as she drank it in, solemn-eyed, amazed but believing it, believing every word I said.

CHAPTER SEVEN

Until Tricia was seven she slept in a little alcove in my parents'
bedroom – the farmhouse had four bedrooms but with Gran
using one and the roof leaking in another we were short of
space. Unfortunately for her there was a small passageway
leading to her bedroom with a bolt on the outside of the
door and Elizabeth and I sometimes took it upon ourselves
to lock her in when she was supposed to be in bed but didn't
want to go. I remember hearing her crying behind the bolted
door begging to be let out as Mum and Dad watched television oblivious downstairs – or in Dad's case slept in front of
the television. I remember Elizabeth bending and putting
her mouth to the keyhole and hissing 'go to bed' while I
leaned against the spindles at the top of the stairs.

It is memories like this that haunt me still, years later,
now she is gone. I wish I could not still hear her crying to be
let out from behind the locked door. I would do anything to
change that memory and I try to replace it with a better one.

This better memory is of me and Tricia climbing into the
same bed – my bed. Mum shouts from downstairs, 'Are you
in bed?' And we hold hands and reply 'yes!' without letting

on we're in the same single bed. We giggle and snuggle down in the dark, happy that we are warm and together and, in our minds, getting away with something. My mother must discover her there when she comes to bed because when I wake up in the morning Tricia is always gone.

Our bolting of the door to try to get Tricia to stay in bed probably isn't surprising considering the methods my mother used. She bought a sheet of plywood to put up at the window of our bedroom every summer evening to make it dark – her version of shutters, I suppose – but Elizabeth and I did not appreciate this brown monstrosity and propped it against the tallboy and slid down it until it snapped in two.

The tallboy was ugly as well. It had drawers crammed with material, never used, that burst out if you slid open the drawers and was impossible to shove back in without skinning your knuckles. This tallboy was a far cry from my Cousin Angela's kidney-shaped dressing table that wore a pleated skirt of white and pink roses. My cousin had pink walls to match and a pink bedspread. My cousin was pink. I was not pink. I longed to be pink.

Mum also removed the light bulb from our bedroom so we couldn't keep putting the light on, until one day when I was six years old and Grandma Mary asked me what I wanted for Christmas. In all innocence I told her I was writing to Father Christmas for a light bulb. 'Poor lass,' she said and within a day or two the light bulb had reappeared.

* * *

Tricia had an affinity with animals. As a child she slid off café chairs in search of dogs on leads and cried because the Blackpool donkeys looked sad. We had a dentist with slicked-back hair and a smirk who crept about in brown suede shoes and was known as 'the butcher', but she agreed to go for check-ups so she could watch his tropical fish flit around their glass cube.

She loved horses and read over and over the 'Silver Brumby' books and *My Friend Flicka*, and never missed an episode of *Follyfoot* and *The White Horses*. We spent our early childhood 'cantering' round the farmyard on imaginary ponies, making clip-clopping and neighing noises while reining them in with imaginary reins. Inspired by Harvey Smith and the Horse of the Year Show, we built 'show-jumping courses' round the back lawn from mops and buckets and old crates and bits of fence post, and timed ourselves by counting out loud as we jumped over them on our imaginary ponies. We begged for a real pony until my parents bought us sturdy, stubborn Skiffle – a Welsh cob who bossed us from the moment he arrived.

We never had jobs to do on the farm – there was a strict demarcation of labour, with my mother ruling the house and garden, and Dad and Gran being in charge of the animals and fields. Our duties were to stop mithering, keep quiet, go to school and not show anyone up. The exception was that we had to bottle three or four pints of milk a night, straight from the enormous milk tank in the milking parlour,

Me and Tricia with Skiffle, who bossed us
from the moment he arrived

using a little jug to pour the frothy milk into glass bottles, fix the silver tops on and then deliver them in a wire rack to the old folks in the cottages up the road. We hated this job. It was cold and, in winter, dark. We used a flashlight with a flickering beam to point our way up the pitch-black lane between the high hedges to the cottages, which if it hadn't been dark were so close they would have been in view from the farmhouse.

But having Skiffle could change this – surely it would be fun to deliver the bottles of milk up the road on horseback. We would practically be cowboys! So on his first day with us seven-year-old Tricia mounted Skiffle only to have the rattle of bottles in the metal carrier startle him and cause him to bolt. He thundered up the farmyard, hooves drumming, skidding into the corner of Gran's Dairy, scraping the skin off his shoulder and tossing Tricia into the air milliseconds before she was due to get her head ripped off by the washing line, as Dad ran behind yelling, 'Drop the milk! Drop it!' She crashed to the ground, amid smashed glass and spilt milk and shattered her forearm. Tricia did not consider this any sort of setback to her riding career and the next day she was back in the saddle with her plaster cast on – and we were back walking up the road with the milk.

Riding lessons and cycling proficiency tests were unknown to our parents. Health and safety stretched to telling us to steer clear of the ponds because Ginny Green-teeth lived in there and would drag us in and eat us.

Without an ounce of road sense between us, and only one protective hat, Elizabeth, Tricia and I would set off round the village lanes with one horse, two dogs (including next door's) and two bikes with no brakes. We'd ride as close as possible to the high hedgerows, trying not to land in the ditch, as cattle wagons and tractors roared past.

When it was my turn to ride the horse I gripped onto the saddle for grim death as it slid about because Skiffle had got the better of us again – he would push his belly out and hold his breath when we saddled him up as we struggled to tighten the girth until we thought we'd got it as tight as it would go then as soon as we got on he'd let his breath out so the saddle went loose. He ambled at his own speed, stopping for a mouthful of grass verge whenever he felt like it, tugging on the bridle and dragging the rider half over his head, as we all kept up a never-ending chorus of 'I was Born Under a Wandering Star'.

We taught the horse bad habits and he taught us bad habits. We only realized he was terrified of combine harvesters when we met one in the lane and after failing to jump a field gate he collapsed in a heap of jelly on the roadside, rider still clinging on.

One day we got wind of a 'horse show' in a neighbouring village. We had never been to such a thing, but after all, we had a horse, so off we went, unsupervised. We arrived to find a field of groomed, polished and plaited ponies among lorries and horseboxes festooned in rosettes. The other riders were wearing jodhpurs, jackets, hats and boots and standing about in groups that looked like they'd wandered off Robert Robinson's *Ask the Family*. Skiffle, having more sense than the three of us, stood at the field gate and flatly refused to go in. We pushed, we pulled, we begged and pleaded as our dogs, tails up, sensing sport, wove between his legs. There was no budging him. Faces turned and gazed at this motley gang of kids in jeans and T-shirts and pumps, with unrestrained dogs and a shaggy, stamping pony. We decided to go home.

We smuggled farm cats through the window into our bedroom every night. My mother did not believe in having animals in the house.

Working animals could be companions, particularly to Gran sitting in his dairy every evening in his armchair covered in cats and with dogs nestling at his feet, but animals as 'pets' or animals being pampered in any way was seen as risible. Grandad Ben's sister, Aunty Annie, lived in a bungalow by the sea with a brown poodle called Coco who had his hair clipped into pom-poms and the mere mention of the animal's name was enough to make everybody laugh.

For my mother it was clear: animals made work. She wasn't an animal-lover so for her there was no payback in having them shedding hair or giving birth to litters of kittens within her four walls. When this inevitably happened and our black and white cat, Minstrel, had three kittens in the corner of our bedroom overnight my mother insisted they be removed immediately. I begged for them to stay. They looked so cosy curled up on the carpet in a closed-eyed heap but Mum ordered Dad to take them away. I sneaked into the barn and brought them back. I took a day off school, saying I felt sick, to try to look after them. Through my bedroom floorboards I heard Mum shouting to Dad, 'She's not poorly! There's nothing wrong with her! It's just them kittens!' They were taken away again and the mother cat rejected them and they all died.

There must have been a better solution, surely *anything* would have been a better solution than letting all the kittens die, but this incident sums up childhood on a 1970s farm – or at least *our* childhood on a 1970s farm; namely that you didn't get sentimental about animals; animals fitted in with humans not the other way round; my mother always got her own way; and as a child you had no power or control over anything.

The farm cats drank creamy milk in the milking parlour – there was usually a circle of cats' bottoms sticking up around the rim of a bucket as they clung on getting first go at the cream, before the calves. But the cats were thin and always hungry. They got scraps from the house and sometimes they had clambered up to Gran's chest – clawing up his breeches and weskit – before he got the chance to drop a piece of dangling bacon rind. My sisters and I mixed bread with milk to make a porridge for them but they weren't very interested. I remember feeling so helpless about the cats and anxiously wishing we were allowed to care for them properly.

Sows gave birth to litters of piglets while they were chained in farrowing crates where they spent their lives. There was always a runt of the litter, in danger of getting laid on and squashed. We'd take them out and call them 'Jonathan' – maybe because my mother said if she'd had a boy he would have been called Jonathan. We'd put them in dresses and wheel them round the farmyard in the toy pram along with the broken dolls, which were all armless, legless and shaven-headed with one or both eyes pushed in. If the piglets died they went hard but if we left it a while the stiffness wore off and we could carry on playing with them.

The only animals my mother was fond of were the cows because they gave us our living. When the cows calved, their calves were taken from them after a few hours to be raised separately. I remember driving past the cow pen by the yard gate and seeing the mother cow's sad eyes looking between the slats as she continually shouted for her lost calf. 'What's the matter with her?' I asked. My mother's face flickered. 'She'll soon forget,' she said.

Keeping the rat population down was necessary on the farm but it was another brutal business. When Dad realized there were rats living near one of the pig pens, my sisters and I hung around watching as next door's terrier, Whiskey, was sent down the rat hole to kill the mother. Whiskey dragged her out and shook her, breaking her neck. The nest was then exposed with spades and Norman, our farmworker, stamped with his hobnailed boots on the pale-pink writhing babies, their eyes still unopened, until they were dead.

Encountering this type of cruelty did not harden me but made me increasingly sensitive to animal suffering. Our old collie, Jill, died when I was nine years old and I sat with her on my own on a pile of straw in the pig pen, crying as she faded away. Gran came out as she died and leaned over us, shaking his head, and said, 'She's at' far end.' Dogs and cats got old and they died – there was no talk of taking them to the vet – although the vet often visited the farm to look after the cows because there was money at stake there. But with small animals it was different, and after they died their bodies were taken to the knacker's yard if they were a dog or thrown on the midden for the foxes to eat if they were a cat.

A trip to dispose of a dead animal was unforgettable and yet routine. Calves which were born dead were loaded into the Land Rover and taken to the knacker's yard – a place you could smell before you could see. Men worked there who my sisters and I looked at with suspicion as though they were personally responsible for the piles of carcasses and body parts strewn about and the indescribable stench. Dad used to tell us about 'Fred the Dead' who drove the knacker wagon which went round farms picking up the bigger dead animals. Again you could smell the truck before you could see it. Fred was never expected to wait in line at the fish and chip shop at the end of the day. His order was put together as soon as his van came into view and passed in a hand-to-hand chain out of the door so he could be making haste as soon as possible. Dad remarked that he lived alone in a caravan and, funny, but he never married.

There are relatively few photographs of us as kids because my mother was not interested in photography. Anyway, being able to find the camera, camera batteries and a film all at once must have seemed more trouble than it was worth. There is one picture I find compelling. Why did my mother take it? What made her immortalize this moment rather than any other? It is 1970. I am standing in our farmyard. I have skinny legs and I am wearing a home-made pinafore in pink corduroy. My hair is tied up with a big red ribbon. I look clean because I've just got home from school. Behind me is the great stone barn and in my hand is a dead duckling, which is yellow and dirty and stiff.

I am trying to cover my face but you can see I am crying.

Tricia stands beside me and gazes into the camera. She is only three and is filthy, having trailed round the farm all day with Dad. Her blue patterned dress and red cardi are smeared with dirt. So is her face. It looks like my mother has cut her hair – possibly with the aid of a bowl.

I have fished out the duckling from the mud between the cobbles to save it but it is too late. Ducks are bad mothers. They traipse about the farm with a line of ducklings racing to keep up behind them as one by one they get picked off by the dog or stuck in the mud and abandoned.

I remember the moment after the photo was taken Dad came out of the barn carrying two buckets. Dad was always carrying buckets; big metal buckets full of milk or food-pellets or water, buckets that crashed when he put them down and with handles that clattered – a noise that rang right round the farmyard and into the house.

My dad carried lots of buckets; that's why his arms were so long. He said he was goalie at school because he had the longest arms in the village.

He put his buckets down, took his cap off and wiped his head with it round and round – a sure sign he was agitated – then put it back on, nudging it back and forth, back and forth, trying to get it comfy.

'Don't bother about that,' he said, nodding at the duck-ling, and he laughed a bit and shook his head. 'It's only a duck. There's plenty more where that came from.'

It wasn't only my parents who had a hard-line attitude to animals. In the front sitting room of my grandparents' house – in the room where we would later view Grandad Ben's body – there was a boarded-up fireplace hidden by an embroidered screen. A bird once flew down the chimney and we could hear it trapped, fluttering in the dark, unable to escape. Grandma Mary said she was waiting for Grandad, who would remove the wooden panelling and rescue the bird when he finished milking, but when he came inside he sat at the great oilcloth-covered kitchen table and stirred his strong tea and ate his roast beef and pickle and buttered bread and when we mentioned the bird fluttering in the dark he acted like he hadn't heard. Grandma turned back to her plastic pail of peeled potatoes and got to work peeling some more, her fingers red-raw in the freezing water. I wondered why Grandma did not insist. Could she not raise her voice against Grandad? It looked like Grandad laid the law down and yet Grandma loved him very much.

Did Grandad ever rescue the bird? I don't know. I was taken home and not told.

My grandparents, Mary and Ben, met each other when Mary was seventeen years old, delivering milk with a horse and cart in Rochdale. It was icy and she got her cart wheel stuck in the tram track as the horse's hooves slipped and slithered on the cobbles. Ben offered to rescue her to which she replied, 'I can manage, thank you.' Within months they were married and a few months after that my mother was born – the first of eight children over thirteen years.

Mary had been raised by her grandmother following scandalous court proceedings involving Mary's parents, Amy and Spencer Holt, which were reported over an entire broadsheet page of the *Rochdale Observer* in July 1923. ROCHDALE DIVORCE CASE REMARKABLE EVIDENCE said the headline, with subheadings also screaming in capital letters 'Struck With a Horseshoe' and 'Allegations and Denials'. Spencer sued Amy for divorce and custody of eight-year-old Mary because Amy had given birth to Mary's illegitimate half-sister Peggy while Spencer was in Canada, having abandoned her, their child and their farm for another woman. Spencer denied being an alcoholic; he denied being in Strangeways Gaol Hospital three times with DTs; he denied a string of eyewitness accounts that he beat Amy, kicked her, tore her clothes off, stole her money and threatened to murder her; he denied being constantly drunk and so filthy he was verminous; he denied attacking her when she woke him from a drunken stupor to help get the hay in until she was forced to defend herself by hitting him with a horseshoe; he denied leaving all the farmwork to her, even when she was pregnant, and only returning home to sell another cow and take the money; he denied his wife 'lived a life of hell'. But ultimately it did not matter that he denied it all because His

Lordship, the judge, said that even if all allegations against Spencer were true, 'the misconduct of the husband had nothing to do with the misconduct of his wife' before concluding that Spencer was entitled to his divorce and custody of Mary, on the grounds of Amy's adultery. Mary was immediately removed from Amy's care and handed over to her grandmother.

Spencer had had the benefit of an expensive private education at Rossall on the Fylde coast – I have what I assume is his school photograph in which he looks like a prig in knee breeches and a shirt with a starched white Peter Pan collar. He had plans to be a vet but he abandoned his veterinary studies and became a drunk and a gambler, a wife-beater and a wastrel which Mary's husband, Ben, most

Amy and Spencer: at whose hands she lived 'a life of hell'

certainly was not. Mary said she had never had a proper home until Ben gave her one. On the back of photographs of her and Grandad Ben, Mary always labelled them 'Us two'.

In my early forties I started looking into my family history; trying to work out where I'd come from; who we were; who I was. I asked my mother for the copy of the *Rochdale Observer* report which I knew she had. She refused. 'I *knew* these people,' was her opaque yet emphatic response. I was infuriated. What right did she have to keep this information from me? I tried reasoning with her – her grandparents had been dead more than fifty years, no one was judging her grandmother now; by today's standards Amy had suffered a terrible injustice. Mum would not listen and

Grandad Ben and Grandma Mary – 'Us Two': a love match

retreated behind the *Daily Mail* to indicate that the subject was *closed*.

I felt like ripping the stupid newspaper away but of course I didn't. I gazed at the wall of newsprint, impotently seething. It crossed my mind that sometime over the previous few years Mum had stopped reading the *Daily Express* and instead started buying the *Daily Mail*. I don't know what the *Daily Express* had done to offend her but it must have been bad because, despite having read it for forty years, she never bought it again.

After she died I found the *Rochdale Observer* report among her chaotic papers; share certificates mixed up with computer coursework, solicitors' letters with shopping lists written on the backs of old birthday cards in bold cursive script (*yoghurt, broccoli, mole traps, flour, penicillin, fuse wire*).

The details were even more shocking than I remembered overhearing in a conversation at Grandma Mary's years before, but I suspected the real reason she had kept it to herself was because she hadn't had a clue where it was.

Grandma Mary always referred to the farmers – her husband and five sons and three sons-in-law – as 'the men'. *The men'll be in. We'll have to get back for the men.* Great store was set by having a hearty meal ready for 'the men' at the end of the day when they came in often cold and wet and tired out and bringing a great rush of freezing air with them. Regardless of whether we were out on our annual day trip to Fleetwood Sands, where Elizabeth remembers splashing in the sea as 'jobbies' floated past, or further down the coast towards Blackpool wading in the public paddling pool in Jubilee Gardens, Cleveleys, or shopping for yet more cloth and wool on Preston Market, or wherever we were, the aunts and Grandma always had one eye on the clock in order to get home for 'the men'. Sometimes a meal was 'left for the men'. 'Have you left something for the men?' 'Yes, I've left some beef for the men.' This would be cold meat plated up beside beetroot or pickles in a bowl with a stack of sliced bread and butter, with home-made cake or fruit pie for after with a cup of stewed tea. But this kind of cold offering was seen as a 'poor do' for the men who had been working outside all day and 'leaving something for the men' only happened once in a blue moon.

We were occasionally left at Grandma Mary's while Mum went to sing in a music festival; many of the local towns had such annual events. Mum had a wonderful contralto voice – not unlike Kathleen Ferrier, a near-contemporary of hers who was also from a Northern mill town – and she attended weekly singing lessons and, despite suffering from terrible stage fright, would often win the festival trophy. At times the sideboard at New House Farm was covered in cups and medals from music festivals at Blackpool, Freckleton, Colne, Skipton and many other local towns.

Mum at her boudoir grand piano, a 21st birthday present, 1953

Mum had sung professionally before she got married, doing a season of *Aladdin*, backing Ken Dodd, at the Palace Theatre, Manchester. It was 1958 and after one performance the theatre manager came on stage to announce that the Busby Babes had crashed on take-off at Munich Airport, leaving many of the Manchester United team dead.

She kept a photograph of herself in her dressing-table drawer in which she looked beautiful in her stage costume, a silver dress nipped in at the waist, alongside an embroidered sewing case, an end-of-season gift from Ken Dodd. She decided the theatre was not for her when she discovered the dressing room splattered in blood because another member of the company had aborted her baby in there. She said little about it except that the men in the theatre were *different*, by which I took it she meant gay. There was talk of her getting an Equity Card, somebody suggested she audition for the Bluebell Girls, but she didn't follow these things up, returning to her father's farm and marriage to Dad a year later.

Grandad Ben offered to set her up in a dressmaker's shop because she was a talented seamstress but she turned that down too, saying she was needed on the farm.

Singing classical music remained the love of Mum's life and she practised most evenings on the black boudoir grand piano in the room below our bedroom. She sang Handel and Berlioz and Brahms in English and in German and we liked listening to her as we fell asleep. Our favourite was Gluck: 'What is life to me without you? What is life if thou art dead?'

When I hear that piece now it stops the breath in my throat and I'm whisked back, lying in the dusty bedroom in

Mum on stage with Ken Dodd, Palace Theatre, Manchester 1958

the dark listening to my mother's singing muffled and float-ing up through the gaps in the floorboards.

As we got older it became embarrassing when friends rang up – the telephone was in the lobby outside the piano room – and they would ask: 'Can't you turn your mother down a bit?'

But as little children we were excited by her singing success – for a start it put her in a good mood – and she let us touch her gold, silver or bronze medals in their little plas-tic pouches. It was like she'd won the Olympics. These were the days of Olga Korbut and we were dazzled by such things.

If she was doing well at the local music festival, winning her classes and going on to the finals, she would be late home and when 'the men' came in from milking at Grandma Mary's and found us still there they'd say, in words that make me wince now, 'Where's your mum? Has she run off with a big black man?' and roar with laughter.

Holidays as a family were rare events. There were eighty cows to milk twice a day and dozens of pigs and calves to be fed and watered. The only time I ever cried with joy was when my parents bought a caravan. I was nine years old and thought that now we might go on holiday and be normal. I knew by this time that not all families lived on farms but that even some of the ones who did went away for a day or two now and then to exotic-sounding places like Torquay or Tintagel, or to holiday camps or caravans at less exotic-sounding places like Minehead or Prestatyn. Only the lucky few (in fact no one but the local publican and his family) flew off to somewhere called Tenerife and learned to swim in jewel-blue pools, and came back with their portraits drawn in caricature, and suntans which didn't only cover their faces and lower arms, like a farmer's tan did.

When the caravan arrived my sisters and I waited on tenterhooks. Would Dad take the car to Mitchell's and get a tow bar fitted or would having no tow bar be an excuse to stay at home and watch the shiny new caravan, with its gold brocade sofa and tiny silver sink, rot in the farmyard?

'I'll see,' was all he'd say.

Buying a caravan had been my mother's idea. The whole project had my mother written all over it because she liked to spend a lot of money and make out she was saving it.

Gran was outraged. His only trip away from the farm had been to fight in the trenches in Ypres in the First World War. He cornered me in the workshop where I was risking my finger-ends playing with Dad's four-foot rusty vice and, nodding at the caravan, he whispered, 'How much was *that*?'

I knew exactly how much because I'd sat silently praying, praying they'd buy it as Mum and Dad negotiated with the salesman. 'Six hundred pounds,' I said, and Gran's eyes bulged and he spat out his bacca. It was 1972 and that sort of money could have got us a B&B in Blackpool, lock, stock and barrel, although Gran wouldn't have approved of that either and Mum would rather have *died*.

After a nail-biting wait the tow bar was fitted and we set off with great towing mirrors sticking out the sides of the car, presumably so Dad could check on the stream of cursing drivers stretching behind as far as the eye could see.

We left Lancashire and headed to Scotland, which was exciting and also worrying because it was the first time I'd ever been abroad and Elizabeth said they spoke different there. She said they'd know straight off we were foreign. Definite.

We kept up a steady thirty down the lanes and fifty on the A roads with Dad 'hedge-top farming' – straining to see over the hedges to find out which farmers had mown yet, which had silaged and which had baled.

'That lorry driver's waving,' said Tricia.

'No he's not, he's finger swearing,' said Elizabeth.

We watched with interest and practised.

Are we there yet? No. We were in a big tangled city where the flyovers had views onto buildings too enormous and scary for people to live in, surely? There were no trees. Nothing grew here. It looked brown and dead. 'That's the Gorbals,' said my mother. Maybe it was, maybe it wasn't; maybe my mother thought any run-down bit of Glasgow was the Gorbals. I don't know.

We got to Loch Ness and went for a paddle. My mother paddled with her nylons and shoes on and then tied her tights to the silver lady on the front of the Austin Princess to dry. She bought a tea towel with Highland cattle on to dry our feet but it didn't absorb the water. Her tights flapped and twisted in the breeze as we drove on.

That night we stayed at a caravan park called 'The Battlefield' at Inveraray. I never thought to ask which battle. It seemed natural that places were battlefields because as far as I could see there were always folk battling about something wherever you were. I thought getting married was something you *had* to do as an adult whether you liked it or not. It appeared to me that grown-ups were shackled together to annoy and resent each other; that they were often paired with someone to whom they were fundamentally unsuited. Such was the random nature of married couples. I believed getting married was the price you paid for growing up and some were lucky in this particular battleground while others, it seemed, were not. The unlucky ones fought a largely wordless war which was slugged out around the kitchen table, in front of the fire or on long journeys in the car. Salvos included letting the fire go out on a cold day; changing the television channel without asking; tutting; eye-rolling; slamming doors; pretending to be asleep or staring at the television wordless and grim-faced whilst drowning out the volume by rattling the *Daily Express*.

But for supper at The Battlefield that night there was a ceasefire and we had tinned meat, tinned new potatoes and tinned peas followed by tinned peaches. It was delicious because we cooked it on a one-ring gas stove and ate it on a fold-down table that turned into Mum and Dad's bed.

As the sun sank the midges came out. They ignored me but I watched everyone else scratching their scalps and rubbing their shins. In the morning my mother wiped the windowsill with a white cloth that turned black and muttered, 'I've never seen owt like it.'

We headed down the Mull of Kintyre to visit Grandma Mary's sister, Great-Aunty Peggy, and her husband, Great-Uncle Tom. My mother said not to tell them we were coming so they couldn't make a fuss. When we got there Uncle Tom was fast asleep after his night shift at the bakery and Aunty Peggy was on day shift. When she got home she made our teas. My mum said Aunty Peggy and Uncle Tom looked tired out.

Aunty Peggy was like Mrs Bun the Baker: small and very fat with red hair piled high on top. She said she was fat because the whipped cream and the custard soaked through her finger-ends at the bakery. My mother rolled her eyes and said Aunty Peggy was a romancer. My mother despised the desire to tell a story. Aunty Peggy said they called her 'the English yin' and she wasn't allowed to plant orange flowers in her front garden because some folks round there didn't like orange and they'd get dug up. My mother wasn't in the know about Scotland's sectarian past and she rolled her eyes again: the things Aunty Peggy came out with.

We went for a walk to the harbour. A boat had come in and tubs of fish were being unloaded on the quayside. The local kids were running about. Right in front of me, a girl my age grabbed a flapping fish by the tail and smashed its head against a bollard. Once. Twice. She laughed in my face and I can't remember if it was her or the fish that had rows of little sharp teeth. Dad shook his head, part impressed, part not. 'She's done that afore,' he said.

The next day, heading home, we found a farming museum – a recreation of a country village in times past – which I later described in my school diary as 'a right old village, falling to bits'. It seems at nine years old I had adopted my mother's downbeat tone. Driving through Ayrshire, we spotted Robbie Burns's cottage. 'We'll have a look,' my mother said, 'because he used to be a farmer, you know.' She never mentioned he also wrote a few poems.

We stopped at a hotel for a meal. Mum and Dad ate plates of ham and eggs and chips and ordered us a platter of sandwiches. The sandwiches had no fillings. They were only bread and butter. Elizabeth, Tricia and I searched fruitlessly for a bit of chicken or beef but no, these must be Scottish butties, we thought – this must be how they made them up here – so we said nothing and munched dejectedly. As we finished, the cook dashed out of the kitchen in her overall: 'You've got the wrong plate!'

We headed home, disappointed because Dad said no, he wouldn't drive up and down the A6 to get the holiday mileage over a thousand.

Parents didn't have a clue about fun.

* * *

Days out were so rare I remember them individually.

When I was three years old, Elizabeth and I went with Dad in a borrowed cattle wagon to deliver a cow fifty miles to Great-Aunty Margaret and Great-Uncle Bill's butcher's shop in Rochdale. There was a little window between the front seats and the body of the wagon. I peered through. The cow's eyes peered back, enormous, shining, long-lashed. I knew she was normally with her friends and now she wasn't. We looked at each other for a few moments before we set off. When we arrived the cow disappeared behind the building to the abattoir and Great-Aunty Margaret took me and Elizabeth into the back shop for a plate of roast beef and gravy. Forty-five years later, when I started writing, one of the first stories I got published was about a hitch-hiker who frees a cow from a cattle wagon before it reaches the abattoir.

We once went to Louis Tussauds on Blackpool promenade. My mother declared the place 'nowt but rubbish' and I'm surprised she agreed to set off in the first place. We wandered round the effigies of Cilla Black and Mike Yarwood and edged past the terrifying wizened waxwork of Madame Tussaud herself but Mum finally drew the line at the Chamber of Horrors and refused to set foot in it. Dad said it would be all right – he'd been in there on a choir trip thirty years ago.

Inside, my sisters, Dad and I gazed at waxworks of Bluebeard with his dead wives dangling from hooks, and Dr Crippen burying his wife in the cellar; of medieval torture on the breaking wheel and witches drowning on ducking stools. One tableau was 'After the Dinner Party' and showed a man in a tuxedo weeping next to a car crash containing his wife's body sprawled in her evening dress with blood splattered across her face which was wide-eyed and staring. 'That's what happens when you drive too fast,' said Dad. In the medical section we saw models of pregnant men and syphilitic genitals. This had turned into quite a day out.

My dad hovered at a distance from the display cases. Louis Tussauds seemed to have changed a bit since that long-ago choir trip. We gazed at the exhibits, noses pressed to the glass, for a long time and when we left we clamoured to describe to Mum details of the amazing things we had seen. She rolled her eyes and said, 'I told you it'd be nowt but rubbish.'

Mum, me and Tricia in a Blackpool
photo booth around 1975

If one of us had the nerve to try to join in an adult conversation or be obviously listening and looking interested we were told 'Children should be seen and not heard' or perhaps the Lancashire version: 'Little pigs have big ears'.

You were left in no doubt that you had nothing of consequence to say; any attempt to do so was described as 'butting in' and it was in fact very rude to interrupt the adults at all. 'We are *talking*!' would be the likely response.

Aunty Jenny lived down the lane where she had three brass monkeys on her mantelpiece: See No Evil, Hear No Evil and Speak No Evil. Speak No Evil had two hands clamped across his mouth to keep it tight shut. I used to stroke that monkey. I knew that monkey was me.

The biggest taboo was sex. Although it was acceptable for us to be there when mother rats' necks were broken and baby rats were stamped to death, we were told to clear off when a neighbouring farmer brought his boar round to our sows.

When I was five I realized my aunty was having a baby only months after her wedding and I asked, 'How does God know you have got married?' This had puzzled me for a while. Was there some magical baby-giving quality about wearing a white dress, having bridesmaids or throwing a party in the village hall? Or did something funny go on in the vestry? Mum and Dad laughed. 'She's thinking about it,' said Mum to Dad, and without addressing me directly they went back to drinking their tea.

I returned to the living room humiliated.

When I was seven or eight I cycled up the lane to the shop for sweets and was followed by a gold car. I cycled faster and faster so as not to hold the driver up – I had learned by then that being 'a nuisance' was the greatest sin. I got as close to the grass verge as possible so he could pass. He didn't, but tailed me all the way there. I told no one at the shop because I was embarrassed at having held up a motorist, and my best friend who lived there said she'd cycle back with me, just for the fun of it. Cars were rare down the lane – you were more likely to come face to face with our herd of cows or Dad driving his tractor. On the grass verge halfway home, looming out of the cow parsley, was the gold car parked at a wonky angle. Approaching it we saw a man crouching in the hedge bottom; as we cycled past he stood up and stepped towards us. He was wearing a shirt and tie and was naked from the waist down and as we passed he thrust out his groin. My friend and I pedalled to a safe distance and then stopped and watched over our shoulders as he got in his car and drove away. We looked at each other and said nothing.

That night I told Elizabeth and swore her to silence. Immediately she yelled: '*Mum! Catherine saw a man with no clothes on!*' The next day at the police station the police-woman asked, 'What do you call it? What name shall we use?' My mother folded her arms. 'There are no boys in our house. We don't call it anything.' My friend's mother suggested: 'Shall we call it a willy?' The policewoman nodded and asked, 'Was his willy like this?' She put her arm at one angle and looked for our reaction, then she moved it to a perkier one, 'Or this?' The question dumbfounded me. I didn't know how to describe it; I only remembered it had been very obviously *there*.

The following day in the school yard my friend said her mum had explained to her that the police had asked that question so they could tell if he'd wanted to make a baby or not. The police brought black and white mugshots round – pictures of 'baddies' straight from *Scooby Doo* – which they spread out on my mother's embroidered cushions in the sitting room. They never found him.

One night a few years later, I was delivering the milk to the nearby cottage by torchlight. It was winter and cold so I was wearing slippers rather than being barefoot. A car headed towards me and crawled past. The vehicle pulled up, engine running, forming a barrier behind me between me and home. I looked over my shoulder and in the moonlight I saw the shape of a man get out and stand, arms folded, watching me. I started running – away from him, away from home – bottles clanking in the heavy metal holder, torch-beam not sufficient to see where I was putting my feet, losing both red slippers, one at a time. I got to the cottage, put down the milk and huddled on the doorstep. It never occurred to me to knock on the door and ask Old Mrs Dunn for help. What would I say? After a few minutes I heard the car purr away. When I dared to move I set off home, back down the lane, feet sore from the stones, as I searched for each red slipper by the thin beam of torchlight. I never told anyone.

Living on a farm should have made reproduction an open book. When the AI drove into the yard sounding the horn on his van we all yelled, 'AI's here,' until one day I asked, 'What *is* the AI?' Dad gave a snort of laughter and said, 'Ask yer mum.' I found her in the kitchen and did so and she barked, 'The artificial inseminator!' I knew I had asked too much and again done something shameful.

Oddly, though, there was one subject that was faced head-on – my father couldn't stand to see mentally or physically disabled children on the television and would become instantly agitated and insist the programme be turned off, especially if they were crying or wailing. 'If one of you had been like that you'd have been put in a home,' he said.

Determined that we wouldn't become poor physical specimens he once pointed out that I didn't stand up straight – because of my acute self-consciousness I slouched and kept my head down. Eventually, when I was eleven and growing my fringe right down virtually covering my face like a curtain, he watched me walk through the kitchen and said, 'Can't you buy a back brace for that sort of thing?'

CHAPTER EIGHT

I am not sure exactly when Tricia changed but it was very early on.

I was sitting on the hearthrug in the living room cutting out; cutting out was one of my favourite pastimes.

Mum was a keen dressmaker who bought lots of patterns from the haberdasher's in Lancaster and would then ask if she could take away their old pattern books. These enormous Butterick and Simplicity pattern books became prized possessions. They were filled with painted pictures of models, stick-thin and elegant in up-to-date outfits of all colours and styles – the most admired being the floor-length gowns.

My first job on acquiring a new pattern book was to go through and give all the ladies names, then certain characters could be cut out and made to enact adventures. This game was called 'Ladies' and in truth their adventures were not very thrilling at all, comprising them getting dressed up and going out to 'ladies' evenings' – something Mum and Dad did every so often with Grandad Ben and Grandma Mary as part of Grandad's life as a Worshipful Master in the Freemasons.

What happened at real-life 'ladies' evenings' was a mystery, except the women wore long sparkly dresses, which we called 'beady frocks', and the men wore bow ties and they came back in good moods with menu cards tied with silky tassels: *Celery Soup, Roast Beef with Spring Vegetables, Peach Melba.*

As boring and limited as my cut-out ladies' 'adventures' were, Tricia was always keen to watch and comment on the game and, for me, it was more fun to play with an audience than without so I asked her, 'Do you want to play "Ladies"?'

She did not reply and walked through the living room and headed upstairs. 'Tricia!' I shouted this time. 'Do you want to play "Ladies"?' She usually jumped at the chance. But there was still no reply and I heard the rattle of her bedroom door as it slammed shut.

I stared at the stair door through which she had vanished and I thought: When will the *old* Tricia come back?

I put the scissors down; the game had lost its allure without Tricia. It struck me consciously for the first time that she had changed over the preceding weeks. She was only eight or nine years old but she was no longer the sweet, easy-going, cooperative child she had been all her life and had become increasingly withdrawn; hiding behind her fringe and getting quieter and quieter. I wanted the old Tricia back, the playmate and the friend, the companion who would join in any game – or at the very least sit and watch me play a game.

So I must have been about eleven when it first struck me that Tricia had changed and a guilty part of me wondered if it was our fault – had Elizabeth and I used up all Tricia's kindness and sweetness by taking advantage of it? What had we done to her?

Of course the changes in Tricia were not discussed or mentioned to Mum and Dad. Why would they be? We had been well trained in keeping quiet and 'not mithering'. We had been told to 'dry up' often enough and conversation was not part of our lives; indeed I don't think we ever had a talk about feelings of any kind. And this never changed – throughout our lives, with all the bereavements, ill health, triumphs and disappointments, and even during my mother's terminal illness, we never had a conversation about how we felt. As children the main topic of conversation around the kitchen table was the weather: what the sunshine would allow to happen on the farm today or what the rain would prevent; what the weather had ruined; what it had saved; what we had just got away with. 'I'm glad we've getten that hay baled.' The accuracy of the weather forecast (referred to as t'forecast) was an article of faith. 'What's t'forecast sayin'?' If the adults weren't talking about the weather, they were talking about the light. 'Nights are drawin' in' or 'this time last week it were dark.'

So, conversations about feelings or emotions or worries about anything other than practical things did not happen. Instead there were remarks about events on the farm

– which of course did cover birth, death and sex, although without any emotional content: 'Number 670's near calving', 'old sow's at far end', 'Number 288's riding', 'I'll have to call't AI.'

'Chatting' was not a concept I was familiar with until I began to visit other families, where I realized, fascinated, that they *asked questions* and other people *answered*.

At New House, after giving us our tea, which was always delicious home-cooked food – steak and onions, maybe, or plaice and chips, followed by home-made apple pie – Mum would disappear upstairs and Elizabeth, Tricia and I were left to our own devices until Dad came in. We would play with fire. We'd roll up pages from the *Daily Express* into a long thin baton and light it on the red-hot coals of the open fire, then 'smoke' it, searing the backs of our throats. Or we'd turn off the lights and write messages in the blackness with the smouldering end like normal children did with sparklers. Rescuing the scurrying woodlice from the burning logs was another pastime. If the fire flagged we'd tip red diesel on it from the silver teapot that lived on the hearth and enjoy the flare.

We watched whatever came on television. The television was never switched off. We would have been lost without it because the silence in the farmhouse was too loud. One wet Saturday afternoon I remember the three of us watching the test card.

None of us watched *Coronation Street* but it always seemed to be on, getting on my mother's nerves: 'They'd have us believe there are folks that go to the pub *every night* just to talk rubbish!'

Mum eschewed anything 'popular' – soap operas, ITV in general, Cilla Black, chart music, idle chatter; these were 'puerile' and considered banal and without merit.

Slade's 'Merry Xmas Everybody' shot to number one in the charts at Christmas 1973 and, as Noddy Holder cheerfully told *John Craven's Newsround* that the song had taken twenty minutes to write, Mum walked past and snapped, 'To think Mozart was buried in a pauper's grave.'

Every evening when Dad finished milking and had eaten his supper he'd turn the television channel to *Panorama* or *World in Action* or any other news programme or documentary he could find. He'd fall asleep in his armchair but his eyes would fly open if we inched towards the buttons, stealing over the hearthrug with the hope of finding some sitcom on the other side.

Tricia and I would try to get as close to the open fire as we could but Elizabeth would be stretched across the hearthrug hogging it, warming herself from top to bottom, her skin mottling. Until I was thirteen there were no other heated rooms in the house. There was never enough warmth to go round.

Meanwhile Mum would be in her bedroom – 'I'm going to lie down for half an hour, I don't want disturbing' – or doing battle with the kitchen which always looked like a bomb had gone off sending pots and pans everywhere. 'I'd better go and do an hour in that kitchen,' she'd mutter darkly and we'd feel that somehow it was *our* fault that the kitchen looked like it had been ransacked. She'd crash and bash the pots around for a while only to emerge later with it not looking much different, say she was 'done in' and go to bed leaving a lingering whiff of martyrdom hanging in the air.

The battle to keep the house tidy had been largely lost but there was tension around keeping the place clean. Inside the house were hoovered carpets, mopped floors, bleached sinks and my mother; outside the house were puddles, mud, animals, straw bales and my father. The trouble started at the back door where the two met.

When Dad came in a great swirl of cold and wet came in with him, including bits of straw and muck clinging to his jacket and his flat cap. He'd leave his wellies dripping by the back door and hang his flat cap to dry over the range. My mother would shout, 'Stop bringing the farmyard in with you. You'll ruin my Hoover, you will.'

Sometimes in the milking parlour the cows would splatter muck on Dad's head and we used to wonder how much of the steaming cap was cap and how much was cowpat. One day Mum had had enough and threw the cap onto the fire where it sizzled and smoked as we laughed and my father muttered and cursed: 'What did you do that for?' When he got a new flat cap it fitted like new false teeth – too big, too bright, too new – and we were glad when it got shiny with cow muck again.

This tension around cleaning and tidying the house rose to a crescendo in the run-up to Christmas Day when my mother knew she would be cooking lunch for eighteen of my dad's family. For years the smell of Christmas was tangerines and Windolene and the sound of Christmas was *Carols from King's* on the radiogram, with Mum grimacing and sighing as she shoved boiled veg through a sieve for the soup starter, every bit of her jiggling, a single black curl falling into her eyes despite her trying to blow it away, as she pounded the vegetables to death with the wooden spoon.

My mother was angry that the world contained so much boring housework, but she was keen on healthy eating. She grew her own strawberries, raspberries, gooseberries, potatoes, peas, onions and lettuce. Her proudest boast was serving up a meal and saying, 'This was still growing half an hour ago.' She boiled her home-grown beetroot in a blackened pot on the open kitchen fire, bubbling away like a witch's cauldron.

She was always trying to lose two stones, so sometimes when we tucked into home-made meat and potato pie or gammon and chips Mum would smear Heinz Sandwich Spread on a slimmers' bread roll – an artificial, light-as-air ball that threatened to shatter into a handful of crumbs when she sliced it – and she'd sit at the table chewing on the dusty remains, lips tight-shut and a grim look on her face.

We were given odd jobs like shelling peas and topping and tailing gooseberries, or very occasionally we were allowed to stir bubbling jam in the brass pan or ice a cake, but as a rule if we dared approach while she was clattering in the kitchen we were told to 'stop mithering, you're being a nuisance' or 'get out from under my feet' and she'd turn up Richard Baker on Radio Three. *These You Have Loved* would drown us out; Berlioz and Brahms, Bach and Beethoven swirling in a great crescendo round the plastered walls and oak beams of the farmhouse kitchen.

'I can't hear you,' she'd bellow, turning up the dial on the pale-blue Kenwood mixer.

I think my mother wished we were invisible and often I felt invisible.

As I grew older I found it increasingly difficult to look a camera directly in the lens and I looked away as though if I couldn't see the camera it couldn't see me. When I was in my twenties and doing a degree in journalism I had to create a photographic self-portrait. The finished piece showed nothing but the very tip of my big toe, plus an elongated, unrecognizable shadow flat against the floor and up the wall.

* * *

Because we were kept at a distance in the kitchen I grew up on top-quality food, with hot meals every night, but left home at nineteen unable to make a baked potato, let alone shortcrust pastry or Yorkshire puddings. Domestic Science classes at secondary school had taught us little besides how to make lemon biscuits and Melting Moments and, more bafflingly, the chemistry behind washing powder. I ended up reliant on a series of boyfriends to teach me how to make meals. I still remember them for what they taught me to cook as much as anything else: Raymond (spaghetti bolognese full of red wine), Keith (curry with chapattis), Mike (a full roast dinner with all the trimmings).

Growing up we had a 'playroom', a lean-to with damp stone walls and floor that turned our toys rotten – or at least the ones at the bottom of the heap. And they *were* in a heap. When Mum shouted, 'Get this living room tidied up before I break my neck,' we'd grab the dolls and the plastic animals and the colouring books and stagger to the playroom door and throw with all our strength, chucking the stuff onto the great mouldering compost heap of toys. Once in a blue moon we'd sort it out, which was daunting as the toy compost was head-high. Nothing had a home; there were jigsaw pieces mixed with Monopoly money mixed with skipping ropes and dolls' clothes, and unidentifiable bits and pieces that could have been anything from anywhere. We'd excavate the heap, dragging out armless dolls, legless dolls with insulation-tape bikinis, naked dolls with shorn hair, and line them up like refugees in the wonky cupboard. Eventually we'd reach the bottom of the heap to reveal the stone-cold floor with the wood beetles and the silverfish and Mum would tell us to think ourselves lucky, there used to be cockroaches under the rush matting in the kitchen before she modernized with lino at the same time as she'd updated to wipe-clean wallpaper covered in turquoise daisies.

One day we tidied the playroom or did some other task that pleased her and stopped her feeling 'put upon'; whatever it was, on this occasion she was gratified and promised that when we were finished we would all enjoy a KitKat together. KitKats were rare and wonderful things because they were bought and not home-made, but what made this promise so exciting was the prospect of us sitting down in the evening to enjoy the KitKats together and maybe having a *chat* like families did on the television. This would have been quite an occasion seeing as my mother had never given me a bedtime story, read me a book, told me a joke or shared a secret.

I pictured us on the sofa, everyone gathered round talking and laughing – which was possibly an image from a Ladybird book or a sitcom because it wasn't one from real life – but when I went into the living room to take part in this Happy Family scene I discovered three KitKats in a pile on the sofa and Mum nowhere around. I was stricken with disappointment as I realized there was to be no get-together and no family chatting, let alone laughing.

I don't know if Elizabeth and Tricia felt equally crushed – trying to put this desire for a more close-knit family into words was impossible, I didn't understand it myself, and I couldn't have asked them the question. But within five years of this, by the time she was fifteen, Elizabeth had semi-moved out of the farmhouse, spending days on end at her best friend's small and already overcrowded house in Lancaster. So for her I think the answer would have been 'yes'. How did Tricia feel? I wish I could have asked her – but then there are so many questions I wish I could have asked. That night, though, nothing was said as we perched on the edge of the sofa, running our bitten fingernails down the silver wrappings and munching on our KitKats as the television blared.

I was always a nail-biter, biting the nails and the skin to the quick until my finger-ends were sore. When I was ten years old my mother said, 'Stop chewing your nails. I read in the paper it means you hate yourself. Why do you hate yourself?'

After the occasion when Tricia refused to play 'Ladies' with me I kept an eye on her for several weeks but I never saw a hint of the old Tricia. Then one day, with a sick thump of disappointment and a sinking horror, I realized that the old

Tricia had gone and would *never* come back. *This* was Tricia now; withdrawn, quiet, more guarded, harder (if not impossible) to reach. She had gone deep inside herself and distanced herself from us.

Everyone became accustomed to seeing her hiding behind her fringe and we even joked about it, laughing that she was the custard monster as her spoon, laden with Bird's, disappeared behind her wall of hair at the tea table. Nobody talked about what, to me, was a dramatic and terrible change in her.

I have wondered many times what, if anything, specific happened to Tricia when she was so young – maybe only eight years old – that essentially changed her personality. I never asked her. As a child it would have been a question impossible to phrase or utter at all, but as an adult it remained unaskable.

After Tricia died, Elizabeth and I had many round-and-round, how-did-it-come-to-this conversations. We tried to trace her depression back to a beginning point and eventually one of us asked: 'You don't think anything *really terrible* happened to her, do you?' We gazed at each other blankly and shook our heads. It was unthinkable and neither of us believed it.

Two years later, when I was sorting through some of her papers, I discovered a note she had made about a friend who had confided she had been abused as a child and Tricia had

written: 'I can't begin to imagine what she has gone through.'
I took this, rightly or wrongly, as the nearest I was going to
get to confirmation from Tricia that she had not been a similar victim herself.

I was eleven when I brought a secondary-school friend,
Hilary, back to the farm for the first time. Her parents were
lecturers and they lived in a bungalow. They ate Vesta curry
and Cadbury's chocolate rolls at a neatly folding Formica
table in their fitted kitchen and then watched TV in the
lounge on their orange faux-fur modular sofa in front of a
coal-effect fire.

Our kitchen had a huge table constantly laden. There
were great jugs of milk, brought in straight from the tank
with the cream rising frothy and thick to the top – a temp-
tation to the semi-feral cats who clamoured round the back
door yowling for scraps. There were home-made cakes and
pies, often still surrounded with all the baking accoutre-
ments including my mum's mixer, bowls and scrapers.

There was no knowing what you might find on the
kitchen table. I once opened a plastic bag to find a cow's
tongue inside – long and coiled – waiting for my mum to
cook and press it. (I was amazed: so that's what 'tong' butties
were – actual cow's tongue.)

The day I brought my friend home she picked her way
through the meowing cats weaving around each other at the
back door and inched through the kitchen with its wonky

walls and low-beamed ceiling and past the enormous table like she'd arrived somewhere Very Different Indeed.

For the first time I saw my home through the eyes of another.

We went into the living room. She took in the open fire with the teapot of red diesel that we merrily poured over the flames to get them going, the battered leather sofa, the table with my mother's sewing machine and the mounds of home-made dresses in progress, and then she stood stock-still, her eyes fastened on the far corner of the room.

'What is that?' she asked, and I cringed.

Circling gently above the television was a dangling flypaper coated in dead and dying flies. Some still managed to buzz. Others waved their legs.

Where there are animals, there are flies – but my friend did not come from a place where there were many animals or, apparently, many flies.

'It's for the flies,' I said and we both watched it circle.

My mother fought a valiant and ultimately fruitless war against flies, armed with sprays and swatters and fly screens and, *in extremis*, in the height of summer, sticky flypapers. She later branched out into commercial-standard electrical fly-killers which glowed blue and buzzed every time they killed a fly. But nothing was up to the task.

'Oh,' Hilary said, transfixed.

I had a mad impulse to wrench it from the ceiling and thrust it on the fire but I wasn't sure that would help.

'What does it do?' she asked.

How to explain to an animal-lover who had just given a school talk about the affection she had for her gerbil?

'It kills them,' I said.

We watched it circle again in the draught from the ill-fitting window.

'But they're not dead,' she said.

'No,' I said.

This visit wasn't going as well as I'd hoped.

Even so, I knew I should be grateful; I'd got home from school not long ago to find Dad in the yard castrating a pig.

'Shall we go and listen to some records?' I asked.

My friend tore her eyes from the flies and we headed up the creaking stairs to my bedroom. It felt safer in there where I could put a little distance between me and the rest of my family.

Hilary became a regular visitor and considered our house to be a strange and fascinating place. She went home and tried to grow green furry coffee cups like she'd seen under Elizabeth's bed but her mother dragged them out and washed them. She told her mum Elizabeth didn't bother with plugs but stuck bare wires from an electric fire directly into the wall sockets. 'Does her mother know?' her mum asked. When Hilary told me, I laughed and shrugged. Who knew what my mother knew.

* * *

In the days after Tricia died, visitors came one after another and cups of tea were made and we went through the story all over again. This ritual may have helped Dad but I found it exhausting. I hardly had time to wave one group of visitors off before another arrived. People also phoned and texted but I found these easier to deal with because they were shorter and I didn't have to control my face or put the kettle on or hunt for biscuits. I have never felt so drained. I have never had less chance to eat – although that didn't matter because I had no appetite. Sympathy cards were appreciated but the condolence that touched me deepest was from a boy called Stanley who had been at our primary school – a middle-aged man now, of course – and had never moved away from the village or married. His card in a child-like hand said:

Just a short note to say how sorry we both were when we heard the sad news of Patricia's death. She was a lovely well-mannered girl who always spoke whenever I met her either in Garstang or when she rode past the workshop on her horse. It did not matter what kind of day I was having, I always felt better for seeing her. The world would be a better place if there were more like Patricia. Heartfelt sympathy from me and Mum.

'I always felt better for seeing her' touched me because it reminded me of Tricia as a young girl when every day she had made my life better for seeing her.

CHAPTER NINE

In February 2016 I arrived at Hawthornden Castle in the Scottish Lowlands on a writing fellowship. For a month I would live at the castle with five other writers – poets and novelists and a non-fiction writer. We were referred to as the 'Fellows', which should have felt pretentious but didn't. It added to the pressure to get something written while we were there.

We were polite and eager and a little nervous on the first evening. The director, Hamish, invited us for sherry in the dining room, followed by haggis, neeps and tatties for dinner eaten around a circular table, set with pewter goblets and lit by candles in front of a blazing fire. It was very cold. I bagged a chair near the fireplace and was pleased with myself. One young woman illustrator from New York asked, 'So what is haggis? Is it the glands and the sweetbreads from the sheep?' She gestured around her face to indicate 'glands'. 'No, no,' I replied, in an attempt to reassure, 'it's largely oatmeal and herbs and—' I was cut off by a writer of historical fiction from Northern Ireland, who said, 'Yes, it could be the sweetbreads and the glands from the sheep.'

The stay in the castle was going to be an experience.

We were there as guests of Mrs Drue Heinz who was apparently one hundred and one years old. The castle was decorated with prints of people in kilts posing on moors, carved wooden stags and paintings of Truman Capote, Aldous Huxley and other personal friends of Mrs Heinz. I asked Hamish if it was true Mrs Heinz used to have a bright-red private jet – the colour of Heinz tomato sauce – but sadly it was not.

We all applied for our fellowships citing some project we would work on while we were there. Some of the Fellows went off walking all day and wrote about that, others sat in the private library and researched and yet others holed up in their rooms and came out for dinner looking as though they had scaled a mountain.

All the rooms were named after writers – mine was Boswell – and lunch was delivered to my room in a small Fortnum & Mason hamper. It was a sandwich and soup and fruit and I sat on my bed huddled in a blanket brought from home and felt lucky to be there.

My room was at the top of the castle up a spiral staircase, so small I hadn't been able to get my suitcase up it and had to ferry my jumpers and fleeces and extra-warm socks upstairs in carrier bags, sweating and embarrassed.

The last thing I brought in from the boot of the car was a Bag for Life containing Tricia's diaries from the age of fourteen until she died. While I was there I planned to read them and start work on a book called *When I Had a Little Sister*. Although Tricia had been gone for more than two years, her death still felt raw and unbelievable. It continued to make no sense that her life ended in the way it did and when I thought about it – which I did every day – it shocked me all over again. Tricia's life and death seemed like unfinished business. I wanted to explore them and try to understand exactly what happened. Why couldn't we have stopped it? Was it something about us? About our family? About the way we lived?

I was frightened of the diaries. They were a mix of Challenge Duplicate Books, Collins desk diaries, page-a-day diaries, John Menzies notebooks, tiny Paperblanks, and a faux-leather journal with fancy ties; and what they contained was a mystery. Would she blame me and the rest of the family? I was frightened of finding out what she truly thought of us but most of all I was frightened of reading page after page of her black despair and deep depression.

I was also aware they had been written as private documents – how would I feel about people reading my diaries? It would certainly have been a no-no to as much as open one of Tricia's diaries if she had still been alive. But she was not alive. What was the alternative? To ignore them? Still, the thought of reading them felt like breaking a taboo. It wasn't what other people would say that bothered me. I had been as close to her over the years as anyone – this was between me and her. But what would she have thought? These diaries contained the only voice she had left. This was the sole way I could hear Tricia talking, explaining, describing her life. In the back of my mind I always knew I would eventually have to read them.

The diaries were dusty; they smelled of the old farmhouse – damp and with a lingering trace of Tricia's roll-ups. Elizabeth had kept them for the two years and three months since Tricia died. They were stored in her attic until the week before my Hawthornden trip, when she invited her plumber round on the pretence of a broken boiler and sweet-talked him into clambering into her ladder-less, floor-less attic to retrieve them.

On that first morning, waking at the castle, I knew I needed to sort out the diaries and start reading straight away because I had a strong urge to put it off. I did not know if I was brave enough to face it. I placed the Bag for Life on the bed. The room was icy, or maybe it was just me.

I decided to go for a walk around the castle grounds. My body was hot inside my winter coat while my face stung with the cold. The snowdrops were out and they covered the banks in the woods, even at times straying across the well-trodden path where a solitary flower, not even accompanied by any leaves, sprouted, bent low, face to the ground, but gleaming white, alone in the winter sun.

* * *

Before I went on the fellowship I told one or two people I planned to read my sister's diaries while I was there – as though articulating the plan would help me decide if it was a good idea or not. I caught sight of one of them mouthing 'Oh. My. God.' behind my back and maybe he was right; maybe it was foolhardy. Would what I found in the diaries be too much for me? I had been depressed and stressed in the run-up to the fellowship. Two days before I left home a chunk of my hair fell out, leaving a bald patch on the crown of my head the size of a ten-pence piece.

Back in my room, I sat on the bed and bit my nails, or rather I bit the skin around my nails. It was compulsive. As I bit I felt a tightening in my stomach. I knew it was possible I would sit in this tiny bedroom with the view of the old castle keep and the woodland dusted in frost, listening to the wind howling round, for days or even weeks and do nothing but pick at the skin on my stinging finger-ends and feel the tension in my stomach ratchet up.

I leafed through one of the books I had brought with me: *Angelhead: My Brother's Descent into Madness* by Greg Bottoms. There was a review on the inside cover and I copied two phrases from it onto a Post-it note and stuck it on my windowpane. The sunlight shone through the lime-green paper and illuminated the words 'Emotional precision and the satisfaction of hard truth' and I knew that was what I was there to find, that was what this search was now about:

'emotional precision and the satisfaction of hard truth'. I wanted this project to be an excavation.

I rooted in the Bag for Life, my finger-ends smarting from the biting and picking. I found the oldest diary, which began in 1981. I opened it. In a childish hand, written in pencil it said: 'Tricia Simpson owns this book so keep your nose out of other people's business and don't read this.'

I began to read.

CHAPTER TEN

Tricia's handwriting was unmistakable, like the handwriting of most people we know well – or maybe that is no longer the case. It was scrawling and not beautiful, which was odd considering our village primary school taught us that correctly formed cursive handwriting was next to godliness. This was a school where we dipped nibs into wooden inkwells of blue Quink, where your 'f's were double-looped and your 'g's were single-looped, but God forbid that your 't's were looped at all, and where a fresh piece of pink blotting paper was as indispensable as a clean hankie.

Tricia had taken none of these handwriting rules on board. A lot of her writing was barely legible so her words were in front of me but many of them I could not grasp.

I soon realized that at times the only option was to let my eyes relax and skim the sentences and hope to absorb their meaning that way.

The earliest diary was a Challenge invoice book. Many years ago my Aunty Dorothy gave us one each for our birthdays so we could 'play offices'. All my family were in business of one kind or another so playing offices, or post offices, or shops were popular games. Holding a biro was a sign of being a grown-up. So maybe this book was left over from that. Every other page was tissue-thin and it began with a list written in pencil by Tricia when she was fourteen.

Happy Times
1. Smoking in the middle of the night with Elaine.
2. Fry-ups after Winmarleigh Young Farmers' Dance with Elaine.
3. Going to the pictures at Lancaster and giggling at dirty films with Elaine and Christine.
4. Cuddling Elaine and being cuddled by her when things went wrong.
5. Smoking in the Watergate [one of the farm's fields] with Elaine.
6. Getting my bike thrown in the canal.
7. Leading Norman [bull calf] on his halter.
8. Mucking out with Dave.
9. Sitting on the silage between loads with my boyfriend.
10. Walking round the lanes with Sarah and her pony, Misty.

I was heartened to see these first two pages were a summary of her highlights up till 1981. Tricia was someone who did not appear to have much happiness, sometimes for months at a time, especially towards the end of her life, so I felt huge relief about this. Her happy times involved girlfriends, animals, farming and smoking, which came as no surprise. Then I realized that many of her highlights involved Elaine, a cousin of ours who was two years older than Tricia, and I felt sad all over again because I knew what was waiting around the corner.

But the tragedy involving Elaine was still over a year away and the large, pencilled, childish handwriting recorded a merry-go-round of falling-outs and making-ups with a group of girlfriends and boyfriends – and Elaine, who she never fell out with, was there as her co-conspirator all along.

I was taken aback because I remembered Tricia as withdrawn at that time but her diary shows she was very involved with her circle of schoolfriends. Relationships with boys and girls were complicated and erratic and caused her endless angst, but they could also make her happy.

The disco in the local village hall was the scene of much of the drama and was one of many dances in village halls on a Friday or Saturday night for miles around. The disco in our village did not serve alcohol and so attracted a younger crowd. From fifteen you graduated onto village-hall discos elsewhere which served spirits by the gallon to teenagers keen to drink as much as possible, as quickly as possible, as sweetly and easily as possible: gin and orange cordial, rum and blackcurrant, vodka and lime, Pernod and black. Even halves of lager and cider had shots of blackcurrant or lime cordial added to sweeten them up and make them slip down easier.

Mum and Dad had met at a village-hall dance a generation before and not much had changed since. In our village in the 1970s we had eclectic musical taste; we'd pogo to Elvis Costello or rock and roll to Elvis Presley, do the 'Quo' to Status Quo or twist to Chubby Checker. The younger girls gathered round the door to the ladies' toilets, perhaps so they could bolt to safety if necessary. The older, cooler, kids hung about in mixed groups by the stage; circles of girls danced round their handbags; lads – having arrived on their mopeds like a swarm of wasps – wore skin-tight bum-flares and leather jackets and lounged against the curtains having a fag, watching.

The diary contained pages of convoluted relationships within a group of ten or so fourteen-year-olds – boys and girls – all swapping and changing loyalties and vying with each other and falling in and out of love.

May 1981

Things I want

1. To know and to like and get on with P for ever.
2. To go out with M.
3. To know and to like and to get on with C for ever.
4. For C & J to get back together.
5. For P to get his job.

6. For Elizabeth to marry Phil, leave home and have a baby girl.
7. To stay friends with S, P, J, C, H, E, M, S, J, M.
8. To get Nelly [her horse] good and win at Scorton [a local village show].
9. Get my O levels and leave school quick.
10. Get on with Mum and Dad, Elizabeth, Cathy, Gran and so on.
11. Never to hurt anyone's feelings again.
12. To have a baby girl when I am 23.
13. To make people happy.

Tricia had hopes and dreams about her horse winning a show and of seeing the back of school but on the whole she was preoccupied with relationships – family relationships, friendships and boyfriends – and her greatest desire was to 'make people happy'. From being a teenager heavily invested in relationships she had a long way to go to become the woman who by the end had relationships with no one except Dad and her horses.

When Tricia raised the subject of sex it was infused with the casual misogyny and double standards of the time and place:

S is still a virgin, he told me the other night. I was extremely shocked. I told him I was too but he wasn't shocked. Thank God. J is a virgin which shocked me cos he boasted like hell. M is not. He went with XY. He said it was the most boring thing he'd ever done cos she lay there like a sack of spuds.

We received basic sex education in secondary-school science lessons when we were twelve. I remember the young biology teacher twisting the chalk in his hands as he sweated, avoided our eye, and hovered in front of a blackboard with a drawing of a set of fallopian tubes on it. His description of sexual intercourse was so tortuous that one lad put his hand up and asked, 'Do you have to go to hospital to do it, sir?'

'No,' said the teacher, his brow a glassy sheen, 'this is a pleasurable act!'

Whether my mother would have wanted us told it was a pleasurable act I'm not sure. Once we became teenagers our general duty to 'not show her up' expanded to include 'steer clear of sex of any sort and at all cost avoid getting pregnant when you aren't married'.

This expectation was never made explicit, of course. When Mum saw lovebites on Elizabeth's neck she reacted with fury: 'One thing will lead to another. You will RUIN YOUR LIFE.'

When she referred to 'doing something you will regret' we knew she meant premarital sex and we knew the message really was 'do not shame me'.

Fortunately sex was not all doom and gloom. We had 'Sex Education: Advanced' at secondary school, aged fifteen, with the fearsome female deputy head. When she urged us to 'put any questions you would rather not ask out loud into the questions box', someone wrote: 'What you doing tonight, Mrs Yule?'

From my teenage perspective, sex amounted to boys persistently trying to do something that girls might also want to do but were too frightened to for fear of getting a reputation as 'a slut' or ending up pregnant. Sex felt like boys trying to 'get' something that girls were pressurized to 'give'. Boys were gaining, girls were losing. It was a constant battle – often literally a fight as you'd stop a boyfriend pulling your shirt out of your jeans while he simultaneously undid your buttons and groped any bare skin he could find.

When Mrs Yule put the 'childbirth' film on, one of the fifteen-year-old girls fell in a dead faint from her lab stool.

Tricia described friendships as 'perfect' and 'too good for words' and at one point got so intense I was alarmed until I realized she had segued into the lyrics of 'Love and Affection' by Joan Armatrading, jumbled up with 'Will You' by Hazel O'Connor.

Declarations of love were followed by fallings-out when she 'hates' the same people and tells them she never wants to see them again, only to pine for them until they come back. On it went; page after page, month after month, a roller-coaster of emotion and tangled relationships with rivalries and jealousies and longing and heartbreak.

I made a mental note to burn my own teenage diaries.

At that time I was seventeen and studying for A levels but Tricia did not talk to me. Tricia's world was her friends – people I only had the vaguest notion of. All these lads she 'loved' and who were 'beyond perfect' were, from my lofty position as an older sibling, kids I could hardly tell one from another, who turned up on pushbikes, smoked crafty fags in the barn, named kittens they found there 'Benson & Hedges' and 'Lambert & Butler' – names that never stuck – and looked furtive as they scuttled up to Tricia's room.

I had my own boyfriend by then – a boy I was largely attracted to for his family because they welcomed me as part family member, part honoured guest. They made me feel looked after. We all sat in front of the fire and ate cheese toasties and I knew I belonged.

I was used to Tricia being withdrawn from the family. I never thought of her as being *secretive* because it did not cross my mind she had anything to be secretive about. The anguished part of her life was hidden from view – or maybe I just wasn't looking.

Tricia mentioned depression for the first time when she was fourteen. Too young to get served in the pub, she got drunk on dusty bottles of spirits from the family sideboard which contained ancient brandies used for soaking the Christmas cake, Harveys Bristol Cream for visitors on Christmas morning and half-drunk bottles of 'Vintage Port' presumably inherited from various great-aunts' equally dusty sideboards, their corks and screw tops sticky and crystallized. She camouflaged great glugs of these in Mum's Hornsea Pottery mugs or necked them straight from the bottle, only to note: 'Getting pissed didn't help.'

She first wrote about suicide when a male friend, who clearly fancied Tricia himself, manipulated her into finishing with her boyfriend. She was fifteen, and noted in her diary: 'I told him I was going to commit suicide. He made me promise I wouldn't for six months.'

She discussed suicide several times over the following weeks but called it 'the coward's way'.

In July 1981 Mum, Dad, Tricia and I had our first holiday abroad. We went as part of a group with Grandma Mary, an aunt, an uncle, some younger cousins and family friends, for a wedding. At seventeen I was happy to leave my boyfriend for ten days in return for my first trip on a plane and hopefully a suntan. It was a major family event marked by Mum wearing nail varnish for the first time – pearlized shell pink – even though she insisted she could feel it weighing heavy on her fingernails, and Dad getting a new holiday outfit made up entirely in beige, including his first pair of sandals.

On the BA flight, acting as confident and entitled as possible, I was served a gin and tonic then a half-bottle of wine with my steak and sauté potatoes, followed by a liqueur. This was better than a top-class restaurant, I decided, never having set foot in a top-class restaurant. I sipped my Tia Maria listening to Supertramp's 'Dreamer' on the in-flight entertainment while beside me Tricia was refused alcohol. She wrote in her diary: 'I am now in an aeroplane flying over the Atlantic. It's boring. I've been going out with M for 2 days, 18 and three-quarter hours. He's gorgeous.' Not a word passed between us about her friends; there was no mention of the new boyfriend she was missing at home, or that she even had a new boyfriend. I have no idea what we talked about – I do not remember much conversation and none is recorded in my diary.

In Ontario I dashed to don my swimsuit and sunned myself on the balcony of the Beacon Motor Inn. In the following ten days I sampled my first Jacuzzi, swam in the pool, basked in the 'whirlpool', ate pancakes with bacon and maple syrup, attended a Mennonite wedding, saw racoons race across the highway, met a Native Canadian on a reservation, visited Niagara Falls and got up at four o'clock in the morning to see live coverage of Lady Di marrying Prince Charles in St Paul's Cathedral. The Canadian newspaper and television reporters loved it. *It's the wedding of the decade! It's Chuck 'n' Di!*

The holiday wasn't ideal – I had to share a bedroom with Grandma who snored and Tricia who ground her teeth all night – but for me there was enough novelty to make it worthwhile. At the very least it was a change from being at home where my teenage life consisted of watching boys do stuff: watching them tinkering with their motorbikes, watching them tuning their car engines, watching them firing their shotguns at rabbits or pigeons or seagulls; or, even worse, my life then was watching boys watching stuff – watching boys watching other boys play darts, or watching boys watching *Metal Mickey* or *The A-Team* or the wrestling on *World of Sport*. Watching and waiting; those were the hallmarks of my teenage life: waiting for the school bus, waiting for lessons to end, waiting for the phone to ring, waiting to grow up, interminable waiting for life to begin. Yes, for me Canada was a relief from all the watching and the waiting.

Meanwhile Tricia wrote:

This is the worst holiday I've ever been on. It's M's birthday today and I'm sat in Canada bored out of my mind. All I want to do is go home to my friends. I am never going on holiday in a group or with family again.

The photographs show a sweet-faced girl with a shy smile, head cocked to the right, head cocked to the left, sunglasses on, sunglasses off. One photo shows her sunbathing as we were gathered together waiting for the bus. Tricia is flat out on the grass verge with a paperback of Stephen King's *Carrie* resting on her face. The cover depicts a stricken, wild-eyed, dark-haired teenage girl with blood dripping down her face as lightning strikes behind.

I examine each photograph in my album, looking into Tricia's eyes, but in truth she appears no happier or sadder than anyone else and to claim otherwise would be to read into the pictures what I now know. Appearances, as they say, are deceptive and it's clear that at the time I underestimated, or was completely oblivious to, the loneliness and disconnection she felt, thinking of her as quiet or moody, or as merely Tricia being Tricia.

I do remember feeling frustrated that she didn't say much, though, and I asked her, when she was fourteen or so, whether she didn't have opinions about things. She was

Grandma Mary, me and Tricia smiling for the camera in Canada

sitting at the kitchen table eating a bowl of Bird's Custard and she sank further behind her hair and replied, 'Just because I think it, doesn't mean I have to say it.'

Tricia loved music and when a song became a favourite she'd listen to it over and over and write out the lyrics. Her diary contained the words for 'Only the Good Die Young' by Billy Joel and 'Someone Saved My Life Tonight' by Elton John. As I read the diaries, when a song was mentioned I lay on the bed in my tiny castle bedroom and listened to it on my iPod and then it felt like Tricia and I were having a conversation, a get-together to talk about old times, right there, right then. And Elton John sang: 'And butterflies are free to fly, fly away, high away bye bye.'

In the castle, the heating boiler had broken and I was shivering on my bed, in a fleecy blanket. As I turned the pages of Tricia's diary from 1981 to 1982 a folded note fell out. I smoothed it and my eyes skimmed the words. It was dated 'February 4th 1982, midnight', and Tricia was telling her best friend that although this friend had helped her she could not help her enough; she then told her boyfriend she loved him but they were too young. She said she had to do something and 'this way is the best and the easiest'. I realized I was reading a suicide note. It went on: 'Mum and Dad, I can't repay you enough for everything you did for me. I'm very sorry. Love you even though I never told you.'

That final phrase was one of the saddest I had ever read.

My eyes speeded up, flying across the letter; I was searching for my own name. Was there a message for me? I turned the page and there it was: 'Cathy, you always cheered me up. Have anything you want. You've got everything going for you, don't mess it up like I did. You liked me and you stuck up for me. Thanks. Goodbye and love.'

This was a note written thirty-one years before she died, when she was only fifteen years old, yet it seemed like I had been handed a wonderful gift; a message of farewell, from a life when I had a little sister. I read and reread it. I kept on returning to it all afternoon. When I went down for dinner I told my fellow writers about finding the note and one said, 'But that was written a long time before she died.' Yes, I said, but it was a loving message addressed to me personally in my sister's own handwriting and as such it felt precious arriving out of the darkness.

I wondered how many other people had been cheered by a suicide note.

I read it again before bed and listened to Billy Joel's 'Only the Good Die Young'. I was lifted by the upbeat song about young love and each time I pressed 'replay' the ethereal piano chords at the beginning made me think Tricia was there beside me.

I did not know what made Tricia consider taking her own life – or maybe fantasize about such a thing – when she wrote that note all those years ago. In the last entry dated before the note it said: 'I needed love.' It must have been escalating distress caused by her troubled and tangled friendships and an inability to get them into perspective. Her mood turned on a sixpence from happiness to despair and she obviously felt she had no control over her life. She seemed to experience life at the extremes – mostly at the negative extreme.

She was still only fifteen and the biggest blow was lying in wait.

Elaine was our cousin – our mothers were sisters – and she was one of Tricia's closest friends. Elaine was cheeky and irreverent. Down New House Lane there was a malformed tree with big protuberances growing on its trunk which as a young child Elaine christened 'Mrs Herbert' after the vicar's buxom wife. She could be rude but she got away with it because she made people laugh; if Elaine was there you knew you'd have more fun than if she wasn't. Grandma Mary, who physically resembled the Queen Mother, smiled beatifically but Elaine was the only person I remember who made Grandma throw back her head and belly-laugh. Everybody loved Elaine. She was small and blonde and looked angelic, in an extended family tending towards the tall and dark. It was easy to imagine she wasn't one of us at all but that she had appeared in our midst as some kind of changeling. Then, the week before her seventeenth birthday, in March 1982, Elaine collapsed and was taken to hospital where within days she died of a previously undiagnosed neurological condition.

Best friends forever: Tricia and Elaine around 1981

CHAPTER ELEVEN

Tricia wrote:

> *March 15th 1982, 7a.m. approx.*
> Elaine died.
> Too bad to write.

There was nothing more recorded for two months.

The diary picked up again with more boyfriend angst but from then on all entries were laced with misery about Elaine, often expressed in direct messages to her and pleas for her help. 'I still miss you. Guide me. Make me like you: tough. I hope you're happy.' Scores of entries finish 'Goodnight, Elaine, God bless' or 'Love and miss you, Elaine. Goodnight.'

Sometimes there was page after page of what amounted to love letters to Elaine as Tricia poured out her grief and loss. Those passages were intense and I latched onto any mention of normal teenage life: playing her records, youth hostelling with her mates, riding her horse, meeting Steve Wright at the Radio One Roadshow, doing her homework and working weekends at a local hotel. There were welcome mentions of everyday things like watching *Dallas*, *A Kick Up the Eighties* and Steve Davis winning the World Snooker Championships, shopping in Richard Shops and going to Popmobility classes that she referred to as 'Popmo'.

Meanwhile her relationship with her boyfriend had deteriorated and he had become violent – something she wrote almost in passing as though it was of little consequence. 'We had a fight. He hit me hard … I don't really care about him hitting me. It's better than just leaving me.'

She never mentioned this violence to me, just as she never mentioned her ongoing torment about Elaine or her worries about leaving school or the misery of falling out with her friends. What would I have done if she *had* confided in me about the violence? I'm sure I would have confronted him – or perhaps recruited a boyfriend to do it for me – but of course she didn't tell me.

I read my own 1983 diary to understand how I was oblivious to all this misery. I was nineteen years old and in a job I hated, processing cheques at the NatWest Bank. I had got the job because my mother noticed me going through the telephone directory writing to all the banks and building societies in my best cursive script on her pale-blue Basildon Bond. I had laboriously handwritten letter after letter, to a backdrop of the ever-blaring television and the evening news: 'Unemployment tops three million for the first time since the 1930s … one in eight people is out of work … thirty-two people are chasing every vacancy …'

'What are you doing?' she asked.

The next day she phoned the bank manager – farmers were often on familiar terms with the bank manager. 'My daughter has finished her A levels and would like a job … yes, she'll call in tomorrow.' I was assigned to a branch in Lancaster, a high-ceilinged, wood-panelled institution where my first task of the day was going into the manager's office to turn over the blotting paper on his desk, as he held his hands aloft in a helpless manner.

I was relieved to have a job at all. I was enjoying earning and was having a good time with a new boyfriend who Tricia liked, and who would later turn violent towards me.

It seemed I was always out eating, drinking, meeting friends and shopping for clothes. I became closer to Elaine's older sister, Mary, after Elaine died, and we went everywhere together, so as Tricia was left alone, I had more company than ever. I was self-absorbed with no awareness of my little sister's particular unhappiness.

And when my boyfriend started hitting me, I didn't tell anyone about that either. When he gave me a backhander while he was driving the car – my car – and I was in the passenger seat and he burst my nose; when he got me by the throat up against the wall, ripped my earrings out and nearly choked me; when he cried and apologized and promised it would never happen again, I stayed in the relationship and didn't tell anyone about any of that because I didn't have the words and I was ashamed.

I had learned from early on to be ashamed, and shame keeps you quiet.

What's more, physical violence was new to me. I lived in an extended family of big strong men, many of them rugby-league players – men who could have picked up my violent boyfriend under one arm and run away with him – but I had never seen or heard of a man hitting a woman in real life. The atmosphere at home could be difficult – cold and tense – but we weren't hitting each other. Being the recipient of such violence made me feel I'd glimpsed a sordid, depraved world, not one my family would understand and therefore a world in which I was alone.

When I was nineteen I dumped the bank job and joined the civil service fifty miles away and Tricia wrote in her diary: 'I'm the only one left. Now I'll be even lonelier.'

A year later her grief for Elaine remained raw:

> The last time I saw Elaine alive I took her a *Look Now* magazine, a book on Shakin' Stevens and an elephant with a bandage round its trunk. When I left I squeezed her hand and said I loved her. At the door I turned back; she was already asleep.

Tricia regularly visited Elaine's grave with bunches of daffo-dils or lilac or cherry blossom gathered from around the farm. Sometimes on her way to the church she sneaked into the primary-school garden – a garden we were not allowed to play in as pupils – and picked flowers from there. When she got to the graveyard she sat beside the grave and talked to Elaine, which she described as 'having lovely chats', and she sang songs to her including 'Love and Affection' and David Bowie's 'Oh! You Pretty Things', about nightmares and strangers.

This behaviour was not surprising because after Grandad Ben died, when I was ten years old, Grandma Mary put a small marble vase by his headstone engraved 'In Loving Memory of Grandad', to encourage his grandchildren to visit his grave. And we did. We cycled to the churchyard, picking buttercups and cow parsley on the way to shove in the marble pot, flung the bikes on the surrounding graves, and lounged sunbathing and chatting. It was a peaceful spot among the gravestones, surrounded by green fields and sheltered by the branches of an oak tree planted to mark George VI's coronation.

On a grave further down there was often a greeting card, damp and fading – a birthday card or Christmas card from a man to his deceased wife, signed with kisses. I thought of this years later when a caretaker at a Glasgow cemetery told me of an elderly man who visited his wife's grave every day, held his arm out for her ghost, opened the car door for her and drove her home to watch *Countdown*, only to bring her back afterwards.

Occasionally as kids we found the great iron key to the church door, in its hiding place, and went inside and ventured up the steps to the pulpit and had a look at the world from there. Or we tried on the vicar's surplice in the vestry, waving our arms about, imagining we looked like something from a horror film. We met Elaine at the church before going on to the post office to buy gobstoppers and aniseed balls.

Years later, when I was a member of a poetry group, we read Wordsworth's 'We Are Seven', about a child who treats her dead relatives as alive and plays on their graves to be near them. I said, 'Oh yes, we used to do that,' and I was aware of all faces turning towards me.

In 1995, when Tricia was twenty-eight, she wrote a long piece in her diary about the loss of Elaine:

At the funeral I felt so alone, bereft, inconsolable. I remember standing on the edge of the grave looking at her nameplate, throwing some grit onto the coffin. Feeling unstable; looking around for an arm or a face to guide me. Everyone was turned away, clutching their own grief. I stood in the cold, unmoving except for sobs. No one came. I went home. Listened to Diana Ross and the Supremes over and over. Building up walls. Wishing I was dead. Stopped eating. Refused to talk. Dropped out of normal behaviour. Became as grey as I felt. No one could get through. I couldn't smile or talk except in monosyllables. Began to fail exams, not

turn up for classes. Smoke excessively. Having fights
with my boyfriend. Feeling a little closer to death every
time. I would get drunk at teenage discos and cry
wanting her back. My boyfriend and I fought. He hit
me, lots of blows to the head. I was hitting him back, I
got dizzy, saw stars. I left school with 5 O levels and
went to 6th form. Mr Y [one of her teachers] took us
out for a celebration. I was the last one to be dropped
off. He reached over and kissed me. Kept trying to get
his hand up my jumper. I was so ashamed. I knew it
was what I deserved. I hated him. He said I was cold
and he knew I could be warm if I tried. Mr C [another
teacher] was a fine man. He tried to get through to me.
I was very fond of him. He died of a heart attack just as
we left school. Then my pony died and then P [a local
boy] died who was everybody's friend. I struggled
through A levels, got two and started work on the farm.
Dad said there were worse tragedies than losing a friend,
like losing a child or losing a mother.

Reading this I was struck first that she had exchanged
remarks with Dad about her distress. I imagined he found
her crying, maybe cuddling the dog in the barn or with her
face buried in her horse's neck in the stable – she mentioned
more than once crying on Nell, her mare – and asked her
what was wrong, but I doubt the conversation lasted more
than a moment or two.

When she wrote this Elaine had been dead thirteen years and Tricia seemed to be trying to move on. I wondered whether she wrote it as a result of counselling or whether she was trying to deal with the grief on her own by saying good-bye to Elaine in writing.

The other striking thing was the predatory behaviour of her teacher. Tricia told me about this some years after it happened with a look of disgust on her face. I wasn't surprised to hear it – the 1970s and early 80s were a sleazy time when young women took it for granted that opportun-istic men would try to prey on them, regardless of differences in age or status. When she told me I rolled my eyes and said, 'Dirty old bastard,' and she nodded.

Writing about Elaine's death, which had taken place all those years before, Tricia continued:

> Elaine, I have to say goodbye. I turned to you when I
> needed to decide what to do. I don't want to let you go.
> I feel like it's my pain and it's precious, if I didn't have
> that there would be a big space. At least I know this
> pain. If I let go of it something terrible might replace it.'

She also wrote about finding out Elaine had died. I recog-nized the latter part, after the phone call, as a factual account of that morning. However, I was baffled by the opening passage about the 'visitation' from Elaine – was this a piece of imaginative creative writing? Was it fantasy? Or was Tricia convinced that she had had a visitation from Elaine who was in hospital and that she shouldered the blame for giving Elaine permission to die?

I was asleep and partly woke. I felt there was someone there. I realized it was Elaine. She said: 'It's me; I'm fine.' I was pleased she had come, happy she wasn't in pain. I'd been worried. She said: 'I haven't got long.' She said I must listen, it was important. She was going, she said. She had to go and I must let her. She said she had accepted it and wasn't going to fight and I must do the same. 'I don't understand why,' I said. 'I don't want you to go. Try to fight it.' She said: 'No, you must be strong.' She was very firm. She said: 'Stop that right now, I'm going and you must let me. Know that I am happy to go. It's right for me. I have something to go to. I'm not scared. I trust them.' I said: 'OK. I believe you. I don't want you to but I'm going to try.' She stayed for a minute. Then she said: 'It's time. I must go.' We said goodbye and she slipped away. I knew she'd gone but it was OK. I let her go. I drifted back to sleep, at peace. It was OK.

The writing then cut to an hour or two later:

The phone rings. I'm awake. I hold my breath. I must be wrong. Make it a dream. Just stop it. I don't want to let this happen. But I can hear Mum groan. 'Oh no,' she says. Catherine goes downstairs. Mum says: 'Tell Patricia Elaine's dead.' Catherine comes upstairs. She has her hands to her face. I stand at the top of the stairs in my doorway watching her. She looks up and her face is crumpled up crying. She says: 'Elaine's died.' I say: 'I know.' I turn away. I shut the door. I just cry. Aunty Marion takes us to school. I sit in the car and I feel a wall building up. I can tell them she said it was OK or I can hide from them. I hide. The wall grows and my misery is all-consuming. I have no substance, I'm just bones. Grey and empty. I'm numb. No one can get into my mind because it is a void collapsed in on itself. They just blow right through me. I see Mr D. I tell him about Elaine speaking to me. I say it can't be true, she was 16. You don't die for no reason when you're 16. He says you do. I break. Shatter.

I didn't discuss the impact of Elaine's death with Tricia in the months after, and maybe she wouldn't have welcomed it if I had. A year later she wrote about me and Elizabeth 'talking about God and dying' and said: 'It always makes me shake.'

If Tricia had received counselling when Elaine died, to help her express her shock and grief, and her loss and loneliness, and her belief that somehow she was responsible (although when this belief began I don't know), would it have made any difference in the long run? Bereavement counselling was not something that would ever have been suggested in our family – nor, I imagine, in any other farming family like ours. 'Therapy' to the likes of us was not to talk about something but 'to keep busy', so I'd see Grandma Mary, Mum and my aunts furiously crafting or painting or gardening to help them deal with grief, and possibly upping their church attendance, whereas I assumed the men went outside and worked even harder than usual. But Tricia was left to her own devices and, although she loved writing and painting, her own devices too often consisted of withdrawing into herself, smoking and staring into space.

As it was, not only was Tricia not benefiting from counselling but her relationship with Mum was fraught. She wrote: 'Mum sighs a lot. Still not speaking to me after three days.'

Mum used silence as a weapon. Her silence was as powerful as her words which could be fierce, opinionated and dismissive. Silently she communicated her anger and contempt – by expression, by mood, by body language. She could remain silent for hours during the day, withdrawn behind her locked bedroom door. I don't know if the door was actually locked, but it was shut fast and seemingly inviolable and it indicated she was UNAVAILABLE. The room beyond was strictly out of bounds. This silence and absence created a brooding, stagnant atmosphere, a torpor throughout the house that was overwhelming.

Dad worked outside for long hours and when he came in he escaped into sleep in his armchair.

By then I had left the farm and escaped too. So had Elizabeth.

But there was no escape for Tricia yet.

What was Mum so angry about? Everything and nothing. Tiny things and things so enormous she couldn't articulate them. I am not sure what bargain she thought she had struck with life, but life had pulled a fast one. She saw her existence as one of chronic self-sacrifice, and described it as 'just one damned thing after another'. She lived in a welter of resentment, hostility and frustration where we apparently 'had her for a rubbing rag'.

I knew what she *didn't* want – what she had – but I had no idea what she *did* want. This did not stop me feeling I should be able to provide it. I felt a responsibility to make my mother happy. I owed her. None of us deserved her – we knew that because she told us so. In some unarticulated way it was my fault she was unhappy, but I was rendered powerless because while demanding help she simultaneously rejected whatever I offered as not good enough. *If yer want owt doing, yer mon do it yerself!* My mother was disappointed in us and so was I.

I know now that as a child Elizabeth felt the same. She remembers her main feeling associated with Mum being one of guilt. She felt she should have been 'better', more like Mum, and that she was a let-down. She dealt with this by trying to keep out of the way and felt immensely self-conscious – worried about doing or saying the wrong thing. She thinks this made her 'dishonest' with herself – unable to show any weakness and with the pressure on to be continually achieving. She remembers staying with an aunt for a few days and when she was brought home the aunt mentioned that she was worried about Elizabeth being 'over-shy' and hardly daring to speak at all, but Mum would not talk about it.

Mum's anger, whether it was because the house was untidy, or we'd missed the school bus, or something had happened on the farm, had an immediate physical effect on me – I felt my stomach contract, I held my breath, I dry-swallowed.

When I was eleven I started going behind the outhouses on the farm where the rubbish was dumped waiting for incineration. I took glass jars, one after another, and lobbed them against the red-brick wall at the back of Gran's Dairy – lob, smash, lob, smash – and I watched the shattered glass fall down behind the coal heap and disappear.

I was highly tuned to my mother's moods, in a constant state of vigilance for changes, but despite wanting to say the right thing and do the right thing I was unable to use this information for anything other than to worry about it. The bad atmosphere was enormous and wordless – an entity, an oppressive presence. The world was unsafe and wobbly. It was a world of high expectations but expectations that could never be fulfilled.

Years later, when I had children of my own, my mother's brooding silence or clattering anger still had this effect on me. On visits to her house I often took refuge in the bedroom trying to distance myself from her noise or her quiet. I clutched a self-help book, blindly staring at positive affirmations, trying to steady myself, or I muttered the words aloud as though incanting a spell. *All is well. All is well.*

CHAPTER TWELVE

I continued to read the diaries at Hawthornden Castle, all day, every day, for the first week. I took breaks walking in the snow and frost around the castle grounds and into the woods. On one of the castle walks was a great boulder with a flat ledge like a giant's seat, which rested on the riverbank above a sharp slope into the water. Playwright Ben Jonson walked here from London in 1618 to meet the poet, and then owner of the castle, Sir William Drummond of Hawthornden, and they sat on this seat to discuss their contemporary, Shakespeare. Determined to get in on the act, I gingerly lowered myself onto the flat stone. It froze me through my jeans but I sat there doggedly trying to pick up any vibes from the seventeenth century. The idea didn't seem so ridiculous. This was a timeless place, with its landscape of cliffs and gorges and trees that went on for ever. After a few minutes, unable to stand the cold any longer, I rejoined the path and strode up to the castle. There I plunged back into a different time and place – New House Farm in the 1980s.

* * *

In 1984, two years after Elaine died, Tricia started sixth-form college twelve miles away in Preston, studying for A levels in English, biology, economics and art. Our local secondary school did not cater for students aged over sixteen and it was not a foregone conclusion that pupils (even clever ones) would go on to further education. Tricia's final school report noted that after a poor start to Fifth Year her performance had improved and her year head remarked: 'I am sure she will be a good worker when she leaves school.' Many pupils left school for employment in local businesses or family firms – shops, farms, garages; otherwise girls usually went into nursing, hairdressing and catering or the lower echelons of banking or public-sector administration. Boys got apprenticeships at British Aerospace, or as plumbers, electricians or joiners. A number of girls got jobs in the local overall factory, or the mill which produced headscarves for the Middle East; the unlucky ones got work in the 'chicken factory'.

It is clear from the diaries Tricia did not enjoy sixth-form college.

I am unsurprised. Education was a chore for me too until I went back to study to be a journalist, full-time, in my mid-twenties, when I found a passion for learning.

But at this stage, for Tricia, passion was lacking. Her week was punctuated by missed buses, skived-off classes, forgotten assignments, uncompleted homework and days she described as 'struggled through'. There was dread during weekends and holidays because they inevitably ended and the whole dispiriting rigmarole would start again. It wasn't that she didn't want to succeed; in one diary entry she remarked, 'Worked in all my lessons. Felt proud,' and later, 'Art went well. I am elated,' but this was rare. Mainly it was a litany of misery and stress as she wrestled with economic data and the balance of payments, analysed D. H. Lawrence and James Joyce, created artistic compositions of sheep's skulls and fried eggs and dusty mirrors, and studied the workings of the digestive system. She was clever and creative but she was dragged down by sadness and found no joy and little satisfaction in any of it. In February 1984 she wrote: 'Cried about the state of my life. Rang Cathy and she was lovely.'

Leafing through the diaries, I latched onto these positive comments about me and read them over and over again hoping to reassure myself that I *did* do the right thing sometimes; anything to try to assuage the guilt. I wanted to brandish these remarks in people's faces: *See! She thought I was lovely! What happened was not my fault!* But the effects of her positive words didn't last and then I had to go on the hunt for more.

At this time I was living in a council flat high up on Oldham Edge overlooking dozens of mill chimneys and row after row of *Coronation Street* houses. The view from my kitchen window was a Lowry painting. I had been allocated a council flat because I had a civil-service job in the town but nowhere to live, so I was classed as homeless. I had to accept the first place I was offered or drop to the bottom of the housing list. I ended up in a large two-bedroomed flat that I couldn't afford to furnish or decorate. My mother shoved my childhood single bed and mattress in the back of the Mondeo and drove me the fifty miles from the farm. We went to Tommyfield Market down the hill from my flat and bought a second-hand two-ring cooker for £18, including delivery and fitting.

Then Mum said she'd better be heading home to get Dad's tea on the table. I watched from my third-floor window as she pulled out of the car park. She didn't look back.

She said she'd pay to have a phone fitted so I could always call home. When I called home she said, 'What do you want, my tea's going cold.'

It was a hot summer and my milk carton bobbed in a bucket of water as I tried to keep it cool. I had a beanbag, a record player and a table and chair. I had no idea about DIY and nailed up some of my mother's 1960s fibreglass curtains – showing ships in full sail – at the living-room window. One day I got home to find a council workman pulling the nails out so he could fit new frames. He looked at me, part accusing, part pitying, shook his head and said, 'I've never seen owt like it.'

I laughed as though I thought it was funny but I felt small and humiliated seeing myself through his eyes: hopeless, handless, useless.

On one of the first nights in my flat a drunk banged on my front door, jamming his key in and out of my lock. I could see his swaying body through the frosted glass. It did not occur to me to put the chain on and lie low. Instead I opened the door, smiled, and said, 'I think you may have the wrong flat.' He looked at me a bit like the workman; as though it was me who was daft, not him.

Coming from a village, I felt it only polite to get to know the old lady next door. Her flat smelled like Great-Great-Aunt Alice's bedroom. She made me a cup of milky tea and gave me details of her bowels and how the doctor wouldn't listen and the syrup made no difference, and if I had time perhaps I could pop round and wash all the crystal in her glass-fronted cabinet?

There were no carpets and no other curtains in my flat and the walls were painted in the previous tenant's chipped and lurid gloss. The grass-green bathroom had no shower so I jammed a rubber hose onto the taps and washed kneeling down.

Junk mail addressed to strangers piled up behind the door and every day I stepped over it. I drank a bottle of wine a night, sometimes driving to the off-licence to buy a second. I never got rid of a single empty.

By the time Mum and Dad came to help me move out into my own terraced house, a year later, empty bottles of Valpolicella, Bull's Blood and Country Manor were lined up against the skirting board right round the kitchen, the dining room and the hall, and Dad, who'd never seen the flat before, gazed about in amazement, shook his head and said, 'She's been living rough.'

It was little more than indoor camping but that didn't stop me loving the freedom of having my own home, loving that I had escaped.

My car was as chaotic. Taking my boss (actually my boss's boss's boss) out on 'an accompanied visit' so he could assess my professionalism with the VAT traders, he got in the passenger seat and his polished brogues tangled up in a set of suspenders with the stockings still attached that must have fallen onto the car floor, among the de-icer and the sweet wrappers, from a laundry bag en route to my mother's. I laughed out loud and slapped the steering wheel at the sight of his long legs pedalling to break free. He looked at me wiping the tears of laughter from my eyes and then he laughed too.

I invited Tricia and other friends to Oldham for weekends and they scattered sleeping bags on the bare wooden floors. We went to nightclubs called Scandals and Smokies and drank lager and Bacardi and Coke. There is a photograph of me, Tricia and Elizabeth standing outside the bright-orange front door of my flat having returned from the corner shop where we had bought our lunch. This was a shop that sold single eggs and individual fish fingers to its impoverished customers and where tatty bits of meat darkened in a display cabinet as flies washed their wings on the inside of the glass.

In the photo Tricia is carrying a Twix and a Marathon, Elizabeth is carrying a tin of Heinz tomato soup and a Marathon, I am carrying a tin of Heinz oxtail soup and a bottle of cider.

I was lonely so I went to the Citizens Advice Bureau to ask about volunteering. They sent me to the local hospital geriatric department. I reported for duty, to be met by a gaggle of nurses who neither knew I was coming nor what to do with me. One looked me up and down: 'So you want to marry a doctor.' They all laughed. 'Good luck with that! You can be in charge of the Horlicks trolley.' She showed me round the ward, marching into a bathroom cubicle as an old man, not unlike Gran, sat miserably on the toilet. 'All right, Eric?' she said as I smiled vaguely, avoiding his eye, pretending I didn't know what he was doing. They gave me a white coat with a badge saying 'Volunteer'. I took it home after dishing out all the Horlicks and stuffed it to the back of a cupboard, vowing never to get old.

I signed up for art night classes at the local secondary school. Three elderly ladies huddled round their watercolours not wanting anyone else in their gang. The teacher was busy getting his O-level students up to scratch for their exam. I did a couple of still lifes – my car keys and some empty wine bottles – then, feeling like an intruder, I stopped going.

My job was in a male-dominated department. One office was plastered in porn – open-crotch shots – put there as a test, a challenge to the influx of young women joining up. Were we men enough to stick around? I didn't flinch, I didn't complain. I never said a word.

I was living in a grubby town at a grubby time. One day, I went for a drink with colleagues after work to a gloomy basement bar behind the bus station. We were sitting at a table downing fast rounds. I glanced behind my chair and saw a thin pale girl writhing naked on the carpet. She couldn't have been older than seventeen. 'It's the teatime stripper,' said my workmate, obviously familiar with the concept. She must have been performing for a few minutes because her bra and knickers were already thrown onto the tiny dance floor. No one was taking any notice. Her music, which came from a cassette deck plugged in by the bar, was too quiet to protect her. When it ended she grabbed her underwear and scurried through a door behind the bar as the barman gave her a pitying half-smile.

I was nineteen and trying to be treated with respect by the business people whose accounts I checked (often leaving them with a VAT bill). These ranged from shopkeepers to scrap dealers, from builders to bakers to clothing manufacturers. I introduced myself as 'Miss Simpson' and refused to give my first name. It didn't always work. One import/export merchant dropped a paper and, bending to retrieve it, remarked, 'Miss Simpson, why are you wearing white tights?

If you get run over on the way home your bum'll look like two bags of flour.'

I met someone at work but he was married. I became depressed – and at last acknowledged it as such. I had had several similar bouts since the age of twelve or thirteen. I had never said anything. This time it had got worse but still I did not go to the doctor's or confide in anyone. It was the familiar numbness and blankness, that contradictory feeling of being hollow yet weighed down. I was struck by a terrible stillness that was impossible to shake off. I was becalmed but not peaceful. I couldn't read. Everything seemed pointless and overwhelming as I shrank smaller and smaller, feeling nearer to death than to life. There was a tightening behind my breastbone, a nagging nausea, a stone lodged in my stomach and a ringing in my ears. I was always on the verge of tears but never cried. I fantasized about dying and spent several evenings considering how I could make it look like an accident.

I lived day by day with a false smile as very gradually, over many months, the darkness began to lift. Why it lifted I did not know. The pattern over the years had been that as I gave up hope of it ever lifting I'd begin to realize I was looking forward to things again, feeling excited.

But although I had at last recognized depression in myself it did not follow that I recognized it in Tricia. At around this time I noted in my diary: 'Took Tricia out to the pub with me and my mates. She was in a bad mood and hardly spoke.'

As I read through Tricia's diaries I realized that her bouts of darkness had been more prolonged, although there had been some respite – usually demonstrated by a resurgence in her love for painting and horse-riding and (when she was older) travel. But there were gaps in the entries – sometimes for months at a time – and I can only assume these were periods of the most severe depression. So my fear that her writing would be unrelenting descriptions of deep depression were not founded – perhaps because during her worst times it seemed too hard to pick up a pen at all.

When I eventually moved into my own terraced house down the road from the Oldham flat, I stood in the kitchen with its hotchpotch of mismatched units, transfixed by the sound of next door stirring their tea and buttering their toast. I lived only feet from these people but never knew their names. By contrast, on the first night in my house, the lady from the other side knocked on the door. She handed me a bottle of parsnip homebrew. 'I'm Clarice,' she said. 'And my man's Bob.' She was in her sixties, five feet ten, with bouncy grey curls, slacks, a pinny worn thin, and bright-white trainers.

Clarice took me to the Sun Inn. She was loud, outspoken and funny and had her own spot at the corner of the bar, alongside a man with an ill-fitting prosthetic face, another with a prosthetic leg that he took off as his party-piece, and a woman with a baby called 'Carly' because she got pregnant drunk on Carling Black Label. Clarice made half the pub meat and potato pies and dished them out in battered cooking tins wrapped in plastic bags.

There was a meeting of the National Front in the back room. When one skinhead swaggered past in his tight jeans and bovver boots to look through the window, Clarice said, 'Ah, are you looking for your mummy?' and smiled at him insincerely until he scurried back to the safety of the snug. Clarice was an elderly woman but being with her made me feel powerful, strong and safe.

Within a week or two I was spending every Sunday evening in Clarice and Bob's front room, watching Agatha Christie, drinking gin and tonic and eating chicken sandwiches as the gas fire prickled our shins. We squeezed on the sofa among her knitting bags and with her Siamese cat, Pinkie, surrounded by years of clutter – every bit with a story attached.

Clarice loved to share her secrets, waiting until Bob dozed off in his armchair before telling me what she'd got up to with her lover during the war. 'If I had my time again I'd do everything twice as fast, twice as often and twice as reg'lar.' She approved of the pencil skirts and high heels I wore for work and that I curled my hair and never went out without full make-up. 'There's no point in having your stall set out and your blinds down, Cath.'

I told Clarice stories too. I told her how I had ricocheted from the violent lover via various other unsuitable boyfriends to my current partner who was charming and faithless. Clarice liked my faithless boyfriend. She watched him from behind her net curtains as he drew up in his sports car which was as long as her house, and as he straightened and buttoned his designer jacket before knocking on my door. Life was for living, not for worrying about other girlfriends. You had to enjoy things while they lasted because nothing lasted for ever, she said, shaking her head and topping my glass up from the Gordon's bottle as the ice cubes chinked.

I had found a home.

Maybe it was knowing Clarice that gave me the power to speak up for the first time. I was leaving work one day when a senior colleague leaned into the lift and grabbed my breasts. He did not say a word but withdrew his hands as the doors clanged shut and I descended to the ground alone. It was so fast and fleeting that I might have thought I'd imagined it if I wasn't still stinging. I went to the pub where workmates drank after office hours. I walked in and announced to the bar: 'You'll never guess what, X just grabbed my boobs so hard in the lift it hurt.'

The words were like clean, fresh water in my mouth.

Every face swivelled my way, expressions aghast.

They heard me. They believed me.

The man was made to apologize to me by my line manager, an experience more mortifying than the original breast-grab. 'I've been given the mother and father of all bollockings, Cath,' he said, 'and told to say sorry. I was tempted and I fell.' The incident did not go on his work record. I did not want it to; I wanted to put it behind me. But the important thing was I'd spoken out; for the first time I'd heard myself speak up about an incident that would previously have shamed me into silence.

At the farm the tension between Tricia and Mum often bubbled over because of Tricia's terrible timekeeping. An entry in her diary records: 'Late going for the bus. Mum crashed on canal bridge – bust the lights and buckled the bonnet. Mum started insulting the chap driving the other car.'

And on an icy January morning: 'My birthday. Mum skidded the car right round taking me to bus and shouted at me.' On the odd occasion Tricia was on time it deserved an exclamation mark. 'Got up in time!'

Tricia's bad timekeeping was caused in part because of her poor sleep habits (although she always had a deeply ingrained lack of urgency – which may have been the depression). She'd stay up half the night reading or drawing, and then oversleep the following morning. The sleep habits developed in these years never left her.

Living in the countryside two miles from a bus stop was a trial. The miles of unlit lane between the farm and the nearest town had hawthorn hedges that towered high as though they would meet overhead and swallow you up. The farm, which had been a playground for children, became a trap for teenagers. Asking for lifts to meet friends, trying to get home at all hours and getting to college and school on time were all flashpoints.

I have a reporter's notebook, begun when I was ten years old, in which I interviewed family members about their likes and dislikes. I kept this going for several years and when Tricia was seventeen she listed as her dislikes: 'Wellies full of water, walking home from the bus in the rain and getting stuck in phone boxes with no lift home.'

Tricia began smoking on the school bus when she was twelve and never managed to give up. But why were we on the school bus in the first place? Mum always had to get the car out to run us to the bus stop half a mile away at eight o'clock every morning anyway or we would have missed it. We then sat on the bus in a smoky fug for an hour as it trailed round remote farms and lanes picking up far-flung pupils to get us to school by nine. The bus was packed with smokers and bullies and bullies' victims. We were never bullied but we witnessed it and, despite being terrified, I tried to fight back by shoving a maths compass up the bully's backside as he lumbered down the bus aisle. Why didn't Mum get the car out at quarter to nine and drive us the three miles to school instead and spare us the torment of that bus? One of the reasons was because, of course, we never told Mum about the bullying and the smoking because that would have involved having a conversation.

* * *

Mum had a fearsome temper and never backed down or admitted she was wrong – sending us to school on the bus was an exception to that. When Tricia was in her thirties and struggling for the umpteenth time to stop smoking – with patches or hypnosis or self-help schemes or whatever she was trying now – Mum said, 'Why did I put you on that school bus? Why didn't I just take you to school?'

She lived in fear that smoking would kill Tricia.

As I read Tricia's diary it was easy to forget the pressure Mum was under at that time. In early 1984 her own mother, Grandma Mary, died of ovarian cancer and Dad was diagnosed with cancer in his left hip bone and had to undergo weeks of chemotherapy. He had already survived cancer in his left shoulder blade five years before and would go on to survive this too, but for a while he was very ill and had to undertake an eighty-mile round trip for each chemotherapy session at Christie's Hospital in Manchester which was followed by bedridden vomiting.

Because both cancerous growths had been on his left side Mum was convinced it was caused by the tank of weedkiller he used to carry on his left shoulder as he walked around the fields in the evenings spraying docks and thistles by hand. But this is something we would never really know.

Meanwhile Mum was keeping the farm going, organizing milking morning and night for our herd of eighty cows, and arranging Elizabeth's wedding to Phil, for which she made all four red lacy bridesmaid dresses. It was no wonder her patience was in short supply. Of course Mum's patience was *always* in short supply – except this time she had reason. Tricia was eighteen and did not see it that way. Shortly before Grandma died, she wrote: 'Mum was nasty. She's acting strange. She doesn't like me.'

As Grandma's ovarian cancer took its toll Tricia wrote: 'I wish Grandma could have some of my time – at least she'd know what to do with it.'

Tricia helped on the farm when Dad was bedridden with chemo-sickness – doing the evening milking and feeding the calves. She mentioned Dad's illness but never acknowledged it might kill him. This seemed odd considering Elaine had died only three years before, so you would think death would be uppermost in her mind – until I remembered at the time I too was unable to countenance that Dad, someone who worked incessantly, carried heavy buckets, flung bales above his head and picked up calves, could physically fail, let alone die.

As I read about Tricia's misery with her A levels, about her struggle to motivate herself and of her fear of academic failure, I was wrenched back to the here and now by a text message from my younger daughter, eighteen-year-old Lara. Lara had a place for next year at Glasgow University and already had the necessary Higher exam results. She texted me to say she wanted to leave school for a few months before going to university. What was the point, she asked, in doing unnecessary Advanced Highers? Instead she planned to get a job and sample the world outside education. She needed me to write to the school to support her. With Tricia in my mind, I did it immediately and without hesitation.

On the same day I heard from my other daughter, 21-year-old Nina, who was working in Germany as part of her German degree at Edinburgh University. She told me she was miserable and had left her job as a classroom assistant in order to travel and go to language school in Berlin.

I thanked my lucky stars my daughters knew when to walk away.

Tricia left sixth-form college with two mediocre A levels and started helping out on the farm. As I read her diary for 1986 I realized it was an account of relative stability, with day after day of normal life – a lot of it spent with an old schoolfriend.

> We talked about clothes and men and Michael Jackson and Clouds [a local disco].
> We got drunk on Malibu and talked for hours.
> I sorted her birthday present – £5 for electrolysis and 20 Bensons.

However, she had regular bad dreams: 'Had a nightmare that Elizabeth and Cathy were saying to me: "You don't belong here. You're not one of us."'

* * *

Her self-confidence improved and she put together a model-ling portfolio by a local photographer. She was five feet nine inches tall, slim with long dark hair and striking features. Although she was 'tied up with nerves' having the pictures taken, she 'loved it'. She was delighted with the finished photographs although shocked at the price: '£38 for photo-graphs!' This was a big step for a person who only a year before had dreaded reading out in English lessons because all eyes would be on her.

Little came of Tricia's modelling career, although I watched her once on the catwalk at a fashion show in Lancaster. She looked terrified and gorgeous. She was not as polished as the other models and when she stumbled the room let out a collective gasp. Nevertheless she had a set of beautiful photographs: 'better than I could ever have imagined'.

I sat rugged up on my bed at Hawthornden, amid the ringing silence of the castle (talking inside was discouraged until dinner-time each day), and as I read the entries for these steady months it was hard to believe how her story ended.

As we were clearing out the farmhouse I discovered her modelling portfolio shoved under her wardrobe, thick with dust and curling at the edges. I had forgotten about these photographs, and Elizabeth and I leafed through and marvelled at the beauty of them, both choosing our favourite pictures to frame and put on display. So now a teenage Tricia – beautiful, solemn, ethereal, brooding – looks down on both of us from our kitchen walls and our living-room cabinets and surveys us with a Mona Lisa expression.

In 1986 Gran died a couple of weeks before his eighty-ninth birthday. The following day Tricia made a doctor's appointment and was prescribed antidepressants for the first time.

She was nineteen.

CHAPTER THIRTEEN

I remember being small – maybe five or six – and my sisters and I were perched in the Land Rover beside Dad; three girls sitting in a row on the front seat squashed together waiting to go to the shop for comics and sweets. There was a man in our farmyard – probably one of the travelling salesmen, known as 'travellers', who sold cow feed and fertilizer – and he asked Dad if he and Mum were going to 'try again for a boy'. Dad did a kind of half-laugh and said, 'No, it's too late now.'

I was glad I was not the youngest of the three sisters. I would have disliked never being able to catch up with the older two and I would not have liked to believe I was the third disappointment. My parents never said they were disappointed by having daughters (pronounced 'dow-ters' by Dad) but it stood to reason they wanted a boy to carry on the farm. My mother said that after each birth of a girl the midwife, Nurse Steele, declared, 'The boys will come! The boys will come!'

We were christened Elizabeth, Catherine and Patricia – strange choices for a mother who did not believe in names being shortened. It was almost as though she was throwing down a challenge to the world: shorten these names if you *dare*. We remained Elizabeth, Catherine and Patricia until one by one we went to secondary school where inevitably, to everyone except my mother, we became Liz, Cathy and Tricia.

Did Tricia feel it was her duty to become a farmer and make Mum and Dad happy?

I never felt that pressure but then I never showed any aptitude for or interest in farming. The only mentions I remember of potential careers involved stereotypically female jobs like teaching, nursing, being a secretary or, if you were attractive and glamorous, an air hostess. When I was seven I slid my leg into the old Austen Princess and a jagged piece of rusty metal sliced my inner thigh to the bone. When I came back from hospital after having five stitches and a traumatic tetanus jab my mother declared: 'Well, you'll never be a model now.'

It soon became clear it wasn't working having Tricia employed on the farm.

She was capable, strong and keen to be involved in the business. When she got herself going she was a great help but she struggled to get out of bed in the morning and could be distracted by a cup of tea and a roll-up fag which could easily last an hour as she did the *Daily Express* crossword or gazed into space. She was leaving most of the early-morning milking to Dad who was now sixty years old and who had recovered from his cancer but was still getting regular check-ups.

Mum was the eldest of eight siblings who had been expected to hand-milk cows every morning before walking miles to school and then milk them again after walking home. She was only seven when the Second World War broke out and thirteen when it finished. During the war years she lived on her family farm in East Lancashire and nights were often spent in the cellar following an air-raid warning. She remembered waking in the morning to see a red glow on the horizon. 'That's Manchester,' said her father.

Mum was quick to feel 'put upon' and resented what she saw as Tricia's easy ride, particularly as Tricia did not help in the house. 'I'm sick to death. You have me for a rubbing rag,' Mum would say, 'taking me for granted. I'm working my fingers to the bone.' The atmosphere between them was tense and, although Dad would have said nothing – anything for a quiet life – I can imagine the slammed doors, the thick silences and the banged pots and pans from Mum to make the point that this poor performance from Tricia Would Not Do.

In 1986, with Tricia aged nineteen, things came to a head, and she recorded in her diary: 'Mum blew a fuse about me working/not working. Said I should sort myself out/consider moving out. I've been considering it for months.'

Family friends suggested Tricia do some travelling. They had relations in Vienna with a young daughter – would Tricia fancy six months as a nanny?

She grabbed the opportunity to escape.

Vienna was bitterly cold and covered in snow in January 1987 as the plane landed and Tricia nervously made her way through the arrivals hall to meet Gerrit, Susie and their four-year-old daughter, Tamara, who was holding Tricia's photograph.

Two days after her arrival she celebrated her twentieth birthday and the Austrian family presented her with a copy of *The Times*, a *Woman's Own*, a china ornament of a frog on skis, an English–German dictionary and a birthday card which played 'Happy Birthday to You'. She described herself as 'touched almost to tears'.

They took Tricia along on their family ski holiday to Hinterglemm. Tricia had never skied before but she had spent a lifetime on horseback; she was physically fit and brave and tackled the slopes with the same courage and determination as she would a set of horse jumps.

'These ski boots are killing me,' she wrote. 'I fall over. I get up. I fall over. I begin to get the hang of it. I fall over. I give up until tomorrow and sit in the sun.'

By the fourth day she was 'frustrated we cannot go faster. I break ranks. Nikki shouts "single file, please" but it is too late, I have tasted freedom.'

Tricia was enamoured by Nikki the ski instructor, who described everything as 'Supa!' I am reminded of her wild crushes when she was fifteen and, as she intertwines remarks about Nikki with the lyrics of Abba's 'When I Kissed the Teacher', I begin to feel nervous. 'I could write a Jilly Cooper novel with Nikki as the hero,' she wrote.

The week was a whirl of eating, drinking, laughing and dancing and, as ski school ended, Nikki told her of the most romantic place in Vienna – the Gloriette, a summer house in the grounds of Schönbrunn Palace – and suggested they could meet there when he returned at the end of the season.

Back in Vienna, as she unpacked her suitcases, Tricia wrote: 'Susie is shocked that I don't know how to wash my own clothes. So am I.'

I am reminded of leaving home and being unable to cook a meal. Mum guarded both her cooker and her washing machine, creating a barrier of anger and martyrdom around herself in the kitchen by bashing and clattering and muttering and sighing. She may have hated this role but it was *hers*. Her frustration would sometimes boil over and the worst rows I had with her as a teenager were caused, at least on the surface, by something trivial like leaving a grill on too long, cutting into food being saved for a meal, or generally 'getting under her feet'.

If Tricia had attempted to use the washing machine there were so many mistakes she could have made: putting in too much washing and overloading the machine; putting in too little washing and wasting hot water; mixing the colours and everything coming out brown; using an incorrect programme so clothes didn't come out clean – so many, many things to get wrong.

The upshot was that Mum did all the cooking and washing but resented us for it. 'Leave it alone! *I'll* do it.' This left you beholden and guilty and ill-prepared for adult life and essentially in a position of dependence and powerlessness. It also sometimes left you without clean underwear, which was why I ended up at secondary school on gym day wearing my sister's boyfriend's bright-red underpants which had a target on the front and bore the words 'Ready! Aim! Fire!'

In Vienna Tricia spent a lot of time reading and rereading letters, writing letters and walking to the postbox. 'Walked around the block to post the letters I wrote last night. Everyone seemed to stare at me. I hope I'm not getting paranoid.'

This was the first mention of paranoia – a condition that became such a destructive part of her life a few years later.

She was twenty years old.

She talked about a book she was reading called '*The Screwtape Letters* – letters from a senior to a junior devil'.

'It causes me to question my religious beliefs,' she wrote. 'I will go to church next week.'

I was surprised. I had not realized Tricia *had* religious beliefs.

After she died I found a book of sermons she had bought from a visiting preacher. She had obviously attended an event and purchased his book and he had signed it for her. On her kitchen table there was a note she had written and never posted thanking him. In her chequebook was a cheque stub for £3,000 payable to this man. I contacted him to ask if he remembered Tricia or if he had talked to her of anything significant before she died. On the phone the preacher sounded detached and said no, he had no memory of her. Who did I say my sister was? What was her name again? Patricia? No, he could not recall meeting her; not at all.

Hearing the lack of interest in his voice made me feel raw. My sister was dead and she had thought enough of this man to buy his book, to write him a thank-you letter, to write him a cheque for thousands of pounds, and yet he didn't remember her and sounded as though he did not have the time or inclination to talk to me. I asked him if he had received her cheque and his voice became alert. His memory was jogged. Oh yes, he said, maybe he did remember Patricia. But what was this about a cheque? He had never received a cheque. How much had I said the cheque was for?

I never found the cheque – only the stub – and it was never cashed. If I had found it I would have ripped it up and chucked it in the bin.

At the time I took Tricia's interest in preachers to be a sign of her vulnerability and her illness. She had never talked to the family about religious faith – but, from what she wrote while in Vienna, it appeared I was wrong.

A week after embarking on *The Screwtape Letters* she wrote: 'I find I want religion to be in my life.'

I googled *The Screwtape Letters* and discovered it was a fictional work examining Christian spirituality written by C. S. Lewis. Was this an opportunity for me to make a connection with the young Tricia? It seemed a chance I shouldn't pass up.

With some hesitation I ordered it.

In Vienna the season for masked balls had begun and Gerrit and Susie asked Tricia if she had a man to take. She had not been in touch with Nikki since their farewell on the ski slopes and she was nervous about asking him.

Susie took her to hire a white ball gown and bought her a pair of white shoes. Tricia's nerve failed so Gerrit declared *he* would take charge and call Nikki. 'I am so happy at the thought,' she wrote. 'I can only pray he will come to the ball. To take my mind off him I read Somerset Maugham's *The Summing Up*.'

Nikki did not commit. He told Gerrit he would see if he was available.

As I read the diary I did not know how this story played out, I did not know if Nikki came to the ball, but as I sat cross-legged on the bed in Hawthornden Castle in 2016 flicking over the pages of Tricia's 1987 entries, I urged him to say yes. I longed to shout into the dark, twenty-nine years into the past, to demand he went to the ball and made Tricia happy. Go to the ball! Do the right thing! Do you not know how this story ends? I wanted to rewind time and ensure that the right thing happened, just this once, at least, and make certain that Tricia's dream came true.

Nikki did not come to the ball, and for a moment I hated him. This was like a badly written film script; this story had gone askew. *Surely* the gorgeous hero came to the ball – even if he was late/wearing the wrong clothes/unable to dance. But no; the day before the ball he phoned to tell Susie he was not available and Susie told Tricia.

I have obliterated his number so that I cannot be tempted to try again. At dinner I thought I would have to leave and cry into my mashed potato. I keep thinking of Somerset Maugham's Grandfather throwing a potato at every picture in the room then returning to his meal. It's quite funny really – this poor family only wanted someone to stack the dishwasher.

Gerrit said I must learn in Austria there are ski, tennis and dance instructors, also musicians, who are very bad boys. I said it's the same in England but I wouldn't have fallen for it there.

Tricia was escorted to the ball by a family friend called Clemence.

> He is extremely correct and shook my hand before blowing the snow off his immaculate trilby. He chatted all the way to the ball. I didn't know what to expect. We changed shoes and went into the main hall. Susie and I put our masks on and lined up with the other girls so we could stand on the dance floor and watch the ballet. The ball began after 10 p.m. The old boys went in first wearing their appropriate caps. My heart began to thump as we stood under the flowered canopies, the orchestra playing very loud. Susie said: 'It's a good feeling?' I said no, although it was partly thrilling. She said: 'It is necessary to enjoy this to succeed in life.' I only hoped not to fall over. The girl in front visibly grew inches as we stepped out. I kept my eyes on her back.

There followed dances by the debutantes who all entered carrying three roses and then, according to Tricia, the event became a 'free-for-all'. 'We danced the polka, the foxtrot, the rumba, the tango, the boogie and the English and Viennese waltzes. I was wooden-footed but Clemence was patient. It was great fun because Austrians don't ask you to dance, they say "you dance", and before you know it you are foxtrotting madly.'

They drank glasses of sekt – a sparkling wine – and orange juice on the balcony and gazed down upon the swirling dancers.

They left in the early hours and headed home through the snow.

I visited Tricia in Vienna and went with her to the Sunday service at the Anglican Church. It never struck me she was going to church for any reason other than to socialize with English-speakers. We were all christened at six weeks old in the Church of England and confirmed aged ten; we attended Sunday school and a Church primary school, where we were told a Bible story every morning which we drew in our exercise books. Prayers were a mix of wishes, hopes and thanks. There were prayers at the beginning and end of the school day and before and after our school dinner. *Hands together, eyes closed.* There was no 'hellfire and damnation'; it was a benign sort of religion.

Indeed, telling us the story of the Massacre of the Innocents, our class teacher – spindle-thin Mrs Darlington, in her oddly outdated, high-fashion 1950s dresses – said, 'King Herod was mardy and one day he had a bit of a paddy.'

Religion featured heavily at primary school. There was much hymn singing and silent memorizing of the catechism which, alongside rote learning of the times tables, practising cursive writing and mastering embroidery, filled our late

1960s/early 1970s schooldays. The establishment was ruled by elderly Miss Proctor whose preferences filled the timetable, so of science, rudimentary French or sports there was none.

We attended Sunday services at Easter and Mothering Sunday and for the Harvest Festival – where the women rushed out of the church if the sermon was overlong muttering, 'My beef'll be like shoe leather.' But I thought going to church was no more or no less a part of village life than buying sweets at the post office or dancing round the maypole at the field day. Bible stories and the lives of the saints were good enough tales – something similar to Greek myths or other legends. My mother mentioned God and the Bible in a random, haphazard way – 'Did I hear you call someone a "fool"? The Bible says you shouldn't!' And when

Me and Tricia at Winmarleigh Church of England Primary School

she spilt salt she threw it over her left shoulder 'to keep away the devil'. I never considered any of this meant you actually *believed in God*, or at least not in anything but the vaguest sense.

Tricia was searching for meaning, and one of the places she was searching was at church. Mum and Dad were impressed with her for getting out of bed in Vienna and leaving the flat at all, let alone meeting all these charming Brits who seemed so keen to say hello and welcome us into the vestry for tea and biscuits.

As for the religious aspect; we did not discuss it.

When *The Screwtape Letters* arrived I began to read but it was very dull. I put it down. I picked it up and tried again, but it was still dull. I put it away, leaving the bookmark in to indicate to myself I would go back and try again. But I did not go back and try again. In fact I forgot where I put it. There was no connection to be made with Tricia through C. S. Lewis. Instead I ordered Somerset Maugham's *The Summing Up*.

Life in Vienna involved much eating: of *Semmel* with ham, *Semmel* with jam, pizza, cream cakes, *Kaffee und Kuchen*, first breakfasts and second breakfasts, feasts at the Chinese restaurant, 'vanillas' sneaked to her bedroom, midnight spring rolls brought in by Gerrit and Susie, 'cocoa to settle the schnapps', *Krapfen*, *Knödels* and *Ohne Gleichen*, ices on the Schwedenplatz, 'delicious' cheese sausage from the Sausage Box, and late-night hotdogs after the clubs.

Then everything changed.

In April Tricia attended the Hungarian Ball in the rococo Palais Auersperg, with its gargantuan chandeliers, grand marble hallways and sweeping staircases. A friend plaited her hair and loaned her a dress. She had had months of dancing lessons by now and could confidently waltz around the ballroom with Ludwig, a family friend. Then, as if sent by her very own fairy godmother, she spotted a tall, dark, handsome stranger. 'Soon after midnight I saw him. He had already seen me and we locked eyes immediately.' This young man was an acquaintance of Ludwig who introduced them. 'He is called Patrik and he is what I always wanted.' For a girl brought up on Walt Disney this was a dream come true. They danced all night and parted at dawn with a promise to meet again. She 'walked on air to the car' (I expect her to write 'carriage'), which took her to a friend's house on the edge of the Vienna Woods for breakfast.

Patrik, a Hungarian musician, phoned the next day, and she wrote: 'This is where the fun really starts.'

They wandered together around the coffee houses and parks of Vienna, going to parties and concerts and enjoying themselves. He took her across the Iron Curtain to Hungary where they stayed in a lakeside summer house and where she 'felt guilty about buying cheap clothes and cigarettes for 40 pence a pack'.

'I love life,' she wrote.

Tricia's life had never looked enviable before but it did now.

At this time, for me, a three-year relationship had come to an end and I was heartbroken. Tricia's happiness made me realize my relationships had always been more about painful longing than joyfulness. What's more, my job as a VAT woman was dull. I spent every day visiting traders around the Greater Manchester area – endless red-brick back-to-backs, corner shops and shabby pubs – where I inspected business records in freezing back rooms or in bars stinking of disinfectant and guard dogs under the gaze of a resentful landlady wearing last night's eyeliner. I made my way around the area inexpertly with a Manchester A–Z and one day found myself at an appointment in Market Street, Droylsden when it should have been Market Street, Mottram, or Market Street, Hyde, or any number of other Market Streets. They all looked the same. I remember resting my head on the steering wheel and thinking: How did it come to this?

Despite Tricia's happiness, however, three months later she wrote: 'I must be moving on.'

Patrik was training to be a singer and Tricia admired his commitment and his big dreams and was inspired by him to find a 'purpose'. She told him about her desire to go to agricultural college and be a farmer. 'Having fun and an easy life isn't everything. It's time to get on with my life.'

'And now it ends,' she wrote as she packed her bags after six months in Vienna. 'I am in love. I know we can make it if we try.'

Tricia left the city carrying Patrik's gifts of a copy of *The Neverending Story* and a gold-heart locket on a chain, plus the news from Gerrit that Susie was pregnant again. As she embarked on a 26-hour train journey back to Britain she wrote: 'My work here is done.'

As I read her diary I had the urge to shout into the past: Stay there! Don't come back! *Stay there!*

She wrote: 'Vienna has been wonderful. I want this to be only the start of my life – I hope it has not been the highlight of my life.'

My heart clenched when I read that.

CHAPTER FOURTEEN

It often strikes me that Tricia was what Gran would have called 'a cob lass' – but then I remember that this is what he called me when he found me sitting in the farmhouse kitchen late one night in the pitch black listening to 'Candle in the Wind' over and over again on a scratched record on the old radiogram. I too was an introverted child; quiet, withdrawn and always observing. I didn't recognize what I had as depression until I was in my early twenties. Even then, it took me several years before I consulted a doctor. These were pre-Prozac days and I was given some enormous purple tablets – no mention of counselling. I remember sitting on the bed, clutching the box, relieved that at last I was trying to tackle it. That relief was probably part of the reason the tablets eventually seemed to work.

As a child nobody mentioned it, of course. I don't think 'depression' was a term in general use – not in our lives anyway – and sufferers if mentioned would have been middle-aged and described as 'bad with their nerves' or 'a nervous sort' or 'a bit poorly'. It was not considered something a child was capable of.

I remember sitting on my bed aged thirteen – it was a Friday evening and I felt deep despair that I would have to go back to school on Monday morning. I wasn't being bullied, I wasn't failing, I had friends and I got on with the teachers; there was no particular problem but nevertheless I knew I couldn't do it. I was filled with dread. A terrible foreboding gripped me, tightening the top of my stomach. I felt distanced from reality and I didn't know if or when this feeling would pass. It occurred to me that if I died during the weekend I would never have to go back to school. I decided that somehow that is what would happen. I would die. Relief flooded over me; a feeling of peace and joy, of euphoria at the thought of leaving everything and escaping.

I did not die, obviously. I did not try to die because that feeling of peace and power was enough to carry me through the weekend and into the following week. Just knowing that I *could* die if I chose was enough.

As I look back on this it seems my behaviour – sitting brooding and unhappy in a shut bedroom – was in some way mirroring that of my mother, who was probably sitting alone and brooding in her own bedroom just down the corridor.

As a young teenager I made a remark to a schoolfriend that I thought sounded smart, sophisticated and worldly-wise. I don't remember what it was but it flashed through my mind that I sounded like my mother. 'How cynical,' my friend replied. And I thought, So that's what my mother is: cynical.

Over the years my depression has been the metaphorical 'Black Dog', an expression used, if not coined, by Winston Churchill to describe his illness. My Black Dog has weighed me down, tripped me up, held me back, always lurking – whereas Tricia's experience of depression it seemed was different; she was shackled not to a Black Dog but a snapping, snarling monster that could turn on her with its great jaws and savage her at any moment.

Tricia was often alone in a crowd. She had a separateness about her, a withdrawing, sometimes compounded by a deep and obvious melancholia. We were a big extended family but after Elaine died it seemed Tricia floated alone in it. The exception was with Uncle Gerald. Uncle Gerald was Dad's brother who had development dysplasia of the hip, a condition treatable now but when he was born in 1927 it doomed him to a life with a dislocated hip. He walked with a stoop and a pronounced limp. Despite this he was cheerful and it's hard to picture him not laughing. When I was twelve I wrote a book of one-line pen portraits of my relatives. His entry said: 'Uncle Gerald never complains although he has plenty to complain about.'

He never married and was the only uncle not to run his own farm, instead doing farm-labouring work, woodturning and even washing up in a friend's transport café on the A6. He was also the only uncle not to be asked to be one of our godfathers; a fact no one noticed until we were grown up. He lived in a static caravan for thirty years on a site he found claustrophobic. He once spotted a neighbour peering at him from *underneath* the next-door caravan. One of his closest friends was 'Little Les', a tiny man with a hunched back who used to come to the farm to buy eggs.

With his disability and different lifestyle, Uncle Gerald probably felt marginalized and maybe that's why he and Tricia gravitated towards each other; that and the fact that they were both dedicated smokers ('smookers') – in Uncle Gerald's case of untipped Woodbines.

Uncle Gerald had also been born at New House Farm, and returned every Saturday to mow the front and back lawns and to clip the hedges. He'd stagger behind his great diesel mower which looked as though it was about to speed up and drag him away. Elizabeth, Tricia and I mithered him to death, flinging ourselves in front of his mower blades as we tried to pick all the daisies that stretched across both lawns so we could make daisy chains or put them in jamjars of water before his deafening machine chewed them up and spat them out. He mowed round the flowering currant bush which was known as the 'knicker bush' because it was usually festooned in underwear my mother had thrown there to dry – a less time-consuming option than pegging it on the line.

In between his labours he sat on the old stone bench by the kitchen door and drank a mug of tea and ate a piece of my mother's home-made sponge cake ('a lump of cake'). If he dropped bits he picked them up off the yard and ate them and said, 'You'll eat a pound of muck afore ye die.'

He taught us to mend flat tyres on our bikes by putting the inner tube in a bucket of water and he was always willing to take us – for a memorable time in his three-wheeler Reliant Robin – to buy toffees at the post office.

He was mentioned often by Tricia in her diaries and, although they may not have had deep conversations, Uncle Gerald always provided peaceful companionship. 'Uncle Gerald called round. Looked at the kitten climbing the tree, the robin chirping in another, the horses chatting, the dog playing and it was beautiful.'

In his later years he moved into sheltered housing – a bungalow with a big back garden which he tended with love and where he was particularly proud of his dazzling daffodil display. Having escaped the goldfish bowl of the caravan he was immensely house-proud and was always swapping his Zimmer for a Hoover and vacuuming with the aid of a Shake n' Vac.

When Uncle Gerald died he left his money equally to his nephews and nieces, and some items to his siblings, but the remainder of his personal effects he left to Tricia. These included his prized possession – a glass-fronted cabinet

Uncle Gerald with a cup of tea and a 'lump of cake'

which contained his framed photos, the drinking glasses he won at the sheltered-housing bingo night and his marble mantel clock.

Tricia and Uncle Gerald were mates.

In the days after Tricia died we threw ourselves into the 'arrangements': appointing an undertaker; searching for a will, in case there were any instructions for us regarding her funeral (there was no will and no instructions); consulting with the vicar; setting a funeral date and time; choosing a coffin; choosing flowers, hymns, cars, readings, reflective music, orders of service, coffin bearers, a funeral venue, catering; writing a eulogy; placing newspaper notices; deciding what clothes we would bury her in;

even notifying the council so the bin lorry wouldn't come head to head with the funeral cortège along the narrow lane.

'I don't know how you're doing it,' my aunt said.

Nights are dark in the country and I would wake in the pitch blackness, my face cold with tears and my pillow wet. I was in Dad's bungalow and was aware that down the lane Tricia's farmhouse stood silent, empty and brooding as though inside time was standing still. I tried not to dwell on it because night-time thoughts of my childhood home filled me with horror. Sleeping there again was unthinkable. I had never cried in my sleep before, I had not known it happened outside melodramas – and I would be struck-through again with the horror and the pain of it – a physical pain; a stabbing in my stomach and heart, a breathlessness, a desire to bend double or curl into a ball. The grief was like an assault. I now knew that the worst could happen – indeed *had* happened – and that this was something so bad it could never be put right again.

Two days before the funeral I sat alone in the farmhouse to soak up the last echoes of Tricia before she left for good. I picked up a notebook I'd given her for her birthday eleven months before. On the first page Tricia had written 'My little book of help myselfs'. In it she had gathered quotes and drawings to help keep her spirits up and to remind herself of the good things about being alive.

On the first page she had sketched some theatrical curtains open and a spotlight shining on an empty stage. A comedy and a tragedy mask spoke in unison: 'Let's begin.' Further on she had drawn pictures of her animals: 'Billy got a start', 'Ted just watched', 'Sasha didn't care'.

Then I found a passage she had written six months before her death during a peaceful spell in early summer as she sat at the back door of her beloved New House Farm on Uncle Gerald's old stone bench overlooking the garden and Gran's Dairy and the fields up to the village church:

Sitting in sunshine watching swallows dash around. They barely have time to chirp. A big boy blackbird alarm-calls. The lilac is out fully now, late this year but here now and scenting early. The longest day is yet to come and it is looking like a sunny summer. Relax. It's lovely. A little plane flying low is the only sound not natural.

Pale blue sky, a slight breeze, lambs calling and birdsong. Time to breathe.

Turn my face into the sun, eyes closed. The colour is hot-pink, mood-lifting and smile-inducing. It's happy-making sitting here on the old bench. I think of Uncle Gerald and feel he's here.

We covered her coffin in red roses. I wrote a eulogy I didn't know if I would be able to read. Elizabeth said she would read the extract from Tricia's notebook. The day before the funeral Elizabeth and I went to St Luke's, the village church, and let ourselves in through the great oak door with the giant metal key we used to find as kids. We stood at the lectern and faced the empty pews and, fighting the urge to whisper, we practised hearing our own voices ringing round the cavernous space saying words we never thought we'd utter. I glanced through the Victorian Gothic window and saw the grave was already dug and covered over with wooden boards, the mounds of earth hidden under sheets of green plastic grass.

I found a photo I had taken of Tricia posing with her sheepdog, Roy, in amongst the cows, to put on the front of the Order of Service. On the back we put a line drawing she had done of herself in her boiler suit leaning on a gate, entitled 'Lady Farmer Having a Think'. We chose 'From a Distance' by Nanci Griffith as the music to carry the coffin into church and 'Tennessee Waltz' by Eva Cassidy to carry the coffin out of church and round to the grave – both recordings were found near her CD player in the days after she died. For the reflective music we chose the Brahms 'Lullaby' – after all, she was still our little sister.

All these decisions seemed to be of the utmost importance. There was almost nothing we could do for Tricia now, so what we could do had to be right.

I was warned that after the funeral I would begin to feel anger towards Tricia because she took her own life. But the anger never came.

Tricia with Roy: the picture on her funeral order of service

CHAPTER FIFTEEN

I got into a routine at Hawthornden. After a morning walk I'd return to my room and read more diary, make notes and lie on the bed staring at the ceiling as I sank into the stirred-up memories. Sometimes I was so lost in the stories I felt I was time travelling. As the days passed more diaries were stacked on the 'read' pile which began to tower over my stash of Cadbury's Creme Eggs and chocolate digestives.

When Tricia came home from Vienna she threw herself into her HND agriculture studies at Myerscough College five miles up the road from the farm. As well as tackling the academic and practical assignments she joined the social activities – selling rag mags in fancy dress done up as a squaw (although on the first day when it was raining she only sold two – both to Dad) and going to the rag ball. 'Did a conga between Mr Parrot and Mr Bowden.' She was attending lessons in stock handling, machinery and computers and for her first term delightedly reports: 'Failed nothing!'

Six months after leaving Vienna and Patrik, she returned to them both for Christmas.

The visit began well: 'I got my holiday spirit singing "Away in a Manger" and skipping gaily down the Viennese street.' Patrik went out late on Christmas Eve and came back with a bundle of three Christmas trees which they put up around the old high-ceilinged flat, decorating them with candles. But by Boxing Day she had detected a change in atmosphere and the next day she wrote: 'I think Patrik just suggested we pack it in. He has gone off … it has only barely sunk in what is happening.'

Over the next few days, as Patrik sloped off 'to work' (he didn't; Tricia followed sometime later and found he was not there), he received many late-night phone calls and she soon realized he had another woman whom, when she asked him outright, he admitted he 'didn't know if he loved or not'.

Tricia waited in his flat during his disappearances and wrote page after page describing her crushed feelings which merged with song lyrics – veering from despair to fury to acceptance to sorrow to vindictiveness. 'I think I have felt it all in the last few days,' she said, adding: 'It is better than feeling dull which is how I felt before.'

Full of regret, yet angry, she threatened to kick him, whereupon she wrote: 'How can you take a man seriously when he says: "Do not kick me in the eggs"?'

I thought to myself: Oh, please, kick him in the eggs.

Patrik told her she was welcome to stay in the flat for the rest of her two-week holiday and he would move out. 'We looked at each other over the coffee cups and under the lightshade. I felt sad. "Now it is over," I said. "Now it is really over." And he said yes.'

She wrote out lines from 'Innocent When You Dream' by Tom Waits: about a lover's gift of a locket, broken promises and broken hearts. In my castle bedroom I supposedly could not get the internet, but I had discovered if I stood by the window it was sometimes possible to get access, so I moved across the room and googled this song. I had never heard it before and when Tom Waits's gravelly voice and jaunty accordion struck up, the lyrics were such a perfect and sad accompaniment to this story that I felt a sob grab my throat, and I thought: Why is life *never* like a storybook?

Tricia contacted Gerrit and Susie who, true to their heroic status, took her back to Hinterglemm on a skiing holiday they already had planned.

Seven days later, on her way home to Lancashire, she sat on the floor at Euston Station and cried. She talked to a fellow traveller also heading home from a 'thumbs down' Christmas and she noticed her fingernails were bitten so badly they 'look like all ten have been trapped in a tractor door'.

When she got home she told Mum about Patrik and Mum replied, 'Good, I never liked him.'

I was sorry it had turned out the way it had, but unsurprised. My heart was still broken from my own collapsed relationship months before. I had even transferred my civil-service job to the Midlands and bought a new house to escape it – neither of which had helped. 'Are you running to someone or away from someone?' a colleague asked on my first day. Didn't all love stories inevitably end in disappointment? Meanwhile, Elizabeth was married with two baby sons, Christopher and Kieran, born only fifteen months apart, so Tricia's love life barely registered; she had too many nappies to change.

Tricia returned to college for her second term which must have seemed more important than ever. She studied 'dairy, sheep and pigs', 'crops and grasses', 'nutritional chemistry and conservation', 'management' and 'farm mechanization' and much more.

She lived away from home for the first time (except for Vienna), in halls of residence five miles from the farm, which meant 'no rows' with Mum and Dad. She was keen to impress them with her commitment to farming but the depression was back.

She did not care for herself very well – smoking heavily, living on cereal and staying awake half the night. She dragged herself out of bed late, missing lectures, or went back to bed for chunks of the day where she slept grinding her teeth so badly she snapped her gum shield and gave herself terrible headaches.

* * *

At the end of her second year at agricultural college Tricia set off on another adventure when she won the BP Travel Award. For this she was to go and live and work on an Israeli kibbutz for six months to study the milking herd's nutrition and output.

I was delighted for her. Having fallen so firmly on her feet in Vienna, I was sure she could make a success of Israel. It seemed fitting that she should be doing something so adventurous – hadn't Tricia always been the brave one? Anyway, it would get her away from home with its oppressive atmosphere, and that had to be a good thing.

Meanwhile, because this was a trip organized through college and was associated, in some vague way, with a company as big and important as BP, Mum was reassured. She cut out the story about Tricia's award from the *Blackpool Gazette* which showed Tricia, smiling shyly, posing with our cows and with the collie, Roy, on a bit of old rope.

To enable her to go Tricia decided she must sell her horses, Amy and Nell, as Amy needed to be broken in and properly trained. 'I sold out. My horses are gone. I can't stop crying … one of the worst weeks I've ever experienced.'

That line brought back a familiar feeling of anger and frustration. Anyone would think she had been forced to sell her horses rather than that she had made a decision for their good and for her own. Why did she act the victim? Why wallow in self-pity, rather than objectively stating she had sold her horses to allow her to travel for six months? As I read through the diaries I encountered this attitude again and again. Whether she was declaring that friends 'always' let her down or that Mum 'never' understood her, there was a lack of ability to get her own situation into perspective and to get a balanced view of her life. Her language in the diaries was absolute – 'the worst', 'utter despair', 'total nightmare' – and yet in real life she had indicated this not with words but with body language. She had hunched and huddled and hidden in plain sight; she had moved slowly and silently among us, creating guilt and that same feeling of anger and frustration that you could do nothing to help.

Through her first two years at agricultural college she had a supportive boyfriend – a fellow student. She brought him to the farm to meet us, and so he could try some of Mum's delicious food. We were relieved to discover he was cheerful, undramatic and friendly. He was the son of a doctor from a rural community – both factors which impressed Mum, and made him a good catch (although Mum would never have used that expression). He was handsome with reddish-brown hair, and he relaxed among us and seemed undemanding and normal and, well, stable, which made him a reassuring presence to have around.

However, again, Tricia could not resist searching out emotional drama. I learned from the diaries that even while she was going out with him she always had a toxic ex hanging about – one she would obsess about and fixate on. She continually questioned old decisions, rehashing them, going round and round, regretting she had 'lost' these previous partners and longing for a relationship that had never existed – or if it had existed had been terrible.

There were echoes here of her teenage diaries, and the endless making up and falling out and self-pitying, self-indulgent drama which seemed standard fare when she was an adolescent, but when it continued in the diaries year after year, it began to wear my patience thin. You're not helping yourself, I found myself thinking – the very thing you are not supposed to say to a depression sufferer. 'You're your own worst enemy.' I longed to sit her down and have one of the conversations we could never have and beg her to search for peace not drama. To try to calm the chaos. To enjoy what she had rather than continually rejecting it in search of something better.

By the time she headed to Israel she was single again.

Within hours of her arrival at the kibbutz, Ma'anit, in northern Israel – where, from her room, she could hear the crickets 'making that far-away-from-home noise' – she met Eric from Manchester as she headed to the *refat* (the cowshed). They chatted and she noted that he was 'really nice to look at and to talk to. He might also be "a lad", not sure yet.' A couple of days later they talked for an hour round the bonfire, and the next day they embarked on a relationship. 'Haven't felt so good in months.' Two days later she decided: 'He's definitely "a lad".' Three days later she was 'advised' about Eric by some of the others as he danced with another girl all night in the air-raid shelter turned disco. Twelve days after their relationship began she was complaining of Eric being 'difficult and bad to me'. She decided there was no option but 'to play the game', so she was 'a little chilly and uninterested in him'. A fortnight after she had left Britain she was right back on the disastrous-relationship merry-go-round of 'it was so nice when we were friends, if only ...'

As I read this in my cold room in Hawthornden Castle, twenty-seven years later, my heart sank and I longed to prevent her rushing headlong into things, to be calmer, to play it safer emotionally – to just bloody well STOP IT.

Despite the drama with Eric, she settled into kibbutz life, helping with the milking, dancing to James Brown in the cowshed at full blast as she did so; calving cows and feeding calves. She wandered the avocado fields, the banana fields and the cotton fields and drew pictures of the animals. At weekends she went to the old air-raid shelter ('the bomb shelter') which was the kibbutz bar, known as the 'Gold Star', where they drank beer, punch and lemon vodka and danced to 'poxy records', although if she was 'not feeling like a party' it might take her until the early hours to get there.

After a month at Ma'anit, and with her relationship with Eric still on/off, another member of the kibbutz told her that she 'acted like she didn't care for anyone but kissed them all'. She wrote: 'That hurt my feelings.'

She travelled to Jerusalem and was dazzled. 'I am totally in awe of this wonderful city. How did I get here? I have planned it for months but it seems I just woke up here. I feel inspired. This is why I came to Jerusalem. This is why I came to Israel.'

She got up early to walk through the Damascus Gate to buy a breakfast of bread and spice and she marvelled at the Church of the Holy Sepulchre and the Via Dolorosa and the Wailing Wall. She walked in the Garden of Gethsemane and got 'cold shivers' in the 2,000-year-old olive grove. She visited the Arab market and wrote: 'It was dirty, lively, busy, cramped and noisy. I loved it!' Two days later the exploration continued as she went on a volunteers' picnic to the Sea of Galilee.

Six weeks after her relationship with Eric began she wrote: 'He's cold. We don't speak. I've stopped worrying about it.'

Within a month this pattern had repeated itself with another volunteer; the same initial 'I feel alive' stage followed by the almost immediate crashing of hope and the hurt feelings and the soul-searching and the upset and the blame.

Tricia seemed to have this 'all or nothing' approach to many things besides relationships: to drinking, dancing, socializing, sleeping, travelling, cleaning up and eating. 'I devoured hummus in pitta bread with such gusto I think I shocked the café staff.'

She lived life at the extremes; loving it or hating it, avoiding it or grabbing it with both hands, ricocheting from 'I wish I was dead' to 'I feel alive' and quickly back again.

This did not chime with my memories of Tricia at that time, which were mostly of her withdrawn and brooding. But it made me realize again how she had expressed herself differently face to face from the way she did in her diaries and her letters – her letters at the time were amusing and light, occasionally sarcastic and often laugh-out-loud funny. She loved being an aunt and recounted stories of her two nephews: 'Mum phoned to tell me poor Christopher sharpened all his finger-ends with a pencil sharpener!' 'Kieran cries every time something new pops up in his new pop-up book!' And yet her diaries, full of brooding introspection and self-absorption veering off to recklessness, were exhausting to read and left me feeling like a carsick passenger in the back seat with a runaway driver.

She remained at the kibbutz for New Year 1989. 'So that's the end of the 80s. Now my life begins.'

For all her difficulties, her melodramas and her sense of nagging victimhood, it appears Tricia always held out hope of something better, something more.

My own life was on the up at that time too. In 1988 I had left the civil service and gone back to college to train as a journalist. It was an impulsive decision. I had spotted a huddle of journalists standing outside the local magistrates' court. There were women journalists among them. They looked like they were having more fun than me, even though they were waiting for a busted paedophile ring to arrive in police vans. They were wearing glamorous-looking macs. They were writing for a living. I went back to the office and scribbled my resignation in red pen on a bit of scrap paper. 'Are you sure?' asked my boss. 'Are you sure?' asked Mum.

Shortly after, Elizabeth found an advert in the local paper for the National Council for the Training of Journalists one-year course, at Lancashire Polytechnic: *Are you interested in your neighbourhood? Do you like to find out things? Do you enjoy telling stories? Why not train to be a journalist?*

At the interview they asked me: 'Why the career change?'

I said: 'That wasn't my career. This is.'

Tricia sent me a card: 'You'll make an excellent journalist!'

When I had joined HM Customs & Excise five years before, aged nineteen, a sixty-year-old colleague had taken me aside: 'You're lucky to be here, you know. This is a *career grade*' (he leaned forward for emphasis) 'and after forty years you will get a *wonderful* pension.' The smile had frozen on my face. The logo for HM C&E was a portcullis and on the day I left I could practically hear the grating and clanking as it lifted and I escaped.

I loved the journalism course and met Cello, whom I would eventually marry. But first I decided to do a degree in journalism at Birmingham Polytechnic – so by New Year 1989 I had just finished my first term there and was still high on freedom and elated with the joy of learning.

* * *

Back from Israel Tricia went to college in Essex to convert her HND to a BSc.

Her placement was on an arable farm in Norfolk. 'Someone noticed I had a Lancashire accent and commiserated with me.'

She worked on the 'potato team' and on holiday in Greece she sent cheery cards which she practised to make perfect in her diary first: 'Been swimming, sailing, riding a motorbike and climbing a mountain and lots of other things that don't involve potatoes!'

She and her boyfriend smoked cannabis, staying up all night, sometimes still sitting in the pub at half five in the

Tricia in the potatoes

morning, playing cards, and the next day suffering from 'hangovers from hell'.

At times she was capable of taking a step back and looking clearly. She had a dry wit and recorded odd details of life in her shared house. 'We have two Kenneths: a cat called Kenneth with a prolapsed rectum and a person Kenneth. Pussycat Kenneth is much nicer than person Kenneth.'

Despite having boyfriends, she retained her sense of aloneness and separation. 'It's 4 o'clock in the morning and I'm alone with my music and my diary. The cat is stoned again.'

After graduating with her BSc she decided it was time to escape this 'miasma of dirge' her life had become. Away from New House Farm, a life back there had begun to seem enticing: 'I'm going home. I've been dreaming about cats and dogs and, most of all, horses. It could be idyllic. I want to catch a farm cat, tame it, feed it and worm it. Have something to love.'

Her New Year's resolution was 'I wish I could be who I want to be'.

CHAPTER SIXTEEN

As soon as she arrived home, before she had even unpacked her car, she noted she was 'unhappy'. She wrote lists – *Go to Asda, book haircut, help Dad with bullocks in back yard* – but she was unable to get herself going.

Instead she lay low in her chaotic room surrounded by unpacked bags, leafing through women's magazines: 'How to have a happy hubby and 20 ways with a lamb chop'. Remarking, sarcastically: 'Subversive.' Before adding: 'This is pathetic. I've completely flopped in a heap. I've got to get a life. This is a beautiful place but it's tied to the past. I can't be free here.'

Three months later, in March 1993, she took a job in Yorkshire as a field officer with the Ministry of Agriculture, Fisheries and Food. 'It was Roger who taught me the first rule of being a civil servant – how to get your cup of coffee first thing in the morning then stare out the window scratching your arse.'

Despite the jokes she found the job tough, with '12-hour days to stand still' and the office being 'mayhem with farmers everywhere'.

Immediately she was worrying about whether she was good enough.

She stuck it out despite a deterioration which led to a GP referral to an outpatient mental-health team. She did not tell me about this but confided in Elizabeth who let me know.

I was more out of touch with Tricia than I ever had been because I had finished my degree in Birmingham and moved to Edinburgh to be with Cello and to work for a children's charity doing fundraising and PR. Cello and I got engaged at Easter 1993 and travelled down to tell Mum and Dad on Good Friday. 'Funny kind of a day to get engaged,' said Mum. There are great gaps in Tricia's diary at this time and no mention of the engagement. A few months later, when I went to buy my wedding dress, Mum came with me but by then she had begun to feel the stomach pains which were the harbinger of her cancer and she sat in the shop and stared into space. 'You're on your own today,' she said.

Our wedding took place in the village church in May 1994, with the reception in a marquee at the farm. Mum's health had rallied in the run-up and she made all four bridesmaid dresses – for Elizabeth, Tricia and two of my old schoolfriends, Carole and Hilary – as well as organizing to have the farm garden landscaped. Dad got a new suit handmade and wore his gold watch and chain that had belonged to Gran. On the day everything looked stunning. Everyone looked happy. We were all smiling, until the photographer told us to stop because we were spoiling his 'classic' photographs. It was a good day – one in which we had all scrubbed up well. One in which everything appeared to be normal.

How did Cello feel about marrying into my family? He thought there were distinct similarities with his own. His parents had emigrated from southern Italy, where they had worked on the land, to Scotland in 1957 having had the benefit of little education. They did farmwork, then later brewery and restaurant work, while raising three children. His family, too, seemed to operate on a 'need-to-know' basis. Cello told them as little as possible – 'why worry them?' He was a journalist at the *Scotsman* newspaper and during the first Gulf

Elizabeth, me and Tricia, May 1994

War, in 1990, had spent time in the press pack on a mine-sweeper, telling his parents: 'I'm with the Navy on exercises off Portsmouth.' Likewise during his adolescence there had been little discussion of feelings or relationships, only his dad laying down the law: no tattoos, no earrings, no gambling and never, under any circumstances, try homosexuality.

My mother was delighted to welcome Cello into the fold. All those years ago Nurse Steele had promised 'The boys will come! The boys will come!' and now, along with her two grandsons, they were here.

Eventually, Tricia decided enough was enough with her job and, at the age of twenty-eight, having done just over two years with MAFF, she decided she would have to go home to work with Dad after all. As she left she noted that she had realized her colleagues were not her friends. 'They can only think of themselves … Can't wait to go now.'

These words filled me with dread as I read them and, even though it was way past changing anything, I felt a tightening in my chest. Losing trust in friends was a hallmark of the years to come when paranoia dripped into her life, poisoning everything.

She went home with hopes of modernizing the farm, shaking it all up. But how realistic was that when Dad was still working and had been running New House Farm all his life and Mum was still ruling the roost inside?

There was a routine on the land governed by the seasons, a routine dependent on the weather that dated back for ever. The farming calendar started with slurry spreading in January and February to get the grass to grow, then rolling, to smooth the ground, and tilling to fertilize it in March. The milk cows were 'turned out' in April from their winter housing into the fields to graze and in May was the first crop of silage (cut grass fermented and stored to feed the cows in winter). In June and July there was 'topping' thistles and dock leaves, the first cut of hay – mowing, turning, baling and carting – and the second cut of silage. In July and August it was time to make haylage – feed for the horses – and mow the second cut of hay. Hedge cutting was in September and 'at t'back end' the cows came in for winter in October. All year round the cows needed milking twice a day and there was a staggered programme of calving so that calves were born throughout the year and not all at once. When the calves had been born their markings were sketched so they could be registered as pedigrees with the Holstein Friesian Society, and they were ear-tagged as identification for MAFF. Bull calves were raised for several months and then taken to market to be sold to farmers who fattened them up for beef.

Despite farming being set in stone in many ways, Tricia wanted to make the job her own. She planned to computerize the books, get to grips with the cash flow, create a business plan, monitor the milk performance, take over the purchasing and generate income from the unused barns. Her enthusiasm bubbled over: 'I'm in love with music again. Music in the milking parlour, music in the car, music in my room.'

She got a new horse, Hattie, and began piano lessons, playing simplified pop and jazz on Mum's old grand piano. She loved the farm cats and the dog – and yet the danger signs were there because at the same time she began to brood about one of her friends sabotaging her romance. 'I feel betrayed, let down. Like I never even knew her.'

Although her mood extremes are obvious in her diary, in real life she was often quiet, reticent, downbeat to the point of being morose. She was like a nocturnal creature reluctant to come blinking into the sunshine.

Cello would prompt me: 'Have you called Tricia?' But I put off phoning because I felt the dead weight of Tricia's depression as soon as I picked up the receiver. I hesitated because I could sense my own depression circling. Phoning Tricia might ease my conscience for a minute or two but afterwards I felt a bit more depleted – it was mentally taking one step forward and two steps back. So I put off calling and resented my husband for suggesting it. Why was it my job? What could I do?

Years later when I discussed this with Elizabeth, who had gone on to work with carers, she nodded sadly and said: 'If only I knew then what I know now about the help that's available for families. But back then I knew nothing.'

When I did phone Tricia, the communication was usually one-sided. Either she enthused about her horses, talking of them as her 'babies' while asking me very little about my own two young children, or, more usually, she said nothing and I talked to myself; faux-calm, faux-cheerful, pretending by the skin of my teeth that we weren't having a fake conversation because no other kind of conversation was possible. I could hear her silent misery and resentment. I wonder now why I didn't come straight out and admit we were living in a horror story. Spell it out. Say: 'God, isn't this awful and I've no idea what to do.' But as the heavy silence leaked from the phone I felt compelled to keep the pretence up that everything would turn out all right if we could only be a bit braver for a bit longer.

The guilt was enormous: guilt that I couldn't help; guilt that I couldn't make her happy; guilt that I wasn't as unhappy as she was; guilt that I was me and she was her.

As I read the diaries it seems unbelievable that I didn't have a proper conversation with Mum and Dad about Tricia's health, until I remember the oppressive terror of the time centring around Mum's illness. Mum's poor health rumbled on for years – having been ill during the search for my wedding dress in 1993, she did not seek a diagnosis for several more years and tried to treat her symptoms with healthy eating. Any awkward subjects only added to her discomfort and, anyway, I didn't have the words.

* * *

One of the only times I found the words to try to debate something with Mum was in 1998 when Mum and Dad began to plan a new dormer bungalow near the farm as their 'retirement home'. There is little mention of this in Tricia's diaries, but being reminded of the frustrations of that time brings back strong memories for me. A derelict red-brick cottage, built for farm labourers, stood on the site, and I pleaded with Mum not to knock it down. I suggested they develop this old cottage to keep their new home in character with the lane. Mum got plans drawn up to incorporate the original cottage, but, ultimately, her heart was set on a new bungalow with fancy underfloor heating, a conservatory (referred to as a garden room) and more light fittings than you could shake a stick at, and when my mother had set her heart on something *that* was what happened. I begged her several times down the phone to keep the cottage but was met by a stony silence. I felt outraged and disappointed. I accused my mother of planning to vandalize the lane. I threatened never to go home again if they knocked the old cottage down. It was very rare – if not unheard of – for me to put my views forward as forcefully as this, but keeping the spirit of the lane intact was important to me. Despite my fury and frustration, my mother would not discuss it with me.

She knocked it down.

She paid two of my cousins to come and dismantle it slate by slate, brick by brick, and then mentioned in passing over the phone that the cottage had gone. I was flabbergasted and disgusted.

In her diary Tricia noted wryly: 'The field opposite the new bungalow site is called The Big Pasture so perhaps they could call the new house "Pasture View" or failing that "Pasture Best".'

The next time I visited I saw the scar on the lane-side where the cottage used to be and I rescued two chimney pots from the stacks of red bricks and other debris. I loaded them in the car and took them back to Scotland where I put them disconsolately outside my front door with plans that never materialized to fill them with plants.

For once my mother had taken some photographs – of my cousins perched on the rooftop waving as they flung the slates down. I saw these prints but passed no comment. I never mentioned the old cottage to my mother again.

At the same time my mother was at last being investigated for her stomach pains. Her GP suggested she was suffering from stress and gave her Prozac. I was visiting. My mother brought the tablets home, took them out of her shopping bag, glared at them, glared at me, and then flushed them down the toilet. Further tests, which seemed to take months, revealed she had non-Hodgkin's lymphoma.

Maybe my mother knew the fight with her own body was a fight she was doomed to lose so she was determined to win any other fight on offer; or maybe she wanted to make her mark on the world while she still had the chance. I don't know; but the new dormer bungalow began to take shape as my mother's health deteriorated.

Over the years, when Cello and I and our two children, Nina and Lara, travelled down from Scotland to visit Mum and Dad in the new bungalow (or, after Mum died, just Dad), we would always take enough food to cook a meal for everyone, including Tricia. It would be something simple: bangers and mash or salmon and salad. We'd phone the farmhouse to invite Tricia to eat with us – sometimes she'd answer, sometimes she wouldn't. Sometimes, on what felt like blessed days, she was in good spirits and would come and take the children for jaunts round the fields on the quad bike, telling them stories of the horses and her dog.

Tricia with Nina, Lara and Joel: a popular aunt

But most of the time her voice would be hesitant and distant – I always suspected I had woken her or disturbed her when she wanted to be left alone. I'd ask her to join us and she'd reply 'I've got to have a shower' or 'I've got to wash my hair' or sometimes 'I've got to have a brew and a fag.' The excuses were not elaborate. We'd plate up her food and watch it go cold, feeling irritated, until we gave up waiting and ate without her.

We would tell the children that Tricia wasn't well, without elaborating. I must have assumed it was obvious that she was depressed – which of course it wasn't. Lara says now that she thought Tricia had one bad cold after another throughout her childhood. *Tricia's ill again?*

If she turned up she often ate alone, standing at the kitchen surfaces scooping it up quickly with a fork before coming into the living room to perch on the settee arm for a short time, semi-detached from the conversation. Occasionally she chatted normally – telling funny stories and making us laugh with her mimicry – but at other times she gazed into the distance looking as though she was not of this world. When this happened her mental pain was manifest. She looked haunted. We made small talk and tried to reach her with questions about her animals or the stables business she was setting up in the old milking parlour, but she was often unreachable; alienated from everyone and everything.

At times there appeared to be a delay between words reaching her and her brain decoding them. Her movements

Lara, me, Tricia, Nina and Elizabeth, 2006

were slow and nervous. Sometimes her face twitched and her words came out in a stutter. When she had gone Elizabeth would say, 'That's the medication,' and I felt despair about what Tricia had lost. 'But she'll go back to normal when she's off the meds, won't she?' I'd ask, and Elizabeth, a midwife, would shrug and look doubtful and we'd sit in silence.

We covertly scrutinized her for weight loss because that was an indication she had stopped taking her meds. If she was heavier than usual she was probably taking them. We daren't ask her. She took exception to being policed. I could understand how infuriating our interference must seem but we were desperate to stop the cycle of taking meds – feeling better – coming off meds – becoming ill again.

Ultimately she was an adult with the right to make her own choices even when that left us in a quandary. I took her to the supermarket after she had been very ill and she picked up a bottle of vodka. I said, 'I thought Dr Beckett told you not to drink with your meds.' '*I know*,' she replied, clutching the bottle to her, 'and he is *so sweet*,' and she gave me a look as if it was almost unfathomable, the sweetness of Dr Beckett, then sailed off down the aisle, with the vodka in the trolley and me trotting behind.

Occasionally on our trips to Dad's she would not answer the phone or even the door and we'd end up going back to Scotland without seeing her at all. Did we blame her when she left meals we had cooked to go cold or refused to leave the farmhouse? Did we blame her for casting a pall over the whole place the entire weekend?

Yes, at times we did. We knew she was depressed but we'd say: 'She's got to help herself.'

I once felt so frustrated with her for not answering the phone that I marched down the lane determined to make her talk to me. I knocked on the farmhouse door but got no answer. I knocked again and again until a hot fury overwhelmed me and I began hammering with all my might on the glass conservatory door, yelling, 'Tricia! Tricia!' Pain shot through my hand. I was filled with rage. She *would* talk to me; I was utterly unwavering. I felt I would knock the door down if I had to in order to get her to face me and talk to me.

Eventually she staggered to the door, dragging a dressing gown around her, bleary-eyed – she had obviously been sleeping. 'What is it?' she asked, clearly thinking someone had died or I'd lost my mind. Deflated, I felt stupid. 'I wondered if you were OK, because you didn't answer the phone.' She looked at me like she didn't believe me and muttered did I want to go in for a coffee, but I could see she'd rather get back to bed. I said no, it was fine, I'd get going. I headed back up the lane dejected, having achieved nothing.

Where had that wave of anger and anguish come from? Perhaps I needed to acknowledge how nightmarish this situation was and, denied the chance to talk about it, I screamed and banged instead.

Or was there a part of me envious of Tricia's licence to withdraw from life? I had two small children (one as-yet-undiagnosed autistic), a husband who worked long hours, a journalism business to help run (both Cello and I were now freelance) and my own depression to keep at bay. Maybe locking the door and refusing to come out looked like an easier option. Life was full of seemingly intractable problems – Mum's illness, the struggle for Nina's diagnosis – and maybe there was a quality of escape about Tricia's existence that was attractive to me. Illness brought her fewer demands.

* * *

The family gathers for Dad's 80th, but Tricia is missing

Tricia's withdrawal reminded me of the Victorian poet Elizabeth Barrett Browning, the eldest of twelve children, who took to her bed aged fifteen with head and spinal pain and immersed herself in writing. Being unburdened with the domestic duties of her sisters she was able to produce a huge body of work. Her illness gave her permission to escape into her mind and the imagination. When she was forty she rose from her couch and eloped with poet Robert Browning to Italy where she had a happy marriage and a son.

There was sometimes a suggestion that Tricia was 'doing it on purpose'. Did we think that because she was suffering she wanted to make us suffer too? Or that she was using her depression to manipulate us? I would argue that she was ill, that she couldn't help it, but occasionally I had to fight back a sneaking suspicion that she was making our lives more difficult intentionally.

On one visit in 2006 I wandered down to the farmhouse and found Tricia sitting outside on Uncle Gerald's old stone bench having a roll-up. I sat opposite her on a rickety wooden bench and tried to start a conversation, telling her what the kids had been up to, what plans we had for the weekend. Chat with Tricia was often forced. She was rarely vocal, although on a good day she could tell a great story. Today was not a good day. She was taciturn and obviously miles away. I asked innocuous questions about her animals. She wouldn't look at me and gazed hard at the horizon. I asked about the stables business. How was the set-up going?

Silence stretched until she blurted out that she couldn't make proper plans because she didn't know how the farm would be split after Mum and Dad died. 'It's impossible! How can I organize anything? It's not fair!' This subject was a lethal combination of death and money and was the ultimate family taboo. I wouldn't have dared raise it, certainly not with Mum and Dad.

The worry about the future of the farm and whether it would stay in the family or be sold, and if it stayed would she be able to farm it, and how a business, buildings and land could be split between three siblings became an obsession with Tricia. Having been back at the farm for over ten years she felt it was hers – she had taken emotional owner-ship of the place and resented me and Elizabeth having any entitlement, or even, it seemed at times, just visiting it.

I didn't have the answers so I blurted out a few platitudes. 'You'll be all right. It'll get sorted out.'

She became agitated, twisting in her seat, dragging her long hair over to one side of her head, then flinging it to the other. She swung round to stare at me with an expression of contempt. 'You and Elizabeth, YOU just want what you can get. You're not interested in this place.' She jumped up and flung her arms above her head. 'You're after everything! You're ganging up against me!' She started tearing at her hair in a frenzy. 'I'll end up with nothing. You'll have everything. EVERYTHING!'

As I watched, open-mouthed, it flickered through my mind that she was possessed by another force. I stared at her, lost for words. She was delusional.

Something shifted in my brain – like those optical illu-sions where faces become vases and vases become faces and which once seen cannot be unseen – and the situation flashed into focus. With clarity I realized: My sister is raving. My sister is mad. *This* is what madness looks like. I had a vision of ranting witches being burned at the stake in the Middle Ages; women who were probably mentally ill. 'No, no,' I muttered, 'you're wrong. That's not true,' but I was shot through with horror and disbelief tempered with the knowledge that I *must* believe it because I had seen it.

I had witnessed something that had changed my world for ever.

Eventually I said I'd better get going and I left her dragging deeply on her fag, sitting back on the bench, gazing angrily across the fields. I walked back up to Dad's, the beautiful lane with the towering hawthorn hedges and the bordering fields of grazing cows offering no comfort today, as the cold shock continued to reverberate through me.

In the car on the way home to Scotland, as the girls sat in the back listening to music on their headphones, I told Cello, 'I think Tricia is mad. I saw it; I saw madness in front of my eyes,' and he looked at me and he nodded and the words hung in the air as we drove up the motorway in silence.

After Tricia died I found many bits of paper around the farmhouse showing calculations where she had been working out how she could keep the farm and all the land while allocating something to me and Elizabeth. This subject had haunted her for the last fifteen years of her life and it became no more open even when Mum knew she had cancer and was dying. It was unimaginable to Mum that soon she would be gone but the farm would not and somebody else would be in charge. If the subject was raised – and I was not brave enough to raise it although both Elizabeth and Tricia tried – Mum would bash the *Daily Mail* she was reading and pull a face implying there was disgusting greed afoot. My mother was not going to have any power or control wrested from her.

How simple it seems, the idea of sitting down and talking, but it was not simple, it was very complicated; in fact it was impossible.

CHAPTER SEVENTEEN

Tricia had first told me she was being watched years before in 1998. It was a local tenant. She said she'd spotted him bobbing down behind the hedge trying to keep out of sight and another time she'd seen the glint of his binoculars from up the lane as he spied on her. This man seemed a sad figure to me; maybe he had a crush on her? He didn't seem to be frightening or hostile or an unstable sort; indeed when we had a power cut at the farm he came over with a variety of leads and generators to help and we sat disconsolately watching him try and fail to boil a kettle.

We all agreed he was a nuisance for bothering her by bobbing about behind hedges with binoculars, but maybe he was birdwatching? Maybe she should ignore him? Nevertheless we were glad when he moved away. It never occurred to us back then that she was mistaken and he hadn't been spying on her at all.

It was a long, faltering journey, often heading down cul-de-sacs, from thinking my little sister was unlucky and a bit moody to thinking she was insane.

* * *

Depression has been described as an absence of feeling but one thing that always made Tricia feel was animals. The doctors thought it unlikely she would harm herself because of her animals. She cared for all creatures – losing sleep over accidentally pouring water on a spider in the sink. Animals should have been her salvation. On her last day at agricultural college she found a baby bird stunned from flying into a window. She held the bird in her hands as it came round and watched it sit on her finger for a few seconds before flying away. 'Like my relationships with men,' she wrote. 'They alight in my life for just a few seconds before flying away.'

Tricia only thought I was spying on her once when my mother was dying. She asked me: 'The last time we were on the phone, were you taping our conversation?' She was standing at Dad's garden gate about to head down the lane to the farmhouse. This question must have been burning inside her because she blurted it out over her shoulder as I stood on the doorstep waving her off. I walked a little nearer. Had I heard right? Her words hit me hard. If she thought I was spying on her she must be getting worse; in fact she must have got very bad indeed.

'No, I didn't tape the conversation,' I said. Then, taking my courage in both hands, I added, 'It's your illness that makes you think that.'

She looked at me and I could see the same sad and lonely expression from when she was a little girl. Slowly she nodded and cast her eyes down and turned to walk away. 'Take care of yourself,' I shouted after her and she did a half-nod and kept on walking. She cut the loneliest figure I have ever seen. I was terrified of what was happening to my little sister. Where was she going? How much worse was this about to get? But if *I* was frightened, how much more terrified must she have been? What must it be like when you don't know what is real and what is not? When you don't know who to trust, if anyone? When you can't even trust your own brain to tell you the truth?

I went into the house and told Cello what she had said and we looked at each other in despair. What could we do? Who could we turn to?

We felt alone with it because the problem had never been acknowledged properly; because Tricia didn't want to talk about it; because if you mentioned it to Dad he went deaf; because if you mentioned it to Mum she took a turn for the worse and put her head back against her armchair and closed her eyes; because I lived 170 miles away and for days or weeks at a time I could pretend it wasn't happening at all.

People often said to me: 'It must be so difficult living that far away.' I would go through the charade of agreeing – yes, it was really hard living all that distance away – and yet inside I knew it might only be those 170 miles that were keeping me sane.

* * *

Elizabeth remembers at that time 'swinging all over the place' in her understanding of the situation, never fully grasping what was happening, thinking a lot of the things Tricia told us due to her paranoia were true, or sometimes thinking she was 'miserable and awkward' and 'doing it on purpose'. She felt that the situation was very divisive. Maybe at times it was clearer for people outside the family to see. Elizabeth recalls Tricia driving down to be at her fiftieth birthday party in Cheshire, in 2010. Tricia sat quietly all night looking haunted and frail and one of Elizabeth's friends went to sit with her. Afterwards, this friend told Elizabeth: 'Never say your sister doesn't love you. What she went through to be here tonight ... never say she doesn't love you.'

Reading the diaries became more frightening as Tricia's illness worsened.

I took regular breaks from them and wandered the castle grounds and gorged on the home-made biscuits, supplied each day by the castle chef, to give me strength.

In 2003 Tricia wrote: 'Did that conversation actually happen? I know things. Then I don't know them. Something then nothing – gone on a coffee and a cigarette.'

As I read I felt breathless, imagining 'reality' constantly distorting and changing before Tricia's eyes.

She also wrote: 'If anything happens to me look to X [a local man]. He's nasty and wants me out of here and out of farming.'

She believed other professionals were acting against her, losing her business deals over land and costing her money. She agonized over this, writing her suspicions down but never in enough detail to check out the truth. She lived in a maelstrom of bitterness and paranoia. I had no evidence as to how many of her suspicions were true but I reminded myself that just because you're paranoid doesn't mean they're not out to get you. The trouble with Tricia's anxieties was there was usually a basis of truth – something real that kicked it off – but the worry then got bigger and more elaborate. It became hard to know where truth ended and delusion began.

'I am in a shark pit,' she wrote a decade before she died.

For years I believed every word she said. When she told me about being victimized and cheated she was convincing because *she* believed it, so every word rang with sincerity and I'd feel my blood boil with frustration and anger that people could be so cruel to my little sister.

In 2006 she phoned me, upset. She said a local man had tried to rape her. He'd walked straight into the house because, as was not uncommon around there, she often kept the door unlocked. She was standing in the living room and he had forced her backwards onto the sofa and tried to ram his knee between her legs. They struggled. After several minutes she managed to fight him off by slamming her heel down hard on the top of his foot, bringing all her considerable force to bear. He staggered away cursing and name-calling.

She was distraught and so was I.

My husband phoned a friend who knew the local man and asked him to tell the man to never go near Tricia again. I could detect the shock in our friend's voice as he heard the story and his difficulty believing what he was hearing. 'I'm gutted about this,' he kept saying, 'I'm gutted about this,' but he promised to approach the man and tell him to keep away.

The only possible reference to this in Tricia's diary is: 'When does a rape end? When he gets off you? When he leaves the house? When you wash away the evidence or when your body heals?'

It wasn't until years later that I wondered if the assault actually happened. That thought never entered my head when she told me – which is strange considering I knew how suspicious she was of me and my sister and how she believed we were trying to cheat her of her place on the farm. She was so convincing; to her these insults and dangers were real and so that's how they came across to us.

Years later Elizabeth said, 'We heard all those stories about Tricia's former friends and how they'd done her down and insulted her and taken advantage of her generosity and we believed every word; meanwhile what on earth was she telling them about us?'

*   *   *

I rarely spoke to Dad on the phone until my mother was dead. It was as though the phone was not his territory, it was hers. If he answered it, he would hand over the receiver like a hot potato.

When I spoke to my mother she wanted to hear about some triumph or other of the kids. When they were babies she would phone and ask: 'What can they do this week that they couldn't do last week?' She wanted to know what clever, witty, funny thing they had done that she could boast about. It took ten years to get my elder daughter Nina's diagnosis of autism, despite first taking her to the doctor's when she was two years old, so I had more pressing problems than whether my mother was impressed or not, yet it was exhausting fielding her expectations.

It had always been exhausting fielding her expectations. When I phoned to tell her I'd got a first-class degree she replied, 'Oh, good. What's a double first?'

Her constant prodding and probing for details of my child's accomplishments added to my sense of failure. I told a friend and she looked at me like I was daft. 'Lie to her,' she said. It seemed so obvious when someone else pointed it out.

I tried to tell my mother that I thought there might be something different about Nina but she didn't seem to hear me. I got pregnant with Lara when Nina was two and she said to someone else in front of me: 'See, it can't be so bad if she's having another.'

Mum and I phoned each other; we spoke, but we didn't communicate. When I asked how Tricia was I had to decode the answer by Mum's tone. What I really wanted to know was: is she acting crazy? I never asked a straight question or got a straight answer. I had to gauge the situation from the hums and haws and asides.

I only found out that Tricia had 'locked them in the house to keep them safe' because Elizabeth told me. Mum never mentioned it. Details were hazy as Mum did not want to talk about it, but it is a mark of how worried she was that she told Elizabeth at all. It seemed Tricia had been in their new bungalow with them, locked the door and removed the key and refused to give it back for maybe half an hour. She thought there was danger outside but it was unclear what she believed the danger was.

I told a psychiatrist friend, who said it has been known for mental-health patients to kill people 'to keep them safe', and I felt my scalp fizz and my heart turn over.

I asked: 'What should I do?' He gave me advice that made perfect sense until I tried to put it into practice. Tricia should have a mental-health social worker, he said; find out their name. Make sure she has an assessment of need. Be persistent. Make contact with the crisis team. Identify the consultant. Ensure she has a social-circumstances report. Keep in regular contact with her entire team. Get regular feedback.

Tricia was registered with an outreach mental-health team and I phoned them to ask for advice. After much chasing around and ringing and re-ringing I was told they could not speak to me – Tricia's health was a private matter and I could not be involved. Tricia had made it clear they were to share her details with no one. They said they would listen to what I had to say but they could not respond. I told them about Tricia locking my parents in the house and asked if they thought my parents were safe. They said they were not at liberty to divulge anything.

I was furious. We wanted to help but we were not allowed. Tricia's paranoia – the reason we were not allowed to be involved with her care – was part of the very problem we were trying to help with.

Frustrated, I decided to *make* them listen and I jumped in with both feet. Did they realize Tricia thought a male member of their staff was going on home visits to the farm to try to have sex with her? Tricia had said so to me and I had let it pass, suspecting it was unfounded paranoia. Now I repeated it. How did *they* like being suspected and insulted? The woman's voice grew interested. Tricia had said *what*? There was not only interest but urgency in her voice now. Oh dear, she said, oh dear. They'd make sure only female staff members visited in future.

* * *

Tricia was beautiful and funny and kind and when she was well there was no one you would rather be with. She was attractive and never found it difficult to get a boyfriend. In her early thirties she was engaged twice to caring men who loved her, but both engagements were short-lived. It seemed that when people got too close she became suspicious. Were they only after her for the farm or for access to the farming life? Were they only trying to use her? She did not mention either of the engagements in her diaries, bar this comment: 'Catherine went to see Mary Wesley at the Edinburgh Book Festival. She said she had the most beautiful hands full of diamond rings. Well I'm two down, only three to go.'

Tricia's last romance was around the time my mother died. I never met him but for a few weeks she was full of it – until the relationship imploded. I was in the kitchen with her making a cup of tea when she mentioned her new man wore handmade leather brogues. He left behind a pair when he stayed, she said; very expensive, they were, very smart. But he had stood her up on their last date. What had she done? I asked. She laughed. 'I sliced the leather brogues up with a Stanley knife.'

I stood, my mouth agape, watching Tricia stirring her tea, smiling.

I phoned the medics again. What if Tricia got pregnant? It would be a disaster. I asked if they could advise Tricia about this, discuss it with her? The woman did a snickering laugh. 'She's an adult!' she replied. 'There is nothing we can do about that.' She laughed again.

I knew Tricia was an adult, but if she got pregnant whose job would it be to look after the baby if she was too ill to do it herself? Not this laughing woman's, that was for sure. I pictured the sliced-up brogues and I thought: Fuck you.

There were periods when Tricia was not depressed or suffering from paranoia and when she felt joy at being on the farm. 'Heaven is New House Farm,' she wrote. 'The lobelia is beginning to flower, the lawns are mown, the cows are milking well, Mum and Dad are happy and all is well.'

Tricia loved bringing the cows up from the fields on her quad bike with Ted, her Labrador/collie cross, slipping from side to side in front of her, which she described as 'like balancing a bag of ferrets on a see-saw'. Sometimes he ran beside her. 'He turns to smile as he trots next to me and this makes me smile too.'

But by 2005 farming was harder and less profitable, Dad was almost eighty, Mum was seriously ill, and Tricia was struggling to get up in the morning and keep going through hard, cold winters. The morning milking was done by a woman from the village – a loyal and lovely person – but the situation was precarious. What if something happened to

Dad? Tricia had wanted to be a farmer all her life but the combination of economics and circumstances had got too much. Mum, Dad and Tricia decided the cows must go. This was a huge decision considering the family had been milking cows for generations.

The Friesian cows were pedigrees, with the pedigree name 'Crimwin'; 'crim' from Crimbles Farm where Gran used to farm and 'win' for the village of Winmarleigh. There was Crimwin Clair, Crimwin Daisy, Crimwin Bessy and Marion and Milkmaid and Joy, Crimwin Joyful and Crimwin Bettina and many others. As the cows had calves they were named after the mother: Crimwin Marion 2, Crimwin Daisy 3 and so on. These were animals bred on the farm, animals which Tricia and Dad knew individually.

They came to Dad's call, which was a strange 'Owp! Owp!' noise that brought them in a lumbering trot to the gate for milking. Another job we were given on the farm as kids was 'turning the cows'. This meant standing in the middle of the lane beside an open field gate waving a stick as the entire herd galloped towards you (the dog would be hassling the last few and making them dash) and hoping against hope that the bulky, ungainly creatures took the hint and turned through the entrance. Sometimes they kept heading straight for you, in which case you leaped around and waved your stick – if you had one – and made panicked 'Go on! Go on!' noises. Occasionally a cow sneaked past and you would try to outrun it; but you can't outrun a cow, no matter how ungainly and bulky it looks, and the dog would have to hurtle after it, mouth gaping, tongue lolling, to fetch it back.

It must have felt like a bereavement to Tricia for the cows to go but all I felt was relief. I'd had sleepless nights imagining something happening to Dad at the same time as Tricia was ill and getting a phone call: 'There are eighty cows here needing milking. What are you going to do about it?' The thought made my heart race.

Twenty-four of the cows went to Ireland and the rest went ten miles north to Carnforth, to join a herd of a hundred and fifty. One cattle wagon made several trips from the farm to Carnforth and back as Dad and Tricia waited to reload it. It must have been agony for them to watch all these animals they had bred and cared for – generations of work – disappearing by the lorry-load up the A6.

One cow, Flo, could not be loaded safely that day as she was unsteady on her legs and kept threatening to do the splits. As she slithered about Dad said he'd keep her. So as the rest of the herd vanished Flo remained at New House Farm. She had calves for the first two years, living alone in the Dutch barn, and then lived among the apple trees in the orchard as a pet for another six years. A dairy cow usually lives five years; Flo lived fifteen.

Years later, when I asked Dad how Tricia was on the day the cows went, he replied, 'All right.' Coming from Dad, the term 'all right' could mean various things.

'All right' – with emphasis on both syllables both on a high note – means 'excellent'.

'All right' – with emphasis on both syllables both on a low note – means 'they tell me it will do but I am not so sure'.

'All right' – first syllable higher than the second – means 'quite good; they didn't make a fuss'.

Apparently Tricia was this third option on the day the cows went – quite good; she didn't make a fuss.

I don't remember phoning her to check. In my relief that the cows could no longer become an enormous problem, I must have heaved a huge sigh and been too frightened to ask.

With the cows gone, the plans to fit the old milking parlour out as stables for Tricia to manage really got under way. This new business would be financed from the sale of the herd. Mum and Dad signed over the milking parlour and the land around it to Tricia and also gave her part of the old barns (the rest of which would be sold for redevelopment) so she would have a house – a barn conversion – next door to the stables. She was also given several acres so she had grazing and pasture for the horses. From the outside it looked like an ideal set-up yet Elizabeth and I were worried that the responsibility for running a business would prove too much for Tricia in her fragile mental state.

When I mentioned this to a friend of hers I was met with an outraged: 'But this is what she has always wanted!' I argued it would be better to get her mental health steady and then go forward with the business. This idea was dismissed; the new stables were a dream come true for Tricia and they and her barn conversion would make her happy. I did not discuss the situation with Mum and Dad; the decisions had all been made by the time Elizabeth and I were told.

We watched events unfold with foreboding.

I did not know it then, but it was around this time Tricia's diary first mentions being prescribed anti-psychotic medication.

The year after the cows were sold our mother died.

Tricia's state of mind ricocheted from entitlement to victimhood; from feeling aggrieved her efforts were not appreciated and that she was missing out on what was rightfully hers to doing a volte-face and revelling in the excitement of her grand plans for the future.

She had architectural drawings prepared for the barn conversion which spared no expense; it was to be a three-storey, four-bed house with an art studio on the top floor, a study, a garden room, a big garden and a double garage. I made encouraging noises – it wasn't hard; it looked gorgeous – but I worried Tricia's share of the money we had each received from my mother's estate would not cover it. Cost cutting did not enter into Tricia's plans and any doubts expressed about the feasibility of the project – let alone the necessity of bespoke kitchens and log-burning stoves – was met with a suspicious glower.

Meanwhile she made plans for her stables: 'There will be 28 stables and a foaling box and an outdoor manège, a round pen for long-lining and cross-country jumps over 60 acres. An all-weather track round the nine acre [field] and a jump paddock in the meadow. I will spend my days managing the livery yard and bringing on young horses.'

She visited a psychic a couple of weeks after the old milking parlour was signed over to her. 'The psychic asked if I was lucky. I said I didn't always feel lucky but yes. She said you've a lot of money coming your way and it's for you to do what you want with. Enjoy it and have fun.'

The psychic told Tricia there was a man on the horizon who would arrive in the next two months. 'I'm almost there,' wrote Tricia.

In her diary I found a letter she had drafted to Patrik, with whom she must have resumed contact by post: 'Patrik, I'm looking forward to spring and an exciting future. I bought a new car and I've been enjoying driving with music on full blast and not a care to hold me down. Feeling blessed.'

It was shortly after this that she locked Mum and Dad in the house 'to keep them safe'. Elizabeth learned about it when she visited a day or two later and found Tricia so ill

– confused and in a very low mood – that she drove her to A&E late at night. Tricia asked Elizabeth to stay outside during the consultation. After what felt like an age Tricia and the young doctor emerged 'all smiles' and the doctor explained that Tricia was 'simply having a normal reaction to her stressful life'. During the drive home, Tricia told Elizabeth about an unsuccessful love affair – a story Elizabeth now knows to be untrue, but one she believed at the time. 'She fooled me too,' she says. When she arrived back at the bungalow, Elizabeth found Mum, then seriously ill, standing barefoot in her nightie in the cold hall stricken and terrified at what was happening to her youngest daughter.

My mother never spoke of these incidents to me. The next time I saw her she was reclining on her leather chair in the living room, feet up on the rest, her hands partially numbed from chemotherapy, unable to sew any more, unable to concentrate or to read, only able to twitch and to worry. She had a look of grey terror on her face, presumably at the perilous state of Tricia's health and dread at what would become of her when Mum was no longer around to try to protect her.

A few months later my mother was dead.

After Tricia died Elizabeth and I kept saying to each other: 'Thank God Mum's not here to see this. Thank God she's not here.'

*   *   *

Despite my mother's lifelong interest in healthy eating, life's little joke had been to stop her eating almost anything at all by her late sixties when she started having trouble with her stomach.

First she couldn't eat mushrooms, then meat, and gradually the list of foods non grata grew and grew. She would sit, hands pressed on her stomach, staring into the middle distance. Pretty soon all she could keep down was Complan. After years of a home-made, organic, wholefood, fresh diet she ended up existing on a depressing-looking powder she mixed with milk three times a day.

As she was dying of non-Hodgkins lymphoma she rarely talked about it. Years of drowning out communication with household implements wasn't going to stop now. She bought a little whizzer from the Lakeland catalogue to froth up her Complan.

One thing she did say was that she could feel the cancer moving through her body like a stealthy force and could taste it in her mouth like metal. She thought it had a power and a life of its own.

Her bed was brought downstairs from the dormer to a room beside the kitchen.

In the days before she died I discovered some organic vegetable stock she'd made and frozen when she was strong. I defrosted it and fed it to her as she lay in bed. She was happy to eat good food; food she *knew* was good because she'd made it with her own hands.

She didn't want to die; forcing down bio-yoghurt along with her tablets as the nurse shook her head out of my mother's eyeline and mouthed, 'There's no point in taking *them* any more.'

I wasn't going to tell my mother that.

The next day she died.

The final days of Mum's life were more difficult than they need have been because no planning was possible, as even at that late stage death could not be talked about. She would not discuss her decline so we were left dealing with a series of crises rather than being able to manage the process. I didn't know of the 'death acceptance' or 'death positivity' movement then but my mother represented the very opposite. Death acceptance encourages open and honest interactions on the subject of death, rather than fear and denial, to help lift the terrifying silence that can surround it. But with Mum the silence got thicker and deeper as her death drew nearer.

The tension and fear were choking.

Rather than being 'a calm presence in the face of death' we were paralysed and horror-stricken.

This meant we eventually asked for painkillers for Mum only hours before she died, whereupon she was offered Paracetamol by a locum doctor with limited English who had never set eyes on her before. When we insisted on an opiate, Elizabeth and I ended up on a 25-mile wild-goose chase to a Preston pharmacy for liquid morphine only to return to find Mum past swallowing and with the death rattle in her throat.

The day of Mum's funeral was the only time Tricia and I ever fell out.

Elizabeth spent Mum's last night sleeping beside her bed and I spent the night before that with her, lying on a camp bed in the darkened dining-room-cum-bedroom listening for any sound – was she awake? Did she need water? Was she comfortable? Her heels were hurting; I put a cushion under, but no, that didn't help; I moved the cushion so her heels were sticking out of the bed. That helped a little. She was supposed to have a special mattress but it didn't arrive until she had been dead a week, so by the time she died she had bedsores.

Although she never said so, we knew she wanted to die at home and so we were determined to do that if we could. Tricia did not do an overnight with Mum as she lay dying – we didn't ask her because we did not think she was up to it, and she did not offer.

After Mum died Elizabeth, Tricia and I chose the coffin together from the undertaker's brochure, as Dad sat in his armchair repeating: 'Oak, oak. Oak, I think, don't you? Brass handles. Oak.' Then the three of us went to the florist's to leaf through the laminated photographs of false-looking, garish flower sprays and wreaths. We chose a large spray of

'English Country Garden' to cover her coffin: ox-eye daisy, pink roses and freesia and blue hydrangea.

After that, besides a trip to Lancaster for black shoes, Tricia largely withdrew into the farmhouse. Meanwhile I set to sorting out the details of the funeral: I chose one of the hymns Mum had had at her wedding – 'Praise, My Soul, the King of Heaven' – I found a photograph of her as a young woman to put on the Order of Service, I wrote the eulogy, I took her clothes to the undertaker's, I organized for the grandchildren's notes to go in her handbag and I asked my cousin – a classically trained singer – to sing 'I Know My Redeemer Liveth', from Handel's *Messiah*, during the service.

I sat in the farmhouse kitchen to write the eulogy because Tricia was the only person with a computer. She put some music on for me; Eric Clapton's *Unplugged*. I wanted to write something generous, I wanted to write something truthful – but telling the truth does not mean telling *all* of the truth. *She revelled in all good news about her children* was true but I didn't mention that she had driven me mad wanting nothing but good news. *She had a particular love of gadgets. She didn't do anything in a simple way if she could find a gadget to buy, to complicate the process, to clutter up the house and to get on her nerves.* Yes, but no mention there of the fact it was usually *us* who were getting on her nerves, not her gadgets and clutter. *Mum loved shopping; the best of everything and plenty of it. She was very modern and forward-thinking. She embraced technology, going to computer classes until recently, so she could surf the internet for knitting patterns. Not your common-or-garden knitting patterns either, but patterns for fiendishly complicated machines that cost a small fortune and had to have a special workroom constructed all to them-selves.* Spot the omission here to mention that we had now been left with not one but *two* houses filled with expensive cloth and wool and gadgets – mostly unusable – and that we were faced with the job of getting rid of tons of unwanted stuff which was expensive and yet worthless at the same time. But the biggest clue that this was a eulogy with subtext was a giveaway phrase, the one I always listen out for at funerals: *She was a cultured woman with a sophisticated taste in music and was once described as more of a BBC2 woman than ITV. One art she never mastered, though, was the art of compromise. She did not suffer fools gladly …*

There is a particular type of tension that builds up between a death and a funeral. If you loved the dead person the world stops turning, reality recedes, everything is suspended, your breathing is shallower, your appetite disappears, your limbs are weighed down and your movements slower, voices sound distant, world events may be reported on the Ten O'Clock News, but they are not real. The only thing that *is* real is the funeral you are organizing. If your relationship with the dead person was difficult and painful then the grief is further complicated by knowing it is now too late for that relation-ship ever to be rectified.

The tension usually breaks once the coffin has been lowered into the ground, after the vicar (and it is always a vicar in our family, a vicar in a churchyard) has intoned: '… we therefore commend her body to the ground; earth to earth, ashes to ashes, dust to dust …' After this most dramatic moment reality begins to reassert itself, slowly, slowly, bit by bit, and you grasp, blinking, that the world has not stopped turning after all.

At Mum's funeral the intense heat changed things – it was so hot I could feel sweat trickling down my back as I shook hands with the other mourners by the graveside. The tension remained high. It was a record-breaking freakish heatwave – 'the warmest July since records began' – and that added an overtone of unreality to the already disorientating proceedings. Mum was dead; everything was different now. Even the weather was different. I carried one of my mother's white lawn handkerchiefs all day, twisting it damply round and round my fingers, using it to wipe sweat off my forehead and the palms of my hands.

After the wake I decided to go back to the graveyard that evening to see the flowers arranged on the grave and to read the messages on the cards. I also wanted to take photographs of the flowers with my usual desire to understand things by turning them into pictures and therefore stories. Tricia, Elizabeth and Elizabeth's grown-up son, Chris, came with me. As we got in the car Tricia said, 'You don't think I did enough for Mum, do you?'

I had not said a word; I had not uttered one criticism of her. I had not asked for any help, nor implied I should have had any, and I was filled with an enormous fury; I was determined not to be burdened with Tricia's guilt – if she felt guilt that was her problem. It was not my guilt – I had been raised with enough guilt of my own and I would not accept hers.

'I have said no such thing!' I was driving the car, doing a three-point turn in the bumpy field opposite Dad's house that we'd used as parking for the funeral. I slammed the brakes on, revved wildly, shunted the car back and forth with Tricia sobbing and Elizabeth and Chris sitting pale and silent. 'If you feel guilty, feel guilty – just don't blame me!' I rammed the car into first gear and set off at break-neck speed, bouncing out of the rutted gateway, up the lane and to the churchyard, aware that with every slam of the brakes all heads were shunting this way and that in unison. I could hear Tricia sniffling. I got out of the car, slammed the door and marched round to the graveside, as the others followed at a distance.

Mum's grave was not far from the vestry door, under the boughs of the great oak tree we used to sit under as kids. The location was sheer chance but it was the most beautiful resting place surrounded by green. It was so peaceful – in sharp contrast to how I was feeling.

I felt guilty about refusing to accept Tricia's guilt. I felt guilty for suddenly seeing Tricia as an emotional vampire who was trying to take my strength to keep herself going. I felt guilty about overreacting. I felt guilty for raising my voice and screaming at my sister – who was ill, for God's sake. I felt guilty for getting angry on the day my mother was buried. I felt guilty because Tricia was full of misery and angst and I could do nothing about it because I had my own misery and angst to deal with.

I stared at the grave, feeling the world was still suspended, still not happening. Had Mum had a happy life? She should have had although she had never looked very carefree; but then I'd never asked her.

Tricia: a self portrait

Did I ever manage to do the right thing? There were occasions when if I deferred to her on everything I was accepted into her world for a time. When I had children of my own I used to take her to sewing and handicraft shows. I watched demonstrations of sewing machines, overlockers and knitting machines with her and she would enjoy herself and be enthusiastic and spend some money and my guilt would ease for a bit.

A few days after Mum's funeral, having cleared her kitchen, I returned to Scotland with tins of food my father would never use. I got home and decided to make a pasta sauce. I stuck the blade of the tin opener into a can of tomatoes which exploded right up the kitchen wall, splattering the blinds and dripping from the kitchen ceiling. I stood in what looked like a crime scene and examined the tin. It was eight years out of date.

Some months after Mum died Elizabeth told me that during her last week, as she lay on what became her deathbed, Mum had said: 'My life would have been nothing without you three girls.'

'I couldn't believe it,' said Elizabeth.

Ten years later I looked at the photographs of the flowers on the grave that I took on the day of the funeral. I was surprised to find tucked in alongside them an A4 sheet: *Interview with*

Grandma, by Nina Mega, aged eleven. Shortly before Mum died Nina had asked her: 'At what age were you happiest?' And Mum had replied: 'When I had your mother.'

Two months after Mum died, Tricia wrote: 'Is my grief over? I will always miss Mum, and the cows still make me cry, but I hope the losses are behind me for now.'

She adds: 'Uncle Gerald seems to want to upset me if he can.' My heart flips because if she was suspicious of Uncle Gerald she was suspicious of everyone.

These entries are typical: optimism and pessimism almost in the same sentence; highs tripping over lows and vice versa with dizzying speed. As I read I feel compassion for Tricia but I also feel compassion for us – the rest of the family – trying to understand and failing, trying to help and largely failing. No wonder we were confused.

Tricia could seem like an ethereal presence, hardly of this world at all. After Mum died, when Elizabeth's youngest son, Joel, was seven or eight, Tricia sent him a birthday card. Joel lived seventy miles away. It said: 'This card is very late. I did try to phone you on your birthday … I thought I heard you playing a good game but maybe it was someone else.'

Quite quickly the work was completed on the old milking parlour – beautiful new stables were fitted, an outside manège built, the fields fenced off into different grazing areas – and Tricia was in business. The yard was to be a 'DIY livery' – meaning the clients did their own mucking out and feeding of horses. From a distance this looked promising; on bad days Tricia could withdraw into the house but on good days she would have a little community of clients to mix with. Tricia bought two horses of her own: Billy and Sasha.

Unfortunately the barn conversion did not proceed so smoothly. The property developers began work only to stop building and to 'hospitalize' the site – workmen disappeared, then the plant disappeared and then there was nothing left but forlorn bits of scaffolding and a sense of dread and hopelessness. The only movement was the wind stripping the plastic sheeting into ribbons which flapped and rattled as the swallows swooped in and out of the eaves before leaving for their winter homes.

Tricia discovered she was tied into a contract with no opt-out clause or completion date. She continued to live in the farmhouse and every time she glanced out of the window she saw the deteriorating site that should have been her dream home. The weeks rolled by, then the months, the weeks took hold, the years came and went, and eventually the weeds became waist high and claimed the barns back as their own.

CHAPTER EIGHTEEN

Two and a half years after I had filled the memory box with bits and pieces from the farmhouse I opened it.

Contents of the Memory Box
1. Nylon swimsuit with Tricia's swimming badges sewn on by Mum's sewing machine in big zigzag stitch.
2. Baby bonnet, handmade in satin and edged in swan's down.
3. Photographs of Tricia through the decades with people I don't know, in places I don't recognize:
   - on a pebbly beach looking freezing
   - on a sandy beach looking boiling
   - camping with bikers wearing a leather jacket
   - in front of Buckingham Palace in a pink anorak
   - by a shiny red tractor in stonewashed denim
   - sailing from (or to) the White Cliffs of Dover with a blond man
   - at a student party with bottles of German wine and a bowl of custard creams

- walking down a lane in the Lake District with a perm
- wearing black sequins beside a man in a red, white and blue sequined boob tube in a photo marked 'Lively Lady Show Bar, Lanzarote'
- at a Marc Almond concert (or it could be a Marc Almond tribute concert)
- sitting at a French pavement café with a book, a beer and a rucksack wearing a jumper covered in snowflakes
- Smoking a fag against a breezeblock wall.

4. Sketchbook containing Tricia's pencil drawings of her horses.

5. Rosettes from horse shows: sixth place; fifth place; fourth place …

Tricia, a life-long smoker, was still trying to
give up on the day she died

6. Stacks of greetings cards usually showing animals –
   laughing horses, cartoon cows, pigs in hoopla
   skirts – containing loving messages: 'Dear Trish,
   fantastic to see you', 'Dear Trisha, wonderful to
   hear from you yesterday', 'Dear Auntie Tricia, thank
   you for the cheque you sent me', 'Thank you for the
   top … the purse … the bag … the bangles',
   unsigned Valentine's cards, and then further down
   the pile: 'So sorry you have not been well',
   'Sad we do not hear from you any more', 'We miss
   you'.

7. The message tags from the wreaths on Mum's coffin
   which Tricia must have gone back and collected from
   the graveyard after the funeral.

8. Two plaster moulds of Tricia's teeth.

The only thing I removed from the memory box was a
photograph of me and Tricia. We were at a party; it must
have been the mid-1980s. I was wearing a shiny, patterned
top and had unflattering permed hair, too short at the sides.
Tricia was wearing egg-yolk yellow but still managed to look
gorgeous with glossy brown hair. I was saying something and
laughing; she was looking at me and laughing too behind
her hand. It looked a fun moment – one I had no memory
of, but one I wanted to keep.

I gazed at the photograph. I brought it close to my face as
if that might reveal something new, something not apparent

Me, Tricia and a long-lost joke

at arm's length. A faint sound? A waft of perfume? I wished I could remember what we were laughing at. I knew the sound of the chuckle; the one that echoed a thousand cigarettes. I could hear it. I wondered what to do with the photograph and decided as usual I would use it as a bookmark and despite my best efforts probably lose it in yet another book I never finished.

I packed the memory box back up and stowed it in a cardboard suitcase my Italian father-in-law brought with him to the UK in 1957. The stuff inside would never mean more to anyone than it meant to me that day and yet not having Tricia there to go through it with me turned it into a pile of damp paper verging on mildewed and largely bereft of meaning. But not meaningless enough to throw away.

I locked the suitcase. I left the memories to compost. I left the job for the next generation.

Two years after Tricia died, a couple of months before my trip to Hawthornden, I walked into the Oxfam shop. A tune was playing on the shop stereo – a fast and crazy tune that whipped me back to happy times; heady exciting times; the very best of times. I didn't know the name of the tune or the musicians, but I knew this music, every note of it, and I knew exactly where it took me – right back to the farmhouse kitchen on a Sunday in the late 1960s or early 70s.

This tune was the theme of a radio show. Every week when it came on the three of us – Elizabeth, Tricia and I – would dash from the kitchen table into the living room, with Mum and Dad watching, laughing, as we danced hand in hand in a circle, in a mad ring-a-ring-a-roses – round and round and round – until the song ended with a great bang on a drum and we collapsed in a heap on the carpet. The tune only lasted a couple of minutes but they were heady, euphoric, unforgettable minutes.

Which radio show was it? Was it breakfast-time or lunch-time? I couldn't remember, those details had gone, but no music could have transported me back so utterly to another time and place. It felt like an out-of-body experience, a forceful wrenching from the here and now straight back more than forty years.

I stood transfixed; I was physically in the Oxfam shop but my senses were years in the past. I was time travelling as I stood there beside the racks of shirts and jumpers, yet I didn't know what the music was.

An elderly man stood behind the counter, and I asked him: 'What's this playing?'

'This?' he said, cocking his head as though he hadn't been aware of any music. 'Playing?'

'Yes,' I said, 'I was wondering what it was.' I was impatient – I didn't want it to end or the tune, and the memories it was bringing back, might disappear again for another forty years.

He peered under the counter and brought out a CD cover and put his glasses on. He pushed them up his nose then pulled them down again; he examined the cover, the front and the back, and then said, 'I don't know,' and handed it to me.

The CD was called *Take It Easy: All-Time Easy-Listening Classics*. Its cover showed a sunset glimmering across the ocean, the sort of thing they give away with the Sunday supplements. It was hard to believe something so bland was having such a profound effect.

I glanced down the listing and there among the Seekers and the Shadows was track 15, the track currently playing, which was apparently 'A Swingin' Safari' by Burt Kaempfert and His Orchestra. I didn't remember the name but it didn't matter – it was unmistakably our Sunday dancing tune.

'How much?' I asked.

It wasn't for sale, as a matter of fact, explained the man. He blinked at me through his thick glasses, but he could maybe do me a deal at 99p.

I took it home and put the track on my iPod. I pressed Play then Repeat, Repeat, Repeat, Repeat, Repeat, Repeat, Repeat, Repeat, Repeat, Repeat, Repeat, Repeat.

Repeat. Repeat. Repeat.

It wasn't that the mad music was easing the loss of Tricia so much as, for a second or two, it was obliterating the loss altogether, making me feel she was back and young and happy and dancing and laughing and with me hand in hand flying round in a circle, breathless. Making me feel that she had never lost her mind, that she had never died, that there had never been any loss at all.

Repeat.

Walking round town wearing my headphones with the wind and rain lashing my face. Repeat. Wandering with my shopping basket round Lidl. Repeat. Mooching up and down the precinct. Repeat. Unloading the dishwasher. Repeat. Repeat.

One day I realized I'd repeated it so much the tune was losing its power. Burt Kaempfert's crazy piccolo and trumpet and drum were losing their potency, they were losing their ability to whisk me away and let me dance hand in hand with a happy Tricia all over again. Instead the tune was being overlaid with memories of today – of walking round town with the wind and rain lashing my face and wandering with my shopping basket round Lidl, of mooching up and down the precinct and unloading the dishwasher. The euphoria was disappearing, becoming fainter. It was fading back into the past.

In my final week on the fellowship at Hawthornden Castle we had a 'performance evening' when we gathered in the drawing room after dinner with a bottle of whisky to read some of the writing we had produced during our stay. One Fellow was a singer-songwriter and tonight he was to perform for us. He looked at me and said, 'This is a suicide song for you,' and he fixed me with a stare.

He was able to speak many languages and English was not his first language. He explained he'd written it for a friend 'who hung himself up'. The song was a frantic, foot-stomping spectacle which included an everlasting pause in the middle during which he froze and stared wide-eyed at me. I realized how much Tricia would have enjoyed the subversion and the sheer brazen inappropriateness of his performance. In my mind's ear I heard her deep, throaty chuckle – the one that bubbled up from her boots – a chuckle created by thirty-five years of dedicated smoking. I heard her laughing and I felt glad – no, I felt *more* than glad, I felt euphoric – because I knew she was there with me. I sensed one or two of the other Fellows glancing sidelong at me, anxious in case I was upset by the bizarre song, but in truth I was hiding behind my whisky glass because I was struggling not to laugh out loud.

In Hawthornden Castle I had been relieved to close the last diary I had brought with me – the one from 2012 – and take a deep breath. By that point Tricia's words were sparse and there were long, empty gaps that echoed bleakly. There were also comments that showed her paranoia was back much earlier than I had realized – shortly after she left hospital in Lancaster following her last hospital stay when she was sectioned. This highlighted what an impossible and monumental task we had had trying to care for her and made me deeply sad.

However, I hadn't found hatred towards us, her family, or endless unmitigated depression – and both those things were a huge relief. I had done something that frightened me and I had survived. In the diaries I had found flashes of happiness and humour and kind references to myself. Those books, which had seemed such a dark and brooding presence when I arrived at Hawthornden, now felt more nuanced.

Back in the real world I sometimes told people what I was writing. A second or two of silence ensued and I sensed them thinking: Why? What are you going to gain from *that*? Some looked worried, others looked doubtful, and I would ask myself: Why *am* I writing this?

The answer was unclear and confused and as I searched for it I fumbled in circles but I thought it was somewhere in here: to examine the death of my sister, to pin it down, to open it up, to prod at the wound, to put my hands in and grope around and get them dirty, to work it out, to discover and to understand, to find Tricia and to keep Tricia and to never let her go, to work out what went wrong and when it went wrong and how it went wrong, to identify the 'point of no return', and, in all of this, to find and rescue myself.

It was different when I told writer friends what I was writing; with them I saw the thought flash across their face: Now *there's* a good subject.

And, yes, the writer in me thought: This is a hell of a good subject. If writers are supposed to write about what fascinates them and what they are passionate about, then this was the subject for me.

I asked Elizabeth and she said it was a good idea: write it. I didn't dare mention the plan to Dad for months. I didn't think he would object but I also didn't want to worry him. When I eventually plucked up the courage he gave me a questioning look and said nothing. Shortly after, I asked for his help in searching out old photos and papers and he joined in enthusiastically rooting through his desk. At times I went hot and cold at the thought of this story being told because how is it possible to be fair to another person? I could read all the diaries, study all the photos and reread all the letters I wanted, but I could never actually live somebody else's life.

In the end I reasoned it was better to write about Tricia and memorialize her honestly than fall back on the old habit of staying silent. My main goal was to be fair and honest – and to be as honest about myself as anyone else.

A year after returning from Hawthornden Castle I discovered two more diaries in Dad's dining room in a teetering pile of farm accounts – diaries that had come adrift from the others presumably because they were written on A5 pale blue writing-paper pads. As I opened the pads the pages detached in clumps so I handled them as though they were ancient parchment. They dated from 1983 and covered Tricia's A-level summer.

There was nothing very different in them to the other early 1980s diaries I had already read until I came to this: 'Went into Cathy's room late tonight to get a towel. She was asleep. She looked at me without focusing her eyes, just like a baby.'

I decided once again this was Tricia giving me permission to read her words, to search through her life, to look at her closely and to write about her.

I may have been clutching at straws.

CHAPTER NINETEEN

Three years after Mum died I received an SOS call from Dad. Tricia had been discovered by a friend in a state of collapse at the farmhouse, raving and incoherent. The friend had called an ambulance and Tricia had been taken to Blackpool Hospital. Dad did not go with her and this was all he knew. I threw a few clothes into a case, jumped into the car and headed south.

As soon as I arrived at Dad's I received a phone call summoning me to see the friend who had discovered her. She asked me to go to her beauty parlour between appointments.

In her salon I perched on a chair between a table set up for manicures and a pile of fluffy towels as she stood hands on hips facing me.

'If you leave your sister in the farmhouse she will die.'

There was probably more preamble than that but I don't remember it. I recall feeling under attack that my sister was ill and this person was suggesting somehow it was our fault.

'She needs to be in a cottage by the sea somewhere, not in that dark, run-down, horrible farmhouse.' (Maybe she didn't use the words 'dark, run-down and horrible' but I felt they were implied.)

The friend was correct in saying that living alone in the farmhouse could not have been helping Tricia's state of mind. This was something that concerned us all but for us to suggest that Tricia leave it would be feeding into the very paranoia that was destroying her life: the belief that we, her family, were trying to take everything from her. But I didn't want to talk about Tricia's paranoia. It was too painful and it felt disloyal and anyway I didn't understand it properly myself.

'She will never agree to leave her dog and cat and horses,' I explained; which was true and was easier to articulate. I quaked at the thought of suggesting to Tricia that she leave her animals and her home; I couldn't imagine doing it and nor could I imagine Dad allowing the suggestion to be made.

The friend waved away the idea that she wouldn't leave her horses. Tricia needed to go away; somewhere completely different, start afresh, renew.

I kept my voice steady. I knew this friend cared for Tricia and had her interests at heart, even if I believed she didn't know what she was talking about. 'She needs to get treatment in the hospital and then come home to what she loves,' I said. 'She needs to stay near my dad and near her doctors. She needs her horses and dog and what's familiar.'

The friend did not appear to believe for a minute that Tricia could love living on her own in the depths of the countryside in a farmhouse with 1980s decor and that stank of stale tobacco. She clearly believed that, familiar or not, Tricia was only at the farmhouse because she was trapped with nowhere else to go and that for some reason her family were against her and refusing to help. And it's perfectly possible, of course, she believed this scenario because Tricia had told her so.

I made a calculation: should I divulge private information or allow this friend to think Tricia was trapped by her family or abandoned by them (or somehow, inexplicably, both)?

'She's got a bank account with £50,000 in it that my dad gave her. She can afford anything she wants.'

This was obviously news.

The friend bustled about preparing for her next client; the meeting was clearly at an end.

'You need to go and get her some nice new cotton pyjamas for the hospital,' she said. 'And I've bought her a book of poems.'

I thanked her for getting in touch and for the poetry. I headed to the draper's for new cotton pyjamas. I felt hurt; criticized and blamed for Tricia's illness. I didn't know if that was because Tricia had criticized and blamed us or whether it was the friend's reading of the situation. What I did know was that despite the accusatory and defensive tone of the conversation we were on the same side – Tricia's side.

I made Dad's tea before we went to find Tricia at the psychiatric hospital. I told him about the visit to the beautician's and her suggestion that Tricia should be staying in a cottage by the sea. He looked at me like it was me who should be in a psychiatric unit. 'Bloody rubbish,' he said.

Every day I drove my dad seventeen miles to the hospital in Blackpool in the searing heat – an overwhelming, oppressive heat that made your clothes stick to your back.

As I drove I recalled my mother's dire threat whenever we got on her nerves as kids: *You lot will drive me into the Royal Bloody Albert!* The Royal Bloody Albert was in fact the Royal Albert Psychiatric Unit – a forbidding Gothic building like a haunted castle from a fairy tale that we used to pass on the back road to Lancaster, on our way to the dentist. When I was a child it repelled and fascinated me in equal measure and I'd swivel on the back seat of the car as we passed by so I could stare at it for as long as possible. What was this place of mad people where we were going to drive our mother? What was this place of turrets and towers and glinting windows and a big locked gate? It was as foreign to us and as distant as Timbuktu. Some people called it a mental hospital but most people back then called it the 'loony bin' and in my mind's eye I pictured everyone in it drifting about in Victorian nightshirts.

I don't know what I thought went on under the fascinating clock tower of the Royal Albert Hospital but I don't think it can have been any more shocking than the unit Tricia had been consigned to in Blackpool in 2009.

I will never forget my first visit.

It was a locked ward so there were buttons and buzzers and intercoms to press and a wait at the door before Dad and I could get in. We were shown into a side room crowded with Formica tables and leather-look chairs. A sign said: 'Visitors Must Remain in Authorized Area. Patients Will Be Informed You Are Waiting.' Dad and I perched on the edges of our seats and exchanged the odd remark – 'It's hot, isn't it?' … 'Aye, it's hot' – whispering, even though there was no one else about.

The fan whirred. No one came. After a few minutes I noticed a disembodied white hand with chewed nails creeping round the doorframe; it felt up and down for a plug socket and, finding it, clicked off the switch of the fan. I looked at Dad and he faintly shook his head.

Sweat ran down my back. Straight away the heat felt more intense without the whirring of the fan. Through the window I watched a fat pigeon edging towards another pigeon on the hospital roof; he did a mating dance, lowering his head and raising his tail as though in an old-fashioned bow. I longed to be outside feeling the fresh air on my face; I longed to be anywhere but here where it must be edging over 80 degrees, anywhere but here in this locked ward waiting to see my little sister, not knowing what to expect.

The hand crept back. This time the fingers felt around for the light switches and one by one flicked each of them off. The hum of the fluorescent tubes juddered to a halt leaving an echoing space in my head; the room became gloomier although the sun still glared off a Formica table by the window.

The hand was back, flashing the lights on and off. On and off. On and off.

Dad and I looked at each other again and said nothing. Sweat broke out on my scalp. I had an urge to run but I needed to see Tricia. Where was she? Where were the members of staff? How were my elderly father and I being kept hostage by an unseen stranger with chewed nails?

I was working hard to appear relaxed and to hide my fear when at last Tricia walked in looking frail and pale and shaky. The nurse who had brought her smiled hello in an attempt to make all this normal. 'Go and sit in the television room, if you like,' she said and marched off. Tricia turned and led us away and I glanced around trying to spot the owner of the white hand but the corridor was empty. We went into a larger room with a television showing a tennis match at Wimbledon but even the familiar *pock pock pock* of the racket hitting the ball wasn't reassuring in here.

'How are you?' I forced myself to sound calm.

'Can I come home?' Her voice was a hoarse whisper. She was on the verge of tears and despite her five-feet-nine-inch frame she looked small and vulnerable.

'Very soon,' I said, and Dad nodded.

'They'll soon get you right,' he said. 'It'll only take a day or two.'

It was impossible to tell who were staff and who were patients – everyone wore sweatpants and T-shirts. I kept trying to work it out and found myself averting my eyes time and again. One woman walked past in joggers and T-shirt and I noticed a livid gash from her ear to her gullet. It was crusting over. Her chest and arms and neck were covered in healed silver scars in intricate criss-cross patterns. She took a seat nearby and, apologizing to no one in particular, waved her hand around her neck and said, 'Sorry about the state of me.'

A middle-aged woman, small and blonde, in a neat buttoned-up pink cardi, edged closer to us for company and to seek safety. She too was on the verge of tears. 'I'm only in to get my meds right,' she said in the tiniest voice. She looked frightened to death. I nodded and smiled at her and asked her how long she had been here. 'I came today. I'm only here to get my meds right.' I nodded and smiled again – a tight smile, an impossible smile.

'You'll soon be right,' said Dad to the blonde lady. His voice, which is always loud because he is deaf in one ear, sounded even louder on this all-female ward and he attracted attention. Heads turned.

A woman sidled up. 'My name's Linda,' she said. She had scraggy grey hair and was swinging a scraggy grey-haired toy.

She stood very close to the four of us and waved the toy in our faces. She was clearly the owner of the white hand with the bitten nails and I felt my heart clench.

'What's your name?' Linda asked Dad.

'Hello,' he said, not having heard the question, and he raised his hand in a small greeting to her.

'Meet Thalidomide,' Linda said, adding in a little-girly voice: 'See his little stumps.' She waggled the toy's front legs at us. 'You ever had an orgasm?' she demanded of Dad.

I looked about for staff. There were none. Thank God Dad could hardly hear. I felt dismay and anger. How the hell could people heal when they were trapped in a state of fear from this kind of harassment? I knew the woman was ill, she was maybe someone's sister, she was definitely someone's daughter, but I burned with a red-hot anger towards her. She pushed her face closer to mine and sneered: 'What's your name?' She was obviously enjoying herself and I began to hate her.

I smiled and answered in a slightly-too-loud, faux-confident voice. 'Hello, I'm Catherine.' She was delighted to get a response – any response – and turned her attention fully on me, smiling. It was horrifying to be in her gaze.

'Have *you* ever had an orgasm?'

I was back in the school yard at the mercy of some bigger, older kid – the one who pulled wings off daddy-long-legs, the one who no one would stand up to because they were all shit-scared too. Linda was gleeful. I tried to start a conversation with Tricia and the blonde woman but they shrank further into themselves and into their armchairs and became mute, gazing at Linda with dread.

How were we going to leave Tricia here? This place was enough to send *anyone* mad. It would not take long in here to send *me* mad. 'Meet Thalidomide,' said Linda, again, thrusting the toy at me. 'Have you seen his little stumps?'

Except there was no alternative. There was nowhere else for Tricia to go for the help she needed. She was trapped and we were trapped too.

Pock pock pock went the rackets and balls at Wimbledon as the sun beat relentlessly through the hospital windows.

Linda continued to needle and harass, circling our chairs, impossible to put off. Ignoring her was slightly more effective than engaging with her but it only meant she turned her attention to someone else. I carried on a loud conversation about tennis with the others – without knowing or caring anything about it. 'This looks like a close match, doesn't it? Where are we up to now, the quarter-finals?'

Linda sidestepped across to the television and switched it off. My feelings for her crystallized into a sharp dagger of loathing that I longed to stick between her eyes and twist. I wanted to see that leering grin wiped off her sneering face. I looked around. We needed help; but I couldn't go and find it and leave an elderly man and two terrified and ill women to Linda's mercy. Where were the staff? Nowhere.

At the end of the visit I went with Tricia to her bed to unpack the new pyjamas I had brought, along with her toiletries and the poetry book. Again I talked in that over-confident voice, trying to sound as though this was all normal, as though I helped my little sister settle into a locked ward all the time. 'So, you've got everything you need just for a day or two?' I made a useless attempt to arrange her toilet bag and hairbrush in an attractive way on the bedside table. A member of staff strode over and barked at me: 'No razors or plastic bags.'

When we left I said, 'It won't be for long; you'll be home in no time; you're in the right place; the doctors know best' – a series of platitudes, stuff that was sort of true and sort of lying but I was lost for anything else to say.

I gave her a stiff hug. She had lost so much weight she felt like an armful of rattling bones softened only by her baggy T-shirt. We were not brought up to hug or kiss so all touching between parents and siblings felt stilted and awkward at the best of times, which this certainly was not. Dad touched her hand and they also did a stiff, bone-rattling, fleeting hug – and that hug, if nothing else, indicated we really were *in extremis* here.

We left Tricia beside her bed, preparing to be led out to the secure courtyard for a smoke, and Dad and I waited for a nurse to come and release us. There were several locks and codes to be dealt with again and then I heard the sound of the door closing behind me. This was both wonderful because it fastened me out of that place but terrible because it fastened Tricia in. The tarmacked car park with its borders of corporation cotoneaster felt like freedom.

How could Tricia recover in there? Everywhere I had looked there had been pain and distress and trauma – as red-raw as it was possible to imagine. There was nothing comforting or therapeutic in that unit and our sole hope was in the drugs they could provide. How primitive it seemed.

Nearly two hundred years before Tricia's stay in Blackpool, 'asylum' had been offered to the mentally ill at the French institution Charenton, by a Dr Esquirol, whose treatment included recuperative walks, beautiful views, therapeutic activities including a 'salon' for civilized socializing, and plentiful staff to create a healing atmosphere. Even the notorious London madhouse, 'Bedlam', had originally been built with the idea of providing 'health and aire' and music had been used as therapy hundreds of years ago by Ottoman physicians.

To my eye, care of the mentally ill in 2009 in the UK had gone backwards and was basic and cruel and possibly worse than nothing.

We drove home from the psychiatric unit in silence. No words could adequately describe the atmosphere in that hostile, overheated, airless place or capture my misery and fear at leaving Tricia in there. But there was also a vague hope that maybe now it could be different; maybe now the doctors would observe and assess her properly and maybe they could *do something*; maybe now somebody could help her to 'reset' her brain somehow, to get the drugs right so she could live again, be Tricia again. As despairing as I was, there was still a little optimism bubbling somewhere very deep down, pointing out that as this was rock bottom there was nowhere else to go from here but up.

However, as I drove Dad back to the hospital every day that week in the never-ending, remorseless heat, I felt my fragile optimism wavering. Dad remained strong and confi-dent. Was this because he had not fully grasped how ill she was or was he right to stay positive? Was it true that she would be back to herself as soon as they had got the pills right, like he kept repeating? I did not know, but it was hard for me to remain hopeful day after day seeing her in that hellish place and never looking any better.

When people asked how she was I said, 'Her depression's bad,' then, thinking this was not enough, I would add, 'She's had some sort of breakdown.' That was as technical as it got. No one officially used the old-fashioned term 'a nervous breakdown' any more but I suppose that was what I was getting at; using a layman's term to try to describe the horror of a person you love losing their mind.

There were never any doctors around during our visits and the nurses squeaked past on rubbery shoes saying things like, 'She's doing well, she's doing well,' without even breaking their stride. I felt overwhelmed by the problem, lost in the complexity of mental illness and my own ignorance. At times I could see no end to the nightmare.

Over the week Tricia began to tell us about some of the other patients, who I couldn't help but think of as 'inmates'. There was one woman aged about twenty-one who wore a crumpled satin cocktail frock and who walked round and round in endless circles. She had had a baby three weeks before and was suffering from post-partum psychosis – refusing to sit down unless they promised her a visit from the baby. Another woman slumped in an armchair, her bare stomach spilling out over her tracksuit bottoms. She claimed to be three months pregnant but had been on a female-only ward for five months.

To smoke, the patients had to wait to be accompanied in a group into an enclosed outside area to light up and Tricia complained that the other women gathered round her, jostling her, as she filled her roll-up with Golden Virginia because they thought she was rolling a spliff and they wanted one. It was as though she had been transported into some terrifying prison drama.

The only blessing was that Linda had vanished.

Day after day we sat in the airless television lounge wordless with misery. *Pock pock pock* went the rackets and the balls at Wimbledon as the sun beat on.

* * *

Tricia left hospital after a week and went to stay at Dad's while receiving outpatient treatment. I returned home to Scotland to Cello and the children (then aged eleven and fourteen) and to a whole different set of challenges: my autistic daughter was being bullied at school. We did not seem able to communicate with the school: another great bureaucracy, another unsolvable problem.

The world was terrifying and impossible. Everything in it was fragile and hanging by a thread – a spinning, fraying thread; one small tug and the job lot – children, siblings, business, ageing parent, everything – would collapse.

The only way to deal with it was to think only about the things that were right here, right now, right in front of me. The dangling thread was getting thinner and thinner but I was too terrified to look closely.

I phoned Dad regularly to ask how Tricia was. 'Not so bad,' was the usual reply. 'Phone her,' he would say. Sometimes I did, sometimes I didn't. If I did I would end up being pretend-reassuring and I knew we were not really communicating.

I did not think I was doing it right but I did not know how else to do it.

In Tricia's diaries the only mention of the Blackpool unit was written three years later in 2012:

During my stay on the Blackpool Psychiatric Unit it was a heatwave, sweaty and sour. I walked in very reluctantly but without being forced because I thought, probably rightly, that it would help me leave quicker, but I sorely regretted it later. I wish I had bitten chunks out of someone.

CHAPTER TWENTY

In 2011 I was doing an MA in Creative Writing and researching a writing project called 'Body Disposal for Beginners' in which I planned to organize my own funeral. Even though I'd left home a long time before, when I was nineteen, the love of a farm runs deep and New House still meant a lot to me so I decided to visit it to look for a potential burial plot.

It was Boxing Day when I got there – a bright clear day, the peace broken by the shooters blasting at the ducks in the field opposite and yelling at their dogs as they raced around searching for the fallen birds.

Dad, by then a widower of four years, was sitting in his armchair working his way through a plate of warmed-up Christmas dinner. I told him what I'd come for. He pretended not to hear. I ploughed on. 'It's some research I'm doing; I'm trying to find a good place to be buried.' He squashed another sprout onto his fork. He scowled at his plate. The lunchtime news blared from the television. He turned it up.

I felt a bit mean; Dad was old. He never talked of death; he acted as though by mentioning it you were inviting it in. This was not a suitable topic of conversation for him; not on Boxing Day, not when he was eating his warmed-up Christmas dinner, not ever.

I decided not to mention it again but to go down to the farm and investigate.

New House Farm has a Georgian frontage with six windows and a front door but the back kitchen is very old – it was probably once a one-room dwelling – and has walls a foot thick. I approached from the front and rapped on the living-room window. I was wary; in fact, although I wouldn't have admitted it at the time, I was intimidated. I had known for years that Tricia had bad days and good days but at times it felt like the best we could hope for were bad days and slightly better days. On bad days she might stay in bed and not open the door or she might open the door but be monosyllabic and give off waves of deep despair and resentment – and sometimes waves of what felt like hatred. It was hard to bear.

But that particular day must have been a rare good day because I could see her vacuuming, singing at the top of her voice to the Dixie Chicks and dancing with the Hoover while wearing her vest and joggers. I rapped again but she couldn't hear me and she carried on singing and dancing, flinging the Hoover's electrical cord from side to side as she sashayed round the living room. I banged once more, so hard it hurt my knuckles, but the music must have been turned up to deafening proportions and she couldn't hear a thing.

I picked my way round to the back of the house. I walked alongside the hedge where in the dusty hedge bottom we used to bury the baby rabbits killed by Glen.

Glen was our farm dog when we were little. In spring he'd nip baby rabbits on the back of the neck and bring them home. We'd wrestle the little dead bodies off him, tapping his nose and yelling, 'BAD DOG,' and then bury them using a bent spoon or a plastic spade and with all due ceremony in the hedge bottom. We'd say a few prayers and fashion crosses out of twigs and string and arrange daisies and dandelions around the grave with an old jamjar of ferns and celandine – only to come back an hour later to find the grave dug up, the body gone and Glen in the back garden with soil on his nose.

I waited for a break in the Dixie Chicks and hammered on the back window and finally Tricia heard me and I got inside. She offered me a coffee and while she put the kettle on I explained I was looking for a place to be buried. She raised her eyebrows a bit but did not ask: 'What craziness is this?' She nodded at the farm map hanging on the kitchen wall. We took it down and cleared a space among the mugs and the ashtrays and the papers on the kitchen table.

I told her the council had advised me against home burial in case circumstances changed and someone had to dig me up. She nodded and thought about that, then said: 'Do you remember how we used to bury all those rabbits down the side of the house and Glen used to dig them up?'

'Yes,' I said, 'I remember that,' and we surveyed the map in companionable silence for a few minutes, thinking about growing up at New House which on good days had had a magical quality to it. As an adult Tricia recalled her childhood in her diaries: 'Summers with cut grass, errant dogs and ponies with fat bellies. Bike rides and cat hunts. Keep the Kettle Boiling and Tin-Can-a-Lurkey [swinging and chase games].'

The farm map showed the fields had names like 'Big Pasture', 'Jack's Pasture' and 'Green's Field'. We got down to the task in hand and I explained about the legal water stipulations – burial grounds must be at a certain distance from water sources – and Tricia found a ruler. Because of her work for MAFF she knew how to read maps and use grid references.

There were no wells, boreholes or springs, so we could forget about those, but there was a brook running down one side of the farmland, so we had to avoid that. I didn't want to choose a plot far from the house because it was the farmhouse I felt the affinity with, not the more distant fields. We examined the map, working away from the house. There were lots of ponds – at the front, at the back and to the side of the house – so the garden was out of the question. Looking a bit further afield I fancied the orchard. We measured it and right in the far corner it fulfilled all the water stipulations. Tricia checked the grid reference then wrote it down and handed it to me: SD476476, my corner of a Lancashire field; my burial plot.

I had been alert throughout our chat for any indication that Tricia would turn on me for wanting to get a slice of the farm – even if what we were talking about was only a hypothetical exercise for a writing project. It was possible that she would see this as some plot to 'claim' the farm – but there had been no sign of anything untoward.

I thanked her and left clutching my map reference, enormously relieved and heartened that on this occasion at least she had appeared to trust me and had humoured me – indeed had helped me, despite our conversation being about the incendiary subject of New House Farm.

Why did I risk going and asking for her help? The answer was partly because of the memories of rare magical times at the farm as children – usually when we were outside and unsupervised and living in our imaginations – but I think there was also a feeling of 'unfinished business' attached to the farm, a feeling that there should have been more of those happy memories. A sense of dread hung over many of my memories of childhood and, at that time, I still had the urge to revisit and try to rewrite them.

* * *

Three years after Tricia's stay in the Blackpool psychiatric unit she was hospitalized in Lancaster after Dad found her crawling up the lane fully dressed but wearing only one shoe. She was on the grass verge on her hands and knees and hadn't known what she was doing or who he was. As he struggled to persuade her to get in the Land Rover she lashed out with her phone in her hand and, catching the glass, she smashed his windscreen. Dad told me the story later, shaking his head over and over unable to believe it; he normally operated on a 'Keep Calm and Carry On' basis but this had been a situation impossible to pretend wasn't happening.

'I don't know how I got her in the Land Rover. She's so strong.'

I took Dad to see her the following morning in the hospital. The first thing I noticed was that her hands were black and blue. She told me the police put her in handcuffs, taunted and struck her. I took photographs of her fingers swollen like sausages and mottled and red and blue and asked to speak to a supervisor.

A member of staff came in and pulled up a chair in a conspiratorial 'we're all in this together' fashion.

'They can be very strong when they're ill,' she said, with a faux-friendly smile that said: *Get real, we're dealing with mental illness here*. She explained Tricia had struggled and tried to get the handcuffs off in the ambulance as they searched for a bed for her, which accounted for the bruising on her wrists and arms and knees. She denied Tricia would have been taunted or struck and declared the police were very sensitive and experienced in dealing with mental illness.

I was in an *Alice in Wonderland* world where I didn't know whether to believe the nurse or my sister or what to make of the evidence in front of my eyes. Was it right to leave Tricia here looking like she'd been beaten up?

I then discovered I had no option because she had been sectioned; detained under section 2 of the Mental Health Act 1983.

Again I visited her every day for a week. Tricia was allowed off the ward if she was accompanied so we went for walks in the hospital grounds. One day she told me a story about someone dying on the ward. I was horrified; as if the experience of being sectioned on a psychiatric ward was not traumatic enough. A patient had saved up his meds and given them to another patient, she told me. I shook my head. 'How awful!' I said, and she looked over her shoulder to nod at me and gauge my reaction as we picked our way in single file round the building. She continued the story, telling me the undertakers had had to come – at which point an alarm bell went off in my head. Surely the patients would not have seen the undertakers? 'They carried the coffin down the ward,' she said, and my heart tipped and sank. This story could not be true – but Tricia believed every word of it. I did not reply and Tricia turned to scrutinize my expression again. She looked haunted and worried. I didn't want to argue with her, to tell her she was wrong when she thought she was right. I didn't want to underline the fact that again, despite some new meds and close medical care, her brain could not differentiate truth from fantasy.

I had no idea how to handle the situation.

She carried on anxiously surveying my face, trying to read my thoughts.

I changed the subject.

When Tricia had stabilized, and they were preparing to discharge her, Elizabeth, Dad and I went in to see the medics. We sat with Tricia in the café before the meeting of her entire team – consultants, nurses, mental-health workers – and as we waited she told us she finally had a diagnosis: bipolar disorder with psychotic episodes.

She was forty-five years old and it was thirty years since she had first recorded in her diary that she was depressed. 'I decided to tell you because I want you to know I'm not schizophrenic,' she said.

Did she think we would judge her for being schizo-phrenic? Did she consider schizophrenia more of a taboo than bipolar and psychosis? I don't know because, of course, we never asked her. We merely listened and nodded.

I felt reassured because I *had* suspected she might be schizophrenic, and bipolar didn't sound as terrifying as the unknown quantity of schizophrenia. Bipolar, to my unmedical ear, sounded a little nearer to depression, which was a terrible enemy but a familiar one.

Dad, Elizabeth and I were invited in to meet the team before Tricia joined us. It was awkward leaving her in the café to go and talk about her behind her back but we were so thankful to be getting access to the experts that we jumped at the chance.

We explained we wanted to help Tricia but when her illness got really bad she lost trust in us and thought we were trying to do her harm. If the team would talk to us when she was very ill then maybe we could explain to them what was happening in her life and give some context for her fears? The team looked at each other, nodding; yes, so long as Tricia agreed, that shouldn't be a problem.

The relief was overwhelming. At last we were going to be able to help; we were going to be informed and to be fully in the picture about Tricia's health. Our knowledge could fill in vital bits of the puzzle. Even in these desperate circumstances and surroundings I felt happy because I thought we had scaled a huge mountain; everyone had acknowledged that we were all on the same side and at last we would be able to work together.

Before Tricia joined us I asked, hesitantly, had anyone, er, died on the ward last week? A circle of blank faces gazed back at me. So, no patient had given his meds to another patient, who had then overdosed? There were laughs around the table, shaken heads. No, most definitely not.

Tricia warily entered the room and the consultant explained that we – her sisters and father – wanted to be involved in her care and that we wanted to be able to contact her team and liaise with them if we were worried about her and vice versa. Tricia listened in that strangely intense yet quizzical way she had developed – as though the language she was hearing was fading in and out or kept changing to something unfamiliar and foreign. She looked frightened and distant. She nodded: yes, we could be kept informed of what was going on. Yes, we could all work together to get her better.

I could have kissed that consultant; never again would we be in the dark, never again would we feel so cut off and helpless and hopeless; from now on we'd be able to support Tricia properly.

I believed we had reached our lowest point – and it was a point lower than we could ever have imagined – but with everyone pulling together it was going to get better; it *must* get better, surely it could not get any worse.

We heaved a sigh of relief.

We left Tricia in the hospital and she wrote in her diary 'productive meeting'.

How naive we were, how trusting, and what a terrible mistake we had made.

* * *

On 30th March 2012 Tricia wrote in her diary: 'Released on licence from hospital. Fabulous! Food shop, thank-you cards, cleaning and washing with *MUSIC*!!! Broadband, online!'

She bought herself some heavy-duty exercise equipment, including an enormous power plate and a gym-quality tread-mill, and branched out trying new routes around the village with her horses: 'Took Sasha round canal path. He walked under all bridges for first time without me getting off. And without being asked.'

She continued to find joy in music: 'Bought Drifters, Ray Charles, Alison Krauss and Union Station, Dixie Chicks, Puccini.' And she tried hard to stay healthy: 'Every day I must: 1. Write something. 2. Exercise. 3. Spend time with horses. 4. Sketch. 5. Clean something – for example one room, or do a load of washing, or tack or bath horse, or clear out one cupboard.'

And she was making plans: 'To do – get better internet, enter dressage test, buy horse wagon.'

We watched from a safe distance as she got on with her life and we held our breath, not daring to look too closely at the spinning thread.

On the surface everything appeared OK. On the surface.

In fact, as I had learned reading the last diary at Hawthornden, by July, only four months after being discharged from hospital, she had begun to believe her phone was being tapped and she wrote about receiving crank calls. Shortly after that she described how someone had maliciously left a dead rat outside her back door. There followed references to people 'sabotaging her job/business/life'.

She confided these events to no one but her diary, as we, her family, watched through our fingers, hoping against hope that, as she appeared to be all right, it meant she *was* all right. It is hard to look at this diary now. It is bleak. Does it show the point of no return? Was that stay in Lancaster Hospital our last chance to help her?

By the end of 2012 she wrote that a named family acquaintance had proposed and she had accepted. She must have believed it but in fact this person was someone she had not set eyes on for more than twenty years.

But we remained in ignorance. Having seen Tricia's mental health improve enough for her to leave hospital in March 2012, we remained unaware that in fact we were all sitting on a ticking time bomb and the fuse was by now dangerously short.

CHAPTER TWENTY-ONE

Dad's father, Gran, fought in the trenches in the First World War – in the artillery firing the big guns that left him also deaf in one ear. He was injured at Ypres when a colleague shot him through the shoulder as he cleaned his gun without unloading it first.

Because Ypres had been such a significant part of Gran's life – the only time he ever went abroad bar a quick trip to Ireland – Dad was interested in it. I suggested we go with him on a short tour of the Belgian battlefields so he could see where his father fought.

The idea was kicked around for a while until Elizabeth said we'd better do it now or it would never happen. We asked Tricia if she would like to come but she felt it was too difficult having her and Dad away from the stables at the same time.

We booked it for December 2013.

In the run-up to the trip Elizabeth and I both phoned the Lancaster team who were caring for Tricia to let them know and to ask: Was it safe to leave her? Did they think she'd be OK without Dad for four days? Would they be able to put extra support in place?

We were worried because Tricia was clearly very depressed again but we were met with a wall of either silence, or what felt like hostility. The woman who was Tricia's main point of contact was part-time and difficult to locate. Other people either did not know about Tricia's case or would not comment. It felt like trying to make contact with a big black void.

We mentioned that Tricia had agreed we should be involved in her care, and she had said this in front of her entire team at the Lancaster meeting eighteen months before. Nobody knew what we were talking about. They said they could not find a note in the minutes to this effect. Had we filled in the required paperwork? It was no good without paperwork. What paperwork? we asked. We were not told about any paperwork.

The barriers had slammed down again. We were not welcome; indeed we were not legally entitled to know anything. We could speak on the phone to them if we liked and they would listen, but they would not respond.

We were back at Square One.

When Elizabeth eventually got hold of Tricia's lead support worker things became heated. Elizabeth insisted that Dad needed help too – he was old and Tricia's main carer – but this suggestion was not well received.

'I'm here for Tricia,' she said, 'not your dad.'

* * *

We decided to go to Ypres. Yes, Tricia was depressed – but that was part of our life. Tricia would probably always be depressed to some degree. Life had to go on in whatever way we could manage. Dad was already eighty-seven years old. How much longer could we wait?

We left Britain on the Eurostar on 1st December 2013 and every morning and evening of the trip Dad said, 'We should phone Trish,' and I'd call her on my mobile for a few stilted moments. 'Are you OK?' 'Yes, I'm OK.' Her voice was lifeless and dull, but it had been like that for many months and we expected it to be like that for many more months.

On 2nd December we went on a walking tour of Bruges. We saw the bronze sculptures of the Four Horsemen of the Apocalypse: Conquest, War, Pestilence and Death riding his pale horse. We went into the cathedral and lit a candle in memory of Mum.

On 3rd December we visited Tyne Cot Cemetery, the largest Commonwealth war memorial and cemetery in the world, on a day when the mist sank low and hung over the graves, clinging like a ghostly presence. We gazed at almost twelve thousand graves of the servicemen who died at the Battle of Passchendaele; so many that the furthest away faded into the fog beneath the looming silhouettes of the poplar trees and the cross of sacrifice.

We walked in silence past the Stone of Remembrance, engraved 'Their Name Liveth for Evermore', and back and forth along the rows of seemingly endless white gravestones, most of which were for unidentified men and marked 'A Soldier of the Great War. Known unto God'.

At the boundary of the cemetery Dad surveyed the land beyond, hands on hips, and shook his head. The landscape was very similar to our home village: flat with cropped fields. A farmer through and through, he stood with his back to the cemetery and said, 'Land's wet, in't it? Very wet.'

That night we went to Ypres and looked around the In Flanders Field Museum and had dinner in a restaurant beside the Cloth Hall, called De Trompet.

'We should phone Trish,' Dad said.

The restaurant was noisy so I took my mobile over to the window and dialled her number.

She answered. Her voice was faint and slow.

'I'm worried about being here,' she said.

I rested my forehead on the cold glass, covering my other ear with my hand, shouting into the phone: 'We'll be back tomorrow. Just look after yourself and you'll see Dad tomorrow. Take it one day at a time.' I repeated this over and over in desperation, hopelessly, helplessly, because I didn't know what else to say. I didn't know if she could hear me properly and I could hardly hear her – she was so quiet, so lost, so distant.

In the following weeks we would debate what she meant by 'I'm worried about being here'; was she referring to being at the farm on her own or did she mean she was worried about being alive?

It was hard to say because, like so much about Tricia and her illness, we didn't ask her the right questions when we had the chance.

'Look after yourself. OK? Dad'll be back tomorrow.' The noise of the restaurant pressed in all around.

'Yes, OK. Bye.' She was so faint it was as though she was already fading away.

That was the last time I heard her voice. I went back to the table. 'How was she?' asked Dad. 'Quiet,' I said. 'I think she'll be glad when you get home.'

We finished our meal, mopping up the fish sauce with hunks of crusty bread and drinking the remains of a bottle of wine. We were subdued, as we had been for the whole trip, but oblivious to the fact that we were walking blindfold right to the edge of Tricia's life, teetering along a crumbling path, only a step away from the end.

As we left the restaurant, Ypres's magnificent Cloth Hall – destroyed in the First War and painstakingly reconstructed – towered over us; the town skyline of spires, steeples and belfries was hazy and only just visible. Artificial trees festooned in Christmas lights blearily blazed through the fog. Stalls sparkling with fairy lights sold hamburgers and bratwurst, chocolate and jewellery. It was a cold night and we were rugged up in overcoats and hats and scarves as we crossed the marketplace and headed up the Meensestraat to the Menin Gate, the Memorial to the Missing.

Crowds gathered, including groups of schoolchildren in hi-vis jackets. Silent groups waited with wreaths of red poppies and at eight o'clock the buglers arrived and the notes of the last post sounded, as they do every evening, under the memorial arches in memory of the fallen whose names are engraved there. As those lingering, longing bugle notes echoed I felt tears running down my face. I wasn't sure what I was crying about, except everything; I was crying about everything.

Forced smiles under the Menin Gate. Unknowingly, minutes earlier, I had heard Tricia's voice for the last time

I sat alone at King's Cross waiting for my train to Edinburgh – Dad and Elizabeth had got a lift to Lancashire with Johnny – and I dialled Tricia's number. Garstang two-double-three-nine. It rang and rang but there was no answer. I tried again and on the third try I left a voicemail: 'We're back. Hope you are OK. Dad will be with you in a few hours.'

Was a part of me relieved that she didn't answer the phone? Was I dreading having to come out with yet more platitudes of the 'everything will be OK' variety?

I nursed a scalding Costa coffee and heaved a sigh of relief: we'd taken Dad away, we'd given him a break, he'd seen Ypres, and now we were back and everyone had survived; we were all in one piece, we'd got away with it.

When I remember the Belgium trip I don't think of the horse-drawn carriage ride or the chocolate makers. I don't think of the crêpes with ice cream or the merchants' houses lining the canal; no, I think of death: of the Four Horsemen of the Apocalypse and Death on his pale horse; I think of lighting a candle in memory of the dead. I think of the ghostly mist hanging low on the gravestones at the cemetery, and the notes of the last post echoing under the archway. I think of the sense of wasted life at Tyne Cot Cemetery. I remember Tricia telling me she was 'worried about being here'. It feels that the holiday was full of 'signs', or portents of doom, and we missed them all – why couldn't we see the disaster so imminent, the calamitous event that was about to befall us? It seems so obvious now. And yet, surely there had been signs and portents of doom for forty years and we had become blind to them. When I look back at the photographs of our trip I study our forced half-smiles under the Menin Gate and the voice of hindsight sets up such a hollering in my head, like a resounding gong and a clanging cymbal: 'You fools!' it shouts. 'You fools!'

I ended up using the 2014 diary I'd bought as a Christmas present for Tricia as a notebook in which I planned her funeral and kept track of the bewildering maze of paperwork created when a next of kin dies.

When the turquoise notebook was full I did not throw it away because, like all things connected to Tricia, it had taken on an extra significance. I put it in the cupboard. Next to it I filed my mobile-phone bills showing the calls I made to Tricia from the various cafés and hotels in Belgium and the voicemails I left from King's Cross. Why did I keep these when I never kept any other mobile-phone bills? I kept them as proof of our final communication. Proof I had phoned her; proof of the last time I heard her voice; proof I had reached out to make contact with her through the dark; proof I had tried.

CHAPTER TWENTY-TWO

After Tricia died it was necessary to have an inquest because her death fell into the category of 'where the cause of death is believed to be unnatural'.

It was scheduled to take place at Lancaster Coroners' Court in April 2014.

A court official met us and led us past people leaning against the walls in ones and twos waiting for the Magistrates' Court to open; mainly thin, haunted-looking men and one or two overweight women. As we clopped past in our high heels and black dresses (me and Elizabeth) and formal suits (Dad, Cello and Johnny) it seemed odd that all this was happening in the same building.

The coroner looked as you'd expect a coroner to look: steel-grey hair, smart suit, well nourished, thoroughly in command of his courtroom and utterly in his element; a patrician figure.

He explained that the inquest was to establish who had died, where, when and how. It was not to allocate blame.

He began with the timing of Tricia's death and said that as she had been discovered on 7th December that would be the date on her death certificate. I asked if the post-mortem examination had revealed whether she had died on the night of the 6th or the morning of the 7th? This felt important. The coroner shook his head and smiled indulgently, looked amused. This was not like the television, he said. In real life it was not possible to pin the time of death down that accurately.

I felt stupid.

He went on to note that the post-mortem showed there had been no non-prescription drugs or alcohol in her system when she died. We had previously been asked if we wanted a copy of this report. A memory of a television programme about JFK's and Marilyn Monroe's post-mortems – horribly intrusive and detailed – had flickered through my mind. 'No,' I said decisively. 'We do not.'

Tricia's careworker came to the witness stand to give evidence. As she spoke it emerged that during the four weeks before she died Tricia had twice asked this careworker to pass messages to Dad saying she was trying to get well, but the careworker had not passed them on. These were messages from Tricia about her desire to live and how she was struggling but was doing her utmost to stay alive. This was a different kind of communication for our family – something honest and addressing the subject of Tricia's mental health head-on (albeit via a third party) – and yet we were only finding out about it now she was dead.

We listened in disbelief.

Did Tricia think the messages had been passed on and had gone unacknowledged? It was impossible to know or, now, ever to find out.

The coroner asked the careworker more than once why she had not passed on the messages. Did she not have a number to use? Why had she not used it? The careworker said she had been trying to support Tricia in the best way she could: keeping the lines of communication open with her. To which the coroner replied: 'How is that achieved when she has asked you to do something? Is what you are saying that you took a conscious decision not to do what she had asked?' The careworker replied that it had not been a conscious decision – but that she hadn't wanted to worry Mr Simpson; then, at last, she conceded: 'Maybe I should have rung Mr Simpson.' She had been trying to maintain her relationship with Tricia, she said.

Throughout her evidence she wept, wiping her eyes and her nose with a tissue.

The psychiatric consultant who had visited Tricia on the afternoon of 6th December then came to the stand to give her evidence.

The coroner asked about the possibility of sectioning Tricia on 6th December. The consultant said she had seemed better; they had sat round the kitchen table and 'everything was neat and Tricia appeared well'.

I mentioned that I had found the kitchen bin full of Tricia's hair. Had the consultant noticed that Tricia had hacked her hair off? I was rebuked by the coroner for the phrase 'hacked her hair off'. I rephrased the question even though 'cutting her hair off' didn't seem sufficient when she'd probably done it with the kitchen scissors and without a mirror. I asked the consultant whether, had she noticed Tricia's long hair had been cut off, she would have taken that as an indication that Tricia was despairing and self-destructive? The consultant shook her head. She did not know if Tricia had long hair or short hair when she saw her, whereupon the coroner interrupted and pointed out that even he, who was not known for noticing whether ladies had been to the hairdresser, would be sure to notice if someone had cut inches off their hair by themselves! But no, the consultant repeated she did not remember. To cut your own hair off, she said, would be 'unusual but not self-harm'.

The consultant was adamant that when she left Tricia on Friday the 6th her life had *not* been in danger. How could her life not have been in danger, I asked, when by either that evening or the next day she was dead? But the consultant repeated: Tricia's life had not been in danger when she left her on the Friday. I longed to thump the table and demand to know how, *how*, could she keep stating black was white – but the coroner said the point had been made. We must move on. We were not there to allocate blame.

In his closing remarks the coroner said the evidence showed 'a lady who was anxious and worried about things, probably unnecessarily'. He added there had been no recent suicidal ideation and therefore no reason to section her.

He concluded: 'What I recognize from my dealings is that people do things spontaneously on the spur of the moment, without history of any previous similar acts or thoughts or recent history. But what is clear is that what your sister did, what your daughter did, she did of her own volition. Although there is no note of her intention, the fact that she did what she did, the way in which she acted is sufficient for me to say it is beyond reasonable doubt that she decided to end her life.'

We emerged from the inquest stunned. I had been expecting it to provide some sense of an ending, some resolution, but I had been wrong. The inquest had set out to do what it intended: to answer the questions who, where, when and how – but not the crucial why?

I had read before that studies suggest farmers may be three times as likely to die by suicide than the average person. Now, here was our personal catastrophe added to that statistic.

On the way to the car we went into Lloyds Bank to help Dad with some banking – he was trying to close an account and had been finding it difficult to get into Lancaster on his own to do it. The teller took his details and disappeared. She returned for more details which she jotted down and disappeared again. She huddled in a group with two or three others and they looked at us over their shoulders, seeing a group dressed in black, possibly on our way home from a funeral. A different teller came back for yet more details. The original one was now on the phone. By this time we'd been waiting ten minutes; there was an ever-growing queue. 'Is there a problem?' I called under the bottom of the safety glass.

'We can't find your account, Mr Simpson.'

'There's ninety in there,' Dad shouted, bending down and yelling under the partition, 'ninety thousand.'

There was a flutter of excitement behind us as the queue of ladies with shopping baskets and trolleys turned to look at one another and pull 'well I never' expressions. 'I hope they find it,' said one and there was a general nodding and murmur of agreement. All impatience at waiting had disappeared; this was too entertaining.

Elizabeth and I looked at each other and began to laugh, shaking with laughter; we were back down the rabbit hole where the world was a bizarre, topsy-turvy place. Where what you knew to be true apparently wasn't true and people could say anything whether it made sense or not and repeat it over and over again and then *that* became the truth. And anyway what was the point of all these words, all this talking, all these procedures; there was no point because none of it changed a thing.

To the relief (or possibly not) of the ladies in the queue the bank found the missing ninety thousand but there was nothing anybody could do about Tricia.

The misplaced laughter in the bank reminded me of the day Elizabeth, Tricia and I went to buy shoes for Mum's funeral. It was the freak summer of 2006; unseasonably hot, stifling, unbearable. We were in a shoe shop, fanning ourselves, lifting long hair off our necks, trying to stop the backs of our legs sticking to the plastic seats. Rip. Rip. Waft. Waft. Someone said something, I don't remember what, and we all burst out laughing – loud raucous laughs. A passing assistant, arms full of shoes, smiled and said, 'It looks like you three are having a good time. Are you shopping for something special?' And we stopped laughing and looked at her for a second before replying: 'Our mother's funeral.' The smile dropped from her face and she backed off, confused, and that made us start laughing even harder.

Sometimes life makes no sense at all.

There was an NHS investigation into Tricia's death.

A manager came to Dad's house a year after she died to discuss the findings. He appeared friendly enough, sitting down on the sofa, slapping his thighs and asking me in a broad Lancashire accent, 'So you've come down from Skoker-land, 'ave yer?'

But after the disappointment of the inquest my heart was not in this meeting.

The report was full of acronyms: STR, CRHTT, CPA, CC, PIR, CCTT, CBU, ECR, SOPs, one following relentlessly after another. Tricia was referred to as 'the Service User' and the members of staff were called STR Worker 1, Crisis Practitioner 6 and so on. It seemed the report was a construction of impenetrable jargon designed to prevent rather than allow communication. I had to read each sentence several times to try to make sense of it – not always successfully.

I did not have the strength. I nodded as the manager ploughed through paragraph after paragraph but I was not grasping it.

The report was contradictory and muddled but hinted that three weeks before Tricia died she may have attempted suicide by overdose. This was deeply shocking and went against what the coroner had said at the inquest – that there had been no previous suicide attempts and therefore no reason to section her.

However, it seemed the only consequence of the investigation into events surrounding her death was some staff members receiving training in record-keeping and 'following protocols'. In conclusion the investigators, having 'carefully considered all the evidence', 'do not believe the identified care delivery issues contributed to the death of the Service User'.

The manager said he would clarify what exactly was known about the previous suicide attempt – if indeed it happened – and would be in touch. I nodded; I knew he wouldn't, and I knew he knew I knew he wouldn't. 'I will get back to you as soon as possible,' he assured me.

The weeks passed.

He didn't get back to me.

CHAPTER TWENTY-THREE

Throughout 2015 and 2016 I continued my fingertip search for traces of Tricia. I put her name in my Hotmail account and pressed Enter. Tricia and I had never exchanged emails but it brought up every mention of her in my messages since 2008.

To reread myself talking about Tricia in the present tense was dizzying.

How had the cataclysmic events of December 2013 not caused all mention of her to self-destruct and vanish in a puff of smoke?

When Tricia had been dead several weeks it made no sense for Dad to keep paying the phone bill in the unoccupied farmhouse. I called the phone company and they gave me a date for disconnection. Garstang 2339. Garstang two-double-three-nine. This was the telephone number I grew up with; the number I memorized as a child; the number my schoolfriends still remember; the number that for many years meant home and familiarity. This was the number I phoned as a teenager for lifts home at midnight, the number

I phoned to tell my mum I'd passed my degree and later to tell her I was moving to Scotland with Cello and later still that I was pregnant. The number I'd phoned to find out the results of Mum's never-ending hospital tests. The number that in the last few years had meant 'Tricia' and a gripping anxiety about how I would find her: would her voice be the echoing, distant one or the overenthusiastic, young-girl one? The number on which I had last heard her voice from Belgium. Garstang two-double-three-nine.

As the date for the disconnection drew nearer I dialled the number several times to listen to it ringing out in the empty farmhouse. I pictured the phone at the bottom of the stairs and heard the bell, shrill, disturbing the dust, disturbing the quiet. And when I had rung off I imagined the still-quivering dust motes, the sound of the ring hanging in the air for a long moment as a fading discordant echo before the enormous quiet reasserted itself.

Then one day I rang Garstang two-double-three-nine and there was no ringing, only a continuous tone – the number had gone and the connection that had always been there was severed for ever.

After she died we found Tricia's camera in the glove compartment of her old Ford. I took the film to be developed and waited to see what her last pictures would reveal.

The snaps showed the confines of Tricia's life in her final months: the view from the side door of the farmhouse, out of the white plastic conservatory my mother paid a fortune for in the 1980s, and across the yard towards the great stone barn slowly crumbling now, and dying, since the builders stopped building. I inspected the prints in detail. I could see plants growing out of the barn roof alongside flapping plastic sheets shredded by the wind after reroofing work started and then ceased. The buildings that had previously housed bleating calves and squealing pigs were empty and decayed, neither barns nor houses now, but stripped back, naked stones and wood. It must have caused a lowering of her spirits every time Tricia glanced through the conservatory window or went out to her car in the farmyard, to see the farm she loved so dearly mouldering away, and the barn-end unit that was supposed to be renovated into her dream home mouldering with the rest of the buildings.

I also took Tricia's mobile to the mobile-phone shop and asked if they could show me the photographs on it. 'Yes, if you put the password in,' the assistant said. I explained I didn't know the password. 'It was my sister's and she's dead.' The assistant looked embarrassed. 'I'm really sorry,' he said, 'it's against the law for me to open it.' I couldn't help it, I started to cry. 'I'm really sorry,' he said again as I rooted in my bag for a tissue. There was a pause, then he said, 'Hold on,' and casting glances round the shop he took the phone and disappeared. A few minutes later he came back and handed me a copy of a photograph printed on office paper.

It showed the farmyard where among the cobbles, tarmac and sprouting weeds stood Tricia's dog Ted. And there was Dad carrying a newspaper he had just bought for her at the Co-op; every day Dad went to get her a newspaper, a tin of soup, a tin of tuna, a packet of cigarettes or a prescription; whatever she needed. Every single day; faithful to the end.

In the photograph he looks quizzically and a little resentfully into the lens, never a fan of having a camera pointed at him. Surrounded by the dilapidation of what used to be his farmyard, he looks like the last man standing.

Dad and Ted: faithful supporters of Tricia until the end

In the early hours of 7th December 2014, exactly one year after Tricia died, I snapped awake. I looked at my clock: 4 a.m. Every atom of my body was listening. My senses were humming like a tuning fork. This was when she died, I thought. Four o'clock in the morning.

One year later still, as the 6th of December 2015 slid into the 7th, I snapped awake again. It was 3 a.m. No, *this* was when she died, I thought, this was it; three o'clock in the morning.

In 2016, another year on, another 6th of December turned into the 7th. There was another awakening, another jolt. I looked at my clock. It was 2.45 a.m. No, *this*, *this* was the time she died.

And I knew, of course I knew, that I would never know.

Building work began again on the old barns, shortly after Tricia died, and by June 2015 they had been transformed from dilapidated ruins into 'stunning unique barn conversions'. The brochure called them 'Rosemarleigh Barns' even though that had never been their names. Winmarleigh, the actual name of the village, mustn't have been considered attractive enough to potential buyers. After she died we had sold the end unit – the one that was to be Tricia's – to the new developers and that had been completed too.

I had suggested Tricia call it 'Whistledown', after my favourite film *Whistle Down the Wind* and in honour of the cold blast that sometimes greeted you when you turned the corner at the bottom of the yard. According to the glossy brochure it was now called 'The Tack House' and was apparently: 'A perfect four-bedroom home designed for modern life. Large open-plan living areas and spacious double bedrooms arranged over three floors. Light and airy, yet cosy and inviting.'

On the open day for the barn conversions we were invited to go and have a look around. In the old calf pens, which used to have compacted earth and straw underfoot and where you couldn't venture without wellies, it was now a cavernous palace of white walls and beige carpets. We were invited to pull on blue plastic overshoes to protect the interior from our feet, which my mother would have described as 'wrong road up'. The kitchen surfaces were white and shiny and a giant cocktail glass of lemons stood on them as sole decoration.

The barns were redeveloped by a Premiership footballer-turned-property-developer and his girlfriend. She greeted us and offered us prosecco from plastic glasses. She was also shiny and perfectly finished, with flawless skin, white teeth, ombréd hair and a dazzling white top with sheer sleeves and very long shell-pink acrylic nails. I complimented her on what a nice job they had done, and she thanked me with a smile, even though I was in fact a little too stunned to take in whether it was nice or not.

Other people – potential buyers and nosy parkers alike – strolled from room to room, necks craning to take in the sheer scale of the buildings and the height of the ceilings. Where the calves used to jostle to shove their heads through the only window in the great thick stone walls, there was now a wood-burning stove. The circular aperture in the eaves through which the swallows swooped every year to nest in the soaring rafters was now a round glazed window and if you went up to the third floor and stood on tiptoe you could peer through it. The view was of our old Dutch barn which Dad still owned and which stood beside Tricia's stables surrounded by a jungle of greenery, stacks of bales and decrepit tractors, the way it always had.

In what used to be the hayloft – with floorboards so rotten cats could fall right through and bounce on the bales below – there was now a bathroom with white walls and a grey slate floor; there were lit candles dotted about and scattered red rose petals.

From another third-floor vantage point – a space only previously accessible to birds and mice – I could see the old farmhouse in a way I had never seen it before. It was surrounded by lilac trees and old rose bushes and bags of builder's rubble left over from this barn project. The house looked like a wallflower at a disco, standing at the side of the flashing dance floor wearing a home-made frock. It was freshly painted and Dad kept the gardens mown, but it could not compete with the total and utter overhaul that had befallen these units. The farmhouse still belonged to the twentieth century, and the centuries before that, while these buildings had been dragged well and truly bang up to date into the twenty-first.

Tricia had shown us the architectural drawings for this unit several years before when she was in an optimistic phase – when she was still making plans to have an art studio and a garden room and she was talking about kitchen designs and bathroom fittings, before the first builders withdrew. But I couldn't imagine Tricia living here in this pristine palace. Every last echo of the farm as it was had been obliterated by hard shiny white. This was country living scrubbed to within an inch of its life. This was country living without dirt or animals. I could not imagine a pile of wellies by the door, or dripping coats drying near the log burner or my dad's flat cap smelling of manure and steaming over the range.

Despite it being an environment too 'perfect' for Tricia, I felt tears welling up. Why couldn't she have had this life? Why couldn't she be planning to move in here and make it her own? Why did life have to play such dirty tricks? I turned away and pretended to be admiring the view over the fields to the woods beyond.

The outside of the barns was glowing honey-coloured sandblasted stone and the doors were PVC in a fashionable duck-egg blue. The doors and gates and eaves and guttering at the farm had always been made of wood and metal and painted a bright royal blue. This was the one thing I really baulked at. They should still be a bright royal blue – one that slowly faded to denim blue and cracked and flaked until a couple of times a generation it was painted a bright royal blue again. That was what it should have been – what it always had been and what looked right. Duck-egg blue seemed so self-consciously *Country Living*, so knowingly 'good taste'.

We wandered around the other units goggling at the way the past had been so successfully removed. All the memories of the games we played and the adventures we had were only in our heads now, no evidence remained. The great stone barn where the rope swing hung from the rafters was now a luxury unit called 'The Parlour' – presumably a reference to the milking parlour even though no animals had ever been milked in there; the old granary where the hay was kept was now 'Crofters Keep' and my dad's signature on the wall from when he was a boy was well and truly gone (in fact we couldn't even work out whether that wall existed any more). The pig pens were 'Summers End', and Gran's Dairy, where he and his dogs and cats warmed themselves under the pig lamp, had been knocked down and completely rebuilt as an 'eco-house' called 'The Dairy'. It was hard to believe that all this *newness* existed on the same bit of the planet.

I pondered the utter devastation of our past. It was inevitable, of course, when we sold the barns, although at that time the extent of the changes was unimaginable.

I had always loved the old farm buildings as though they were living, breathing things, but at that moment I hoped I never loved another building so that I never had to face losing it again.

A few weeks later Dad's brother, Les, visited. Les was in his late eighties and was also born and raised on the farm. Dad and Les are not sentimental about New House; they acknowledge that times move on and things either progress or stagnate and deteriorate.

We showed Uncle Les the barn development and walked around the outside of the as-yet-unoccupied units, nosying through the windows, faces pressed against the glass, eyes cupped against the sun. Despite Dad having received a hefty cheque for the barns eight years ago, we still felt we had the perfect right to be standing on this ground. We tried the doors and discovered that the barns had been left unlocked and we went inside the biggest one without hesitation. This time there were no blue plastic overshoes or glasses of prosecco.

We recalled a party Elizabeth threw in this barn in 1976 when the old record player was wired up with extension after extension to play Rod Stewart's 'Maggie May' and 'Make Me Smile (Come Up and See Me)' by Steve Harley and Cockney Rebel, and we had stocked the bar, built of bales, with bottles of Martini – Cinzano or Rosso for the beginners; dry for the sophisticates – and tins of Party Seven, and we fried sausages on a barbecue constructed from a stack of old bricks. How did we not burn the barn down? How did we not frighten the animals to death? How were we allowed to do it? The worst I remember happening was somebody crashing their car through Dad's hedge as they drove home drunk and coming back the next day contrite and embarrassed to apologize.

But that was all a long time ago.

Now Dad and Uncle Les gazed around at the acres of white and beige and shiny, shiny surfaces and shook their heads and agreed: 'By 'eck, you can hardly credit it, can you?'

CHAPTER TWENTY-FOUR

As a teenager I read my horoscope every day in the *Daily Express*.

Tricia's diaries contained in-depth astrological lists she'd drawn up showing compatibility between star signs, and there were mentions of visits to 'the palmist'. She believed her disastrous love life was 'all explainable by astrology'. When we cleared out the farmhouse I found a bag of runes and a book on how to read them, which now sits on my bookshelf. Elizabeth took Tricia's book on reading tarot cards. Having stopped going to church for years after returning from Vienna, she appears to have been searching for meaning and answers in other places.

A friend told me she had been for 'a card reading'. She was impressed; the woman *knew* things – my friend nodded her head – oh yes, the woman definitely knew things.

I booked an appointment. I was mostly laughing at myself but a tiny voice kept saying: 'Well if Tricia was into all this maybe she's just waiting for the chance to talk to you. Why not? What have you got to lose?' To which the answer of course was: 'An hour and a half and thirty-five pounds.'

The card reader was a middle-aged woman who operated from a room above a financial adviser in a local market town. She wore crystals in her ears, crystals around her neck ('leopardite: good for speaking out') and on her wrists, and there were little sequins glittering on her jumper. On her window-sill were books including *Working with Guides and Angels* and *The Archangel Guide to Ascension* and the sun shone through the glass illuminating angel transfers stuck on the panes.

She asked me to sign a form which, among other things, stated the angel cards were 'just for entertainment purposes'.

'I don't believe they are only for entertainment purposes,' she said, waving her hand over the form dismissively, 'but it's the law.'

We sat either side of a small round table draped in a cloth and I chose from a pack of angel tarot cards.

She had asked me no questions about myself. Her interpretation of me was from my appearance and from the cards and from, I suppose, the fact that I was there at all. Her interpretation was that I was a woman who had been let down in love and needed to set off on an adventure. She recommended backpacking the Inca Trail in Peru: 'I can see you grabbing that backpack' – she tried to recommend a tour operator who specialized in such trips but couldn't recall the name – 'and swimming in the ocean with a lovely guy.' She then informed me my 'third eye' was closed but only because I had been told as a child not to talk about being psychic or 'seeing auras'.

It seemed, simultaneously, two memories sprang to mind: how I used to read auras in the pub twenty years ago whenever I had too much to drink; and my mother dowsing with a twisted coathanger round the living room looking for a lost watch. I told the card reader about my mother. 'The apple doesn't fall far from the tree,' she declared, satisfied.

After quite a lot of this sort of thing, during which I didn't want to disappoint her by mentioning my husband and the family holidays I had got booked, she asked if I would like to use another pack of cards. I pointed to the 'Angels from Heaven' pack which she had mentioned could get messages from 'the other side'.

'Do you have a question?' she asked.

I hadn't come prepared with a specific question and I was momentarily taken aback. What would I ask Tricia if she was here now?

'Are we doing the right thing with the old farmhouse?' I asked.

The lady shuffled the cards and tapped them with her knuckles. 'This is for Catherine,' she said to them, tapping again. 'This is for Catherine.'

The first card said: *I can see all of your thoughts.* The lady considered this. 'It can be like solving a riddle using these cards,' she said and she shuffled again. The next said: *My mind is free*. She looked at it. 'You know sometimes they, on the other side, don't care about the things we care about. They have no earthly worries. I think the message means it doesn't matter what you do with the house. She is no longer attached to it. Do with it whatever makes you happy.'

She shuffled the cards and put down another.

It said: *I had to leave that way.*

I felt my throat constrict. I knew I was going to cry, but hoped I did not.

She put down another card.

My death was painless. Don't hold onto any guilt.

I could not stop myself crying, even though I felt foolish and despised myself for it. The lady handed me a tissue from a box beside the table, of the type that was so thin it absorbed nothing. She placed the last card.

I wish I had told you more often how much I love you.

She put the pack down and said: 'Do whatever you want with the house. Don't worry and have no guilt.'

I thanked her in a stilted 'that was very interesting, thank you very much' kind of way, accompanied with a too-bright smile, and I shoved the disintegrating tissue in my pocket.

People who grieve often catch sight of 'doubles' in the street – lookalikes of the deceased – the shock of it taking their breath away. Not me. I saw Tricia in Lara's face. The older Lara got, the more similar they became. Sometimes I did a double-take at photographs, unsure which of them it was.

I saw Tricia's smile, I heard her laugh. Lara has the happy side of Tricia and not the sad. History is only partially repeating itself.

Lara set off to Glasgow University in September 2016 with a box of Tricia's old mugs and plates she had brought back from Vienna and Israel.

She posted photos on Facebook of parties in her student halls and I saw Tricia's things as props in the background, taken out of the dusty farmhouse and given a new lease of life.

Tricia's horse, Billy ('proper' name Wainright), is a black thoroughbred, almost seventeen hands, which she bought for dressage competitions. He is elegant and beautiful and highly strung; at once magnificent and yet delicate and fragile. She loved him very much.

In May 2016 I stood at Dad's window looking out towards the lane. A friend of Elizabeth's was riding Billy and she had stopped beside the garden gate to talk to Dad. Since Tricia died Dad had fed and cared for her horses, Billy and Sasha, every day with the help of Laura, a local woman who kept her horse, Sarah, alongside them in Tricia's stables. Billy and Sasha went into the paddock every day with Sarah, for exercise. They were all great pals.

Now Billy was being moved to a stable in Cheshire nearer Elizabeth so she and her friend could ride him every day and give him the handling he needed. It made sense but it felt sad. Billy and Sasha would be separated.

In one of Tricia's diaries I had found a short piece she'd written from Sasha's point of view, called 'My Name is Sasha'. Tricia often wrote passages in the voices of her animals to send to her nephews and nieces.

> I have a friend called Billy who lives next door. It makes me feel safe knowing he is always there and I think he feels the same about me. We argue sometimes, usually if he looks at my dinner I get grumpy but we never fall out. We go into the paddock most days to gallop. We both like to get down on the ground and roll over to scratch our backs. Then we eat the juicy grass.

Now I watched Billy dance in the sunshine; he pranced sideways and swished his tail, keen to carry on. Elizabeth's friend was a good rider: she held him firm; she was in control.

Billy's leaving was the best thing for him, I knew that; he was a big strong horse in the prime of life who needed to be worked. It was a good idea.

Yet it was also a further dismantling of Tricia's life.

I watched Billy set off at a swift trot that covered yards with every few steps. There he went, out of sight; the sound of his trotting hooves faded away soon after and the moment had passed.

I wondered which moments of *my* life I needed to grab and to live so that someone else did not live them for me.

* * *

Two and a half years after Tricia died we put New House Farmhouse up for sale. The smart barn conversions next door were now full of new families and it made no sense for the big house to remain empty.

One day as I sat at my desk an email arrived with the link to the estate agent's particulars and my finger hovered over the Enter button. I daren't press it. I did some breathing exercises: in for five, hold for five, out for five. I gathered my courage and pressed and the glossy photos opened showing a white farmhouse nestling among a jungle of green. A more idyllic rural spot it would have been hard to imagine.

In estate-agent lingo New House Farm was 'a gem', 'a wonderful opportunity' offering 'tremendous scope'. There was no mention of bumpy walls and Anaglypta wallpaper, of squint light fittings or 1970s swirly carpets. Instead there was talk of it 'needing a programme of cosmetic improvement' or – and my heart clenched – a 'complete rebuild'. New House Farm as a pile of rubble; it was unthinkable.

I wondered if the fortune-teller was right. Would Tricia not care what we did with it? The farm was one of the things she had cared about most, to a dangerous and self-destructive degree. I considered it a moment longer. Of course she didn't care; she was not here to care.

It was those of us who remained who were left to care about the bricks and mortar, about the view of woodpeckers from the bathroom window, about the smell of the old tea roses in the back garden, about Grandma Marjorie's lilac tree that tapped on the sitting-room window. It was the ones left behind who needed to let this go.

The next day the 'For Sale' sign went up.

By this time, June 2016, there were days when the numbing shock of Tricia's death seemed to have begun to fade and I realized I had unfinished business with the NHS manager.

I dug out the report.

It was as impenetrable with jargon as I remembered but I was now more able to deal with it. As I read, it dawned on me that Tricia probably did try to die by suicide, by overdose, three weeks before she died. The report said that, when changing her prescription for stronger drugs on 15th November, 'the pharmacist was concerned as the blister packs received back from the Service User should have contained two weeks' medication, however these were empty.' It goes on to refer to the 'possibility of recent overdose'.

Despite eighteen months having elapsed since we last spoke, I decided I must chase up the NHS manager for an explanation. His mobile number was handwritten on the report and I can only imagine his sinking heart as his phone rang and he became aware that a closed case had come back from the dead.

He was friendly and polite; yes, of course he remembered the case and he remembered me. No, it was not a problem; he would retrieve the notes and get back to me as soon as possible.

Two or three weeks later he phoned to say he had a meeting arranged with his manager to find the answers to my questions. He would be in touch to explain what he had discovered.

Shortly after, he texted to say his meeting had been cancelled at short notice due to 'sudden sickness'. I texted him to tell him when I was available to talk. He did not reply. Three weeks later, having heard nothing more, I sent another text but as I sent it I knew I would not hear from him.

I was right; I never heard from him again.

I told a psychiatrist friend about the silence from the NHS. He was in no doubt: There was no way the health authority would talk to me. 'They will not risk saying the wrong thing and opening the door even a chink for you and your lawyers to pursue a claim.'

'But I don't want to make a claim.'

'Doesn't matter. They are not going to say anything.'

I knew what he meant and I didn't have the strength.

It seemed that the facts were these: Tricia had more than likely tried to kill herself three weeks before she died. We were not told about this because of her paranoia which came as part of her illness. We were not aware of how bad her paranoia had got because she was unable to tell us and we were not privy to her diary. Consequently we went on holiday – taking Dad, her main support – just when she needed him most. We were banging our heads against a brick wall with the health authority then and I was doing the same now.

I had a moment of clarity: I had to stop searching for answers as to why it had happened. There were many things I would never know. There were some things I could take a good guess at, but other things, whether I knew them or not, that could never make the difference I wanted. No matter how many traces I found of Tricia, how many letters and photographs, diary entries and mementoes. My search had to end because nothing could change this story. However much I dug and read and considered, I could not find Tricia and rescue her. No facts, no amount of knowing, could bring her back to us.

I needed to put this burden down.

CHAPTER TWENTY-FIVE

After a death there is always *something* waiting in ambush to grab you by the throat and knock the breath out of you – whether it is a line in a book, a scene in a play, a story in a newspaper, or a lyric in a song.

I was on the train heading to a writing workshop listening to Nina Simone on my iPod; she was singing 'Here Comes the Sun'. I misheard the words; thought she was mourning how long it had been since she'd seen a loved one. That was not what she was singing, but it didn't matter, that's what I heard, and so the damage was done as the boot caught me with another blow under the ribs and I was reeling again.

At the workshop we were asked to write five lines beginning with certain words. My words were: 'It is'.

It is 944 days since it happened.
It is always on my mind.
It is common for me to cry on buses and trains.
It is still impossible for me to listen to the Brahms 'Lullaby'.

It is better than it was.

I read the lines out to the rest of the group and I sensed people were reading another story altogether into the words. None of them knew me. None of them knew Tricia. It felt odd that they did not know the story of Tricia because 'The Story of Tricia' had become such a huge part of me. Half of me wanted to explain – 'No, you see, what happened was this …' – while the other half of me hugged Tricia and her story to myself.

I often cried on buses and trains but I did not want it to keep happening.

The following day I was on the train heading to Glasgow. In the early hours I had lain awake with ungraspable thoughts swirling dizzyingly through my mind like the patterns on my mother's living-room carpet and I had taken a Tramadol. The pills were Mum's from when she had cancer; she didn't believe in taking painkillers, not even when she was dying, and had chucked them in the back of a cupboard, so now I kept them by my bed. Just in case. Now, on the train, I put my feet up on the seat opposite, I plugged the headphones of my iPod in and played Mozart's piano sonatas, and with the remains of the Tramadol I floated to Glasgow.

But the world lay in wait.

Months later I was at a poetry reading in a vegetarian restaurant. Could there be a more benign environment?

I had spent nearly three years walling up my grief; laying the bricks so carefully, so skilfully smoothing the mortar. Weeks went by now when I didn't cry. My grief was safe. I believed.

A woman beside me told me she had had a pie for breakfast. 'Sweet or savoury?' I asked. (I was being polite, you understand.) She looked askance. 'A pie! A pie!' she barked. 'A Scotch pie – meat!'

'Oh,' I replied, 'where I come from a pie could be meat or fruit.'

The woman bristled. 'Well this is *not* where you come from, *is it?*'

And just this, this thoughtlessness, this small unkindness, and I felt the mortar crack a little.

Tricia was not here for moral support, she was not here to keep me company, but I could almost hear the crackle of her tobacco as she dragged on her cigarette, a pause as she held the smoke in her lungs and blew it away. A throaty chuckle, then: 'Tell her to sling her hook.'

I did not realize for some time, but it was as though Tricia and I had swapped roles. When I was in difficulties – like here with the pie-woman and at Hawthornden when my colleague sang 'The Hung Himself Up Song' – she was there to offer words of advice and to laugh with me at the absurdity of life.

* * *

In August 2016, we were moving house and my mother's black lacquer grand piano was too big to come with us. This was the piano my mother was so desperate for us to learn to play that she paid us to practise: ten pence an hour – I usually did fifteen minutes, two-and-a-half-pence-worth at once. Elizabeth and I wrote down our practising times on a piece of paper which we stuck behind the kitchen mirror. ('What's that?' asked Gran, in amazement and disbelief, shaking his head, disgusted that children should be *paid* to practise.)

Piano lessons were the only after-school activity my mother took me to, but piano-playing was her love, not mine. I didn't ask to go – I would have preferred art or dancing or almost anything. I was aware that I was a disappointment to my mother whose ambitions were musical. I had a little musical aptitude but not enough. But then my mother, who *could* play, never sat beside me and showed me a scale; she never explained how to read music; she never let me sit and watch her play. She wanted to pay up-front and buy a piano-playing child who mirrored her talent, but it didn't work.

Tricia never got childhood piano lessons; my mother was disillusioned by the third child and would not throw good money after bad so I decided to teach her. She was maybe eight years old. I watched her struggle with a scale and declared: 'Your fingers are too stiff and fat. You will never be able to play.' It took her until she was in her thirties before she regained enough confidence to get a proper lesson.

The piano was my mother's twenty-first birthday present from Grandma Mary and Grandad Ben and was her prized possession. We were only allowed to play it after beginning official lessons – it was off-limits before then. We had to wash our hands before each session and woe betide you if you messed around pretending to be a 'proper piano player' and hammered on lots of keys at once: 'That is NOT a toy!' would bellow through the house.

After my mother died I had the piano brought up to Scotland where it sat majestically in the bay window of our living room, played for a time but eventually abandoned as a musical instrument and used only as an impressive shiny surface for displaying photographs – including one of my mother sitting at the piano on her twenty-first birthday.

It was my first thought when we put the house up for sale: 'What will happen to Mum's piano?' And one of the first things Dad asked when I told him we were moving.

I tried a couple of dealers but buyers for very old, out-of-tune grand pianos are thin on the ground. I fantasized about it being on a cruise ship sailing the world or gracing a drawing room in a stately home, or in a saleroom in New York where reconditioned Rönisch pianos go under the hammer for a fortune. I put it on Facebook – 'Free of charge to a good home'. Many people got in touch. Someone was interested in getting it as a 'surprise' for their parents for when they came back from holiday. Someone else asked about the postage to Australia. It seemed a tall order that a suitable home would be found; it was beautiful but so big. I went hot and cold imagining having to get a joiner to cut it up and take it to the tip. I would be physically sick. Maybe I could turn the legs into gigantic candle-holders; the frame into a bookcase? Lara suggested its six-foot length could become a bed with the extra side bit for the cat.

After only a day or two a family from Glasgow offered to adopt it. They had two children both keen to learn, and the space to house it.

Two men – piano-removal specialists – came to take it away. These men were nothing like Pete and Trev; they were respectful and not intrusive. They worked quickly and quietly – 'one, two, hupp!' – seeming to read each other's minds as they manoeuvred the enormous instrument; removing a leg – 'one, two, hupp!' – tipping the frame sideways onto a stretcher, wrapping it tightly in a blanket and strapping it up with webbing before using a trolley to wheel it outside.

I stood in the bay window – the space now piano-less, bare and enormous. I watched as the piano was inched into the van, the men straining at the weight of loading it without damaging it – putting their backs into it, but gently.

I had a flashback to the day my mother died, of the undertakers removing her body from the bed in the dining room which in her final months had become her bedroom.

We all said goodbye to her. She was lying on her back, hands resting on the quilt, eyes closed, and wearing her home-made cotton nightie; exactly the position in which she had died. Exactly as she had been as we sat around her: Dad and Elizabeth holding a hand each, Tricia and I perched on the bottom corners of the bed. When Dad had said: 'I think she's at' far end.' Exactly as she had been when she opened her eyes a minute later and looked round at each of us and her eyes flickered shut and she let out her last breath.

Before the undertakers disturbed her we withdrew to the kitchen. I made eye contact with Tricia but was frightened by the sadness and shock in her face, which I knew were reflected in my own. We were heart-stoppingly aware that Mum's body was being strapped to a stretcher and manoeuvred away: through the double doors, across the conservatory, out of the French doors, round the house and to the waiting vehicle – whether it was a hearse, a van, an ambulance, I don't know; I dared not look.

I glanced sideways from the kitchen and inadvertently caught a glimpse of the stretcher with her wrapped body being carried down the garden path, past the living-room window. Death is not dignified. My mother would not have approved, even though there was no alternative.

When the undertakers had arrived I'd half-expected her to rise from her deathbed, flap her hands at them and say: 'Get away! I will do it *myself*!'

I could not wait to move house and to begin to build something again rather than this constant taking apart. I knew I would be wary of buying things, though. I wanted to wear my possessions lightly; to be in control of them, rather than they being in control of me. I wanted owning things to feel like wearing a silk scarf rather than lead boots.

The piano-removers' van doors slammed and the vehicle pulled away. I knew I had to be brave, not sentimental. I turned back to the room and a small ball of dust that must have been lurking under the piano pedals drifted and rolled past my feet across the bare bay window like tumbleweed.

The day after Tricia died I had leafed through her desk diary on the kitchen farmhouse table, two pages for a week. It did not seem intrusive to turn the pages because this 2013 diary looked like a public document lying there open on the oilcloth. Thinking back, this may have been an excuse, because Tricia lived alone and would not have expected anyone to read her diary, open or not. Perhaps I just wanted to get closer to Tricia in any way I could.

In the months before her death, alongside details of new clients at the livery yard, the diary included notes about getting the dog clipped at 'Scrub Doggy Dog', her exercise regime ('30 mins on the treadmill, 5 mins on the power plate'), appointments ('choir practice, 6 p.m.') and the weather ('Glorious shining sun'). But later, among the every-day, were other comments: 'Steven is clearly racist', 'stopped

Lottie stealing from me', 'Lynsey is being difficult, bolshy', 'Derek was catty', 'rowed with Julia', 'accosted by thingy', 'rat left on doorstep'.

By the end Tricia was only slipping out of the house to the stables at night to muck out her horses when it was dark and the livery yard was empty. The world was a dangerous place and it was safer to withdraw. She trusted no one; she couldn't help it – all except for Dad, she always trusted Dad.

The doodling began in January 2013 and grew and grew over the following pages. The doodles were intricate drawings in black biro carved into the paper; interlocking shapes that looked like numbers and letters but weren't: triangles, arrows, zigzags. She must have sat for hours at the table smoking, drinking coffee, thinking about the people who were trying to steal from her, accosting her, leaving rats on her doorstep, as she obsessively ground these jet-black marks into the page.

Every Sunday there was an outfit detailed in the diary she would wear for church: 'Black chiffon dress with pale blue jacket and blue shoes.' Sometimes with a separate outfit for evensong: 'Louis Féraud jacket, Mango black split skirt, high heels.' In the last months of her life she had begun to attend church with my mum's sister, Aunty Marion, to sing with the choir, although I don't think she made it every week. This outfit-organization seems to have been an attempt to wrest some control over her life and yet the attention to detail as regards her clothes was out of proportion for attending a service in a small village church. It was noted by the congregation, though, and after she died one or two of the parishioners came to me to say: 'We did like to see her at church. And, oh, she was always so smart.'

Her diary continued: 'Went into Garstang, saw Russell Howard and Joe Turner.' Joe Turner was an ex-boyfriend of hers who I knew was not in Garstang at that time, and Russell Howard is a television comedian with no connection whatsoever to the town. I stared at her handwriting trying to make sense of it. My heart hurt as I realized her psychosis was not limited to paranoia about those around her doing her ill but also included delusions of seeing people who were most definitely not there at all.

By September the doodling was so strong it was cutting through several pages at once and making dents into pages months away. By now she believed not only that she had seen famous people whom she hadn't, but that she was interacting with them: 'Sam Cam very unhappy about applause and positive feedback. Put a complete stop on all positive comments. Boris helping her.' Then later: 'David C and Obama on the telephone.' I stared at her handwriting. How could her brain do that to her?

In October she wrote: 'Harvest Festival: Jessye Norman was there and she came to say hello afterwards. Dream come true.'

Jessye Norman is an American opera singer who has never set foot in Winmarleigh. I gazed at Elizabeth and Chris, who were there with me and who stared at the diary in silence too, and I said: 'Whom the gods would destroy, they first make mad.'

I forced myself to continue to turn the pages.

The week she died was blank except for a margin of doodled arrows drawn on the Friday, alongside the only two words on the page, a small: 'I confess.'

The last time I went out with Tricia was to celebrate my fiftieth birthday. It was three weeks before she died, around the time she thought she'd spoken to Jessye Norman. A fiftieth birthday seemed significant and it didn't feel right to celebrate such a landmark event and not to include her. I was aware that life was passing for us all and Tricia was missing out on much normality.

Dad took me and Tricia out for lunch. He was agitated, shaking his head a little at the state she was in but saying nothing, withdrawing into his deafness. Tricia trembled slightly, stared at the table, nibbled on her food, pushed it round the plate. She seemed frightened, hypervigilant, as though she expected an explosion or a sudden hand on her shoulder at any moment. She was both on high alert and yet not there. She appeared to have shrunk and her spirit had shrivelled as if there was nothing left to say and nothing left to do.

I felt insipient panic – the sense that I was responsible, that I had to make this work, that I had to *do something*. I commented on the food, on the restaurant, on the weather. I asked about her horses.

But there were no words left.

The restaurant was bustling – voices murmured, cutlery clanked, crockery clattered – but within that room there were two realities: everyone else's and ours.

Around our table a terrible quiet settled.

I could not wait for the meal to end. I wanted to run and run and never stop.

I realise now this was around the time she may have attempted suicide by overdose.

We ate in silence.

CHAPTER TWENTY-SIX

Three years after Tricia died I went to the Scottish National Gallery of Modern Art to see the 'Surreal Encounters' exhibition. It contained the painting *On the Threshold of Liberty* by René Magritte which depicted a room panelled with many scenes or windows and containing a cannon. The sign said the painting may have been inspired by a quote from John Buchan's *Prester John*: 'The clear air of dawn was like wine in my blood. I was not free but I was on the threshold of freedom.'

I was struck by this phrase. I read it over and over again and I wrote it down. I wondered did similar thoughts pass through Tricia's head as she smoked those four cigarettes on the bathroom floor on her last night on earth, staring at the black windows or watching the dawn break through the frosted glass? Did she feel the clear air of dawn like wine in her blood? Maybe that's how she considered her decision to die: as taking a step towards the threshold of freedom.

* * *

A few months before I visited the exhibition, journalist Sally Brampton had died by suicide. She had written a memoir of her depression and the press referred to her as having 'lost her battle'. Some commentators objected to the battle analogy. Not me. From where I was sitting, Tricia's life with depression looked exactly like a battle. It looked like vicious hand-to-hand combat while under sniper attack. Living with bipolar and psychotic episodes looked like a dirty business; the disease didn't play fair: you could follow all the rules – take the drugs, exercise, try to socialize – but it didn't let up; it rarely went off the attack and if it did it was only temporary and in reality it was still there lurking, waiting in ambush.

It had been relentless and cruel and attacked Tricia until dying had seemed like the better, or perhaps the only, option; better in that moment to die than to go on living another day fighting. It was a battle – but an unfair battle, a battle in which the odds were stacked so highly against her that after years of combat she had lost hope that it could ever be any different – that it could ever be any better.

By 6th December 2013 Tricia believed she would never be well again and that the terrible fight she was engaged in – day in, day out, year in, year out – was never going to end. This belief is mentioned in her NHS notes. She had lost hope. She believed she was trapped for ever – unless she brought the situation to a conclusion herself.

How I wish she had not believed that – but I cannot blame her for doing so.

In one way the decision was rational; she took control and ended her suffering. In another it made no sense, partly because of Dad and her horses, dog and cat – they needed her day to day, every day. They were *right there*.

But, again, the clue is in the NHS investigation notes: on 3rd December she said she thought people would be better off without her. Once those two beliefs – that she would never get well again and that her loved ones would be better off without her – were at the forefront of her mind I think the decision was made. Unfortunately she could not see beyond her decision to die and understand the devastating and irreversible impact.

When she found the rope and took it upstairs I believe she thought she was not only on the threshold of freedom for herself but that she was also setting her family free. Her death certificate said *death by hanging*. What it should have said was *death by depression*.

Could we have done more? Could I have done more? Yes, of course. We could always do more.

On my first visit to the farmhouse after she died I ran my finger down the slant chip in the paintwork on the stairs where my dad's penknife had cut through the rope. As I walked up the stairs through the space that had held Tricia's suspended body I heard the words from the Bible: *yea, though I walk through the shadow of the valley of death*. I could not set foot upon the creaking stairs without those words resounding, round and round in my head, *yea, though I walk through the shadow of the valley of death*, and continuing to echo as I passed the cupboard halfway up and after I'd reached the spindles at the top of the stairs, including the one that had taken her weight, cracking across the bottom, but not breaking right though and releasing her.

It was the same on every visit I made for months, years. Each time I went upstairs I had the urge to duck as though she was still there, as though it was obscene to walk through the space her body had occupied, and then to glance over my shoulder to catch a glimpse of my little sister. Surely it was impossible for this to happen and it not to leave a livid scar on the universe, an everlasting scream.

But now it feels as though the house has let go. It is empty, of our furniture, of our detritus, of us. Tricia has been gone four years. On my last visit I wandered from room to room and the house felt weightless. It was full of space and light. It was ready for another family.

It was time for me to step towards my own threshold of freedom – freedom from guilt about things I could not have changed, freedom to be who I am, freedom to stop being who I am not, freedom to speak out, freedom to be visible; freedom, in other words, to write this book and in so doing to leave behind a lifetime of silence about Tricia. Then to move forward with a lighter step, glad my own children are outspoken and opinionated, nothing like the shy, tongue-tied child I used to be.

I took a last look around the old farmhouse. Fresh air circulated and the sun streamed through the windows.

A memory came to mind. At the funeral one of Tricia's old schoolfriends told me: 'Tricia said she wouldn't have wanted to be born any other way. She said her lows were low but her highs were high and she was thankful for that.'

I opened the door and the sun was surprisingly bright – it was always cooler and darker inside the farmhouse than out.

I stepped through and pulled the door closed behind me.

I will remember Tricia as the happy child she was; the loving, generous, kind child who empathized so strongly she experienced your joy and your pain, right there, right then. I will remember her as the joyous, excited child who danced in circles to the tune of a crazy piccolo on a Sunday morning, breathless, ecstatic to be hand in hand with her sisters, laughing, looking at us with trusting brown eyes, believing us when we told her we could fly; that if we only tried that bit harder and screwed our eyes shut that bit tighter and wished that bit more, then we could all be *free to fly, fly away, high away, bye bye.*

Tricia, 1967–2013, beautiful always

ACKNOWLEDGEMENTS

Thanks to my little sister Tricia for being my little sister and for the diaries, letters, photographs and memories.

To Dad and my big sister, Elizabeth, for their support and recollections.

To Mum for many things, including the cover photograph.

To everyone at Hawthornden Castle for creating the perfect writing environment.

To Lynsey Rogers and Will Mackie of Scottish Book Trust for their faith in this project.

To my Scottish Book Trust mentor, Kapka Kassabova, for her insights.

To my agent, Joanna Swainson; my editor, Helen Garnons-Williams; and the team at 4th Estate for their help and support.

To early readers, encouragers and advisers: Mary Stewart, Aunty Dorothy and Uncle Dennis, Chris Heathcote, Sam Boyce, Julie Myatt, Frances Hider, Steve Dudhill, Carole Stewart, Hilary Hine, Menna Rowlands, Anita & Doug Clark, Stella Birrell and Edinburgh Writing Pals: Peikko, Ever, Sil, Alison, Mark and Ali.

To Shelley Day, Hannah Lavery and the Writing Mums, Helen Boden, Marjorie Lotfi Gill, Janice Galloway and Jenny Lindsay, whose writing workshops sparked many of the memories in this book.

To Cello, Nina and Lara for everything.